T0318345

The Economics of Saving and Growth
Theory, Evidence, and Implications for Policy

Saving rates display great variation across countries and over time. They are also closely related to growth performance. This volume provides a state-of-the-art account of key variables, institutions, and policies that determine saving. Drawing from a systematic exploration of the existing literature, the collection summarizes current knowledge about cross-country saving trends, the relation between saving and growth, the impact of financial policies and institutions on saving, the effect of foreign resource inflows on saving, and the links between income distribution and aggregate saving. In addition, new research results are presented on the two latter areas. The work has a strong empirical motivation: to help address real-world issues on consumption and saving in both industrial and developing countries, in order to assist in the design of rational and effective macroeconomic policies.

Klaus Schmidt-Hebbel is chief of economic research at the Central Bank of Chile. Formerly with the Research Department of the World Bank in Washington, DC, he has also taught at the Catholic University of Chile, the University of Chile, and Georgetown University. Dr. Schmidt-Hebbel has published extensively on saving, fiscal policy, and pension reform in edited collections and journals.

Luis Servén is an economist with the Research Department of the World Bank. He has also taught at the Universidad Complutense and the Center for Monetary and Financial Studies, both in Madrid, Spain. Dr. Servén has published extensively on macroeconomic modeling, investment, and saving in books and professional journals on international and development economics.

The Economics of Saving and Growth

Theory, Evidence, and Implications for Policy

Edited by
KLAUS SCHMIDT-HEBBEL

LUIS SERVÉN

CAMBRIDGE
UNIVERSITY PRESS

CAMBRIDGE UNIVERSITY PRESS
Cambridge, New York, Melbourne, Madrid, Cape Town, Singapore, São Paulo

Cambridge University Press
The Edinburgh Building, Cambridge CB2 2RU, UK

Published in the United States of America by Cambridge University Press, New York

www.cambridge.org
Information on this title: www.cambridge.org/9780521632959

© The World Bank 1999

This publication is in copyright. Subject to statutory exception
and to the provisions of relevant collective licensing agreements,
no reproduction of any part may take place without
the written permission of Cambridge University Press.

First published 1999
This digitally printed first paperback version 2006

A catalogue record for this publication is available from the British Library

Library of Congress Cataloguing in Publication data
The economics of saving and growth: theory, evidence, and
implications for policy / [edited by] Klaus Schmidt-Hebbel, Luis
Servén.
p. cm.
Includes index.
ISBN 0-521-63295-1 (hb)
1. Saving and investment. 2. Economic development. 3. Economic
policy. I. Schmidt-Hebbel, Klaus. II. Serven, Luis.
HC79.S3E25   1999   98-11639
338.9 – dc21   CIP

ISBN-13 978-0-521-63295-9 hardback
ISBN-10 0-521-63295-1 hardback

ISBN-13 978-0-521-02331-3 paperback
ISBN-10 0-521-02331-9 paperback

Contents

Contents

Contributors

Angus Deaton
Princeton University

Patrick Honohan
*Economic and Social Research
 Institute, Dublin*

Maurice Obstfeld
*University of California at
 Berkeley*

Klaus Schmidt-Hebbel
Central Bank of Chile

Luis Servén
The World Bank

Foreword

Since the 1960s, world saving rates have followed a declining trend, accompanied by an increasing saving disparity across developing regions: saving rates have doubled in East Asia, stagnated in Latin America and the Caribbean, and collapsed in sub-Saharan Africa. Saving rates have also declined sharply in former socialist economies since the beginning of their transition toward a market economy in the early 1990s.

These regional saving disparities have been closely reflected in growth performance: higher-saving regions have also enjoyed faster income growth. High saving alone cannot guarantee the achievement of rapid and sustained growth and the reduction of poverty, but the international evidence does suggest that high saving inevitably accompanies that pursuit. Dissecting this empirical association between saving and growth into causal mechanisms is of utmost importance to both theorists and policy makers committed to achieving high growth and poverty reduction. There is a virtuous cycle in which high growth promotes high saving, and high saving in turn promotes fast growth.

The available evidence also suggests that high saving is associated with good macroeconomic performance and sustainable access to foreign lending. However, the recent turmoil in East Asia also reveals that while high levels of national saving contribute to domestic and external stability, they do not offer full insurance against the risks posed by fragile financial systems or unsustainable exchange rate policies. Therefore a better understanding of the interplay between financial and macroeconomic policies, on one hand, and saving, on the other, is another key priority from the policy perspective.

Against this background, we still have much to learn about how specific structural policies (related to tax incentives, the financial system, or foreign aid) and important structural features (such as the distribution of income and demographic forces) affect national saving levels.

This book reviews some of these issues – and provides some new research findings – at both theoretical and empirical levels. It documents broad saving trends in the world, takes stock of our current knowledge about saving and consumption, identifies major unresolved issues, and provides new results on the effects of foreign transfers and income inequality on national saving.

The volume presents World Bank–sponsored research on why people and institutions save, and why they do not, and why some policies may help, and others do not, in getting virtuous saving–growth cycles under way. A broad audience of academic and applied economists in the fields of macroeconomics and finance, as well as policy makers and development specialists, will benefit from reading this book.

The volume is part of the World Bank's ongoing research program dedicated to understanding better the fundamentals of sustainable growth and development and poverty alleviation. This research program seeks to cross traditional boundaries in economics – in this case bringing together macroeconomists, financial economists, and international economists – and reflects our commitment that the findings be disseminated widely, not only to academics and applied economists, but also to policy makers and development specialists.

Joseph Stiglitz
Senior Vice President
and Chief Economist
The World Bank

CHAPTER 1

Introduction

Klaus Schmidt-Hebbel and Luis Servén

> Attempts by economists to understand the savings and consumption
> patterns of households have generated some of the best science in
> economics. For more than fifty years, there has been serious empirical
> and theoretical activity, and the two strands have never been long
> separated as has happened in so many other branches of economics.
>
> Angus Deaton, *Understanding Consumption*, Oxford, 1992.

Over the past three decades the world has witnessed a steady decline in
its overall saving rate. This trend decline conceals widely diverging regional saving patterns, particularly within the developing world: saving
rates have doubled in East Asia, stagnated in Latin America, and collapsed in sub-Saharan Africa. These saving disparities have been closely
reflected in the respective growth performances: across world regions,
higher saving rates have come with higher income growth.

Why are these saving disparities of any interest? From a theoretical
viewpoint, there is in principle little reason to expect saving rates to
behave similarly across countries. In an ideal first-best world, different
saving rates could just be the result of optimal intertemporal consumption decisions when preferences, technology, demographics, and/or
other factors vary across countries. In the real second-best world, however, intertemporal choices are subject to a host of externalities, market
failures, and policy-induced distortions that in many countries are likely
to cause saving to differ from its welfare-maximizing levels. Of course,
the result need not be too low a level of saving. True, some distortions –
such as too low government saving in a non-Ricardian world, or moral
hazard leading to inadequate private saving for retirement in anticipation of public bailout of the old-age poor – can indeed result in socially
insufficient saving. But other types of market imperfection, such as the
absence of risk-sharing instruments, or policy-induced distortions, such

1

as forced saving schemes, can conceivably lead to saving above socially optimal levels.

Yet the very low saving ratios of many developing economies, particularly among poorer countries, strongly suggest that the prevailing situation is one of socially insufficient saving. Indeed, the direct association between saving ratios and growth rates across countries noted above hints at the existence of virtuous cycles of saving and prosperity along with poverty traps of undersaving and stagnation. This in turn would suggest that an increase in the saving levels of the poorer countries can be important to their higher long-run growth and welfare – a view that remains controversial, however.

Saving is also a central policy concern for reasons other than its direct growth impact. A national saving ratio broadly in line with the economy's investment needs is often viewed as a key ingredient to reduce a country's vulnerability to unexpected shifts in international capital flows. As illustrated by the recent experience of Mexico, low domestic saving can exacerbate the economy's vulnerability to sudden shifts in capital flows, which in turn may be driven by factors such as herd behavior or self-fulfilling expectations on the part of international investors. In other words, under increasing international financial integration, high domestic saving contributes to macroeconomic stability, itself a powerful growth factor. However, the recent turmoil in East Asia also shows that high saving cannot provide full insurance against the risks posed by fragile financial systems or misaligned exchange rates.

This book takes a fresh look at major research and policy issues surrounding private saving (or consumption) in the world. The book addresses two broad questions.

What do we know about saving?

As stated in the epigraph, theoretical research and empirical findings have advanced remarkably close to each other in explaining why households consume and save. This volume provides a state-of-the-art account of the key variables, institutions, and policies that determine private consumption and saving. Drawing from a systematic exploration of the existing literature on saving around the world, the book summarizes current knowledge about cross-country saving trends and correlations (Chapter 2), the relation between saving and growth (Chapter 3), the impact of financial policies and institutions on saving (Chapter 4), foreign resource inflows and saving (Chapter 5), and income distribution and saving (Chapter 6).

In addition, new research results are presented in the two latter chapters. Analytical insights and simulation results on the effects of foreign transfers on national saving are reported in Chapter 5, and international empirical evidence on how income distribution affects aggregate saving is presented in Chapter 6.

What should we know?

The topical surveys and new research presented in this book have been developed with a strong empirical motivation – to help address real-world issues on consumption or saving behavior in both industrial and developing countries. They also provide a candid assessment of what we *do not* but *should* know about saving to assist in the design of rational and effective macroeconomic policies. The chapters in this volume pursue this objective one step further, identifying the major unresolved issues and the methods that should guide future research.

Overview of the Book

Chapter 2 sets the empirical background for the volume. It outlines the major trends in saving across the world and over time, and documents the association between saving rates and major saving determinants, providing the statistical background for many behavioral hypotheses on consumption/saving and related variables explored in depth by subsequent chapters. A critical review of saving data shortcomings and improvements closes the chapter.

The strong empirical association between growth rates and saving ratios across countries and over time remains a major macroeconomic puzzle whose solution has key policy implications, especially for the growth merits of saving-enhancing policies. Chapter 3 presents a rigorous and comprehensive account of the different explanations that have been proposed for this empirical regularity, ranging from the traditional life-cycle model to recent research on less conventional models based on liquidity constraints and consumption habits, and encompassing both the microeconomic and aggregate perspectives. Based on the recent literature and the author's own work, the chapter outlines the research priorities for uncovering the solution to the growth–saving puzzle.

The impact of financial reform on saving remains controversial: some argue that it should result in more efficient intermediation and thereby encourage saving, but recent evidence suggests that the easing of borrowing constraints that follows reform actually discourages saving. Chapter 4 provides a thorough up-to-date account of the existing knowledge on the influence of financial factors and fiscal incentives on the level of saving. It focuses on two main areas: the financial system and its influence on saving decisions, especially through limitations on consumers' ability to borrow; and the institutional factors – from social security arrangements to tax incentives to specific financial instruments – that determine the menu of available assets and their rates of return. The chapter identifies the major unresolved issues and outlines the most promising ways to address them.

The effects of foreign resource inflows on national saving, investment, and growth have been the focus of a long-standing theoretical and empirical debate. The controversy has recently centered on the effects of development aid, which – according to the critics – is almost fully used by the recipient countries to finance increased consumption, that is, to lower domestic saving. Chapter 5 starts with a critical overview of this debate and provides an innovative perspective. The chapter develops a theoretical (exogenous) growth model and applies it to show the effects of foreign aid and foreign lending on an open economy's transition and steady-state equilibria. The model is extended in two directions – adding borrowing-constrained consumers and endogenous growth – and simulated numerically to assess the dynamic effects of foreign aid on saving and growth. The chapter concludes by outlining an empirical version of the extended model amenable for econometric implementation.

The relationship between the personal distribution of income, investment, and growth has received increased theoretical and empirical attention in recent years, but less emphasis has been given to the link between saving and inequality. Chapter 6 aims to fill that gap. It reviews analytically and empirically the links between income distribution and aggregate saving. Consumption theory brings out a number of direct channels through which income inequality can affect overall household saving – positively in most cases. However, recent political economy theory points toward indirect, negative effects of inequality – through investment, growth, and public saving – on aggregate saving. On theoretical grounds the sign of the saving inequality is therefore ambiguous. The chapter presents new empirical evidence based on the thorough analysis of a large, consistent world database on income distribution that has become recently available to applied researchers. The empirical results, using alternative inequality and saving measures and various econometric specifications on both cross-section and panel data, provide no support for the notion that income inequality has any systematic effect on aggregate saving, a finding that is broadly consistent with the theoretical ambiguity.

Preparation of this book has benefited from the collaboration of many individuals. We are particularly grateful to Craig Burnside, Jerry Caprio, Chris Carroll, David Dollar, Sebastian Edwards, Aart Kraay, Ross Levine, Steve Marglin, Branko Milanovic, Lyn Squire, Vito Tanzi, and Michael Walton for discussions and comments on the overall project and specific chapters. Financial support from the World Bank's Policy and Research Department is gratefully acknowledged. Finally, we thank Wanhong Hu, Faruk Khan, and Bo Wang for their outstanding research assistance.

CHAPTER 2

Saving in the World: The Stylized Facts

Klaus Schmidt-Hebbel and Luis Servén

Introduction

The introduction to this book started with the empirical observation that the world saving rate has declined steadily since the 1960s. Increasing regional disparities are hidden behind this world trend. First, the gap between industrial-country and developing-country saving rates has widened. And within the developing world, the saving divergence across regions has grown massively. At one extreme, national saving ratios have risen from 18.3 percent of GNP during 1965–73 to 27.6 percent during 1984–93 in East Asia and the Pacific (without China), and from 25.3 percent to 36.8 percent in China. At the other extreme, saving rates have been declining steadily in sub-Saharan Africa from 10.5 percent of GNP in 1965–73 to 6.4 percent in 1984–93.

These startling trends warrant a closer look at world saving patterns and their relation to other key economic variables. In this chapter we review six stylized facts concerning the evolution of saving rates in the world and its major regions since the mid-1960s. In addition, possible explanations for the stylized facts offered by recent economic theory are briefly mentioned, anticipating some of the issues taken up in depth in subsequent chapters of this book. This chapter concludes with a brief reference to the causal interpretations of the empirical facts.

An important caution concerns the measurement of saving rates. The data used here suffer from most of the shortcomings of conventional macroeconomic data on saving and related variables. These shortcomings are conceptually and practically important, so that a closer look at data limitations and possible remedies is well justified. This is taken up in the methodological appendix to this chapter.

Six Stylized Facts on Saving and Related Variables

We focus next on six stylized facts and world trends concerning country and regional saving rates since the mid-1960s. Two facts relate to the

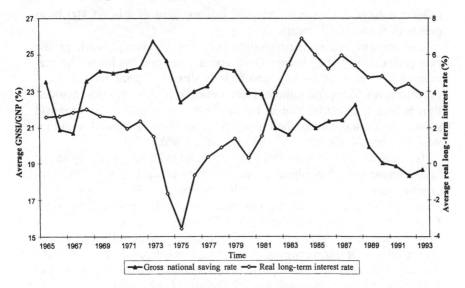

Figure 2.1. World saving and real interest rates (gross national saving rate including net current transfers, 10-year government bond real rates for G-10, weighted averages, 1965–93).

time and regional patterns of world saving rates, and the remaining four refer to the long-term association between saving and other macroeconomic aggregates.

Unless otherwise noted, we use unweighted averages of countries' gross national saving ratios to GNP, but most of the qualitative features described next also hold for alternative measures such as gross domestic saving rates and regional averages weighted by income levels. The basic data are from the World Bank BESD database, based on UN and national sources of national-accounts information. They cover the period 1965–94 and include 113 industrial and developing countries.

The World Saving Rate Has Been Declining and the World Real Interest Rate Has Been Increasing since the 1970s

The weighted-average world saving rate rose slightly during the 1960s and early 1970s to a peak level of 25 percent in 1973 (see Figure 2.1). Subsequently, world saving started a steady decline, to 19 percent in 1993–94. In turn, the average (ex post) long-term real interest rate shows the opposite pattern: from a range of 2–3 percent in the 1960s it plunged briefly to negative levels after the 1973 oil shock, then quickly rose to high positive levels in the early 1980s, and has remained close to 4 percent in recent years. According to the Group of Ten (1995), this reflects a trend increase in the real interest rate of around 100 basis points over the last 35 years.

The contemporaneous correlation between the average world saving rate (respectively, the average G-10 saving rate) and the long-term real interest rate is −.61 (−.56), significantly different from zero at the 5 percent level. The predominant interpretation of this empirical association is that the secular rise in the interest rate is due to lower world saving, which has outweighed a parallel reduction in desired world investment levels (Group of Ten, 1995; IMF, 1995).

Is saving sensitive to the interest rate? The evidence generally shows that interest rates have little or no effect on private saving. Empirical cross-country tests focusing on saving or consumption levels typically show that interest rates do not influence either (Giovannini, 1983, 1985; Corbo and Schmidt-Hebbel, 1991; Deaton, 1992; Edwards, 1996; Masson, Bayoumi, and Samiei, 1995). Other empirical studies that focus on the degree of intertemporal consumption substitution (by examining the rate of growth of consumption) likewise find weak or zero impact of real interest rates (Giovannini, 1985; Deaton, 1989, 1992).

Saving Rates Show Diverging Patterns across Regions during the Past Three Decades

Figure 2.2 (which uses unweighted averages of country data) shows that the trend decline in the world saving rate since 1974 conceals widely diverging regional saving patterns. OECD saving rates have been falling since the early 1970s, due mainly to lower public-sector saving (Group of Ten, 1995; IMF, 1995). Within developing countries (henceforth LDCs) it is useful to distinguish between 11 takeoff countries[1] (defined as those that have achieved high and sustained saving and growth rates during the past two decades) and all other developing countries, excluding former socialist economies (henceforth referred to as transition countries). The large group of non-takeoff LDCs shows a pattern of declining saving rates since the mid-1970s, similar to that observed in the OECD, but reaching a much lower average of 10 percent since 1983. In contrast, the takeoff countries have been able to break through their historically low level of saving (and growth) since the 1970s. Within the takeoff group, the 10 market economies have more than doubled their saving rates since the late 1960s, to reach an average 32 percent in the early 1990s. In turn, China started at rates close to 25 percent in the late 1960s, and has

---

[1] This group includes China and 10 market economies: Hong Kong, Indonesia, Korea, Malaysia, Singapore, Taiwan (China), and Thailand in East Asia; Botswana and Mauritius in Africa; and Chile in Latin America.

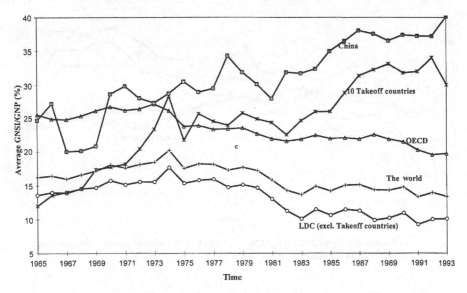

Figure 2.2. Saving rates by world regions (gross national saving rate including net current transfers, unweighted averages, 1965–93).

continuously raised its saving rate until becoming the world record saver at 40 percent in the early 1990s.

Similar world and regional trends in national saving ratios to GNP are observed when regional averages are weighted by annual GNP levels (Figure 2.3) or by population (Figure 2.4). In the latter case, the obvious exception is the world saving rate, which now shows no downward trend from the 23 percent level reached in the late 1970s; this is due to the significant weight given to China's high saving rate, reflecting its large share in world population. These results allow us to return to unweighted averages in what follows.

A large and increasing divergence of saving rates among developing country groups is also apparent from a geographical classification of developing regions (Figure 2.5). Using the World Bank's regional classification, saving ratios have risen from 18.3 percent during 1965–73 to 27.6 percent during 1984–93 in East Asia and the Pacific (denoted in Figure 2.5 by EAP, defined as exclusive of China), and from 25.3 percent to 36.8 percent in China. South Asia (SA) has been the only other developing region where saving rates have shown an increasing trend – but from a very low 9.5 percent in 1965–73 to a still modest 15.3 percent in 1984–93. The Middle East and North Africa's (MENA) very high 29.0 percent saving rate during the period of peak oil prices fell to 19.8 percent during

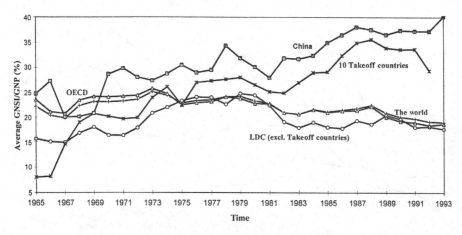

Figure 2.3. Saving rates by world regions (gross national saving rate including net current transfers, averages weighted by GNP, 1965–93).

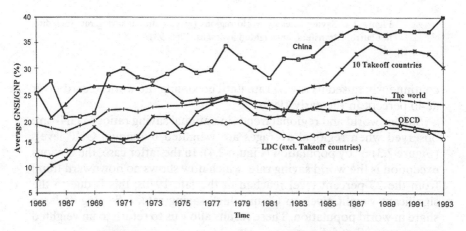

Figure 2.4. Saving rates by world regions (gross national saving rate including net current transfers, averages weighted by population, 1965–93).

1984–93. In Latin America and the Caribbean (LAC), the modest saving rates of the 1960s and 1970s fell even further during the "lost decade" of the 1980s, to reach 13.6 percent in 1984–93. But the most dramatic regional development took place in sub-Saharan Africa (SSA), where saving rates have been declining steadily from 10.5 percent in 1965–73 to an abysmally low level of 6.4 percent in 1984–93.

Saving rates show a wide dispersion across countries and over time within any given developing region. In Latin America, for instance, gross national saving rates shrank in Mexico from 23 percent in 1980–87 to 19

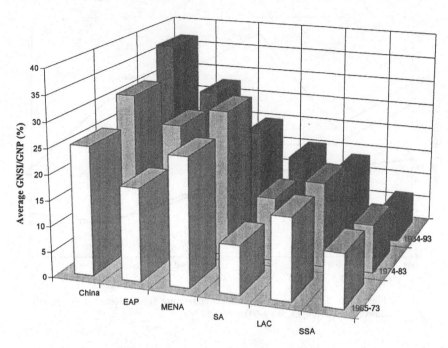

Figure 2.5. Saving rates by developing regions (gross national saving rate including net current transfers, unweighted averages, 1965–93).

percent in 1988–94. Mexico's saving decline reflected an unsustainable exchange rate policy, a loose fiscal stance, and a weak banking system, thus contributing to the 1994–95 crisis. In Chile, however, national saving rates grew from 13 percent in 1974–87 to 25 percent in 1988–94. This saving takeoff reflected a strong fiscal stance, the success of financial and pension system reforms, and high growth, therefore reinforcing the virtuous saving–growth nexus.

Saving rates in transition economies have followed a declining trend since the onset of systemic transformation in the late 1980s (see Figure 2.6). In Russia saving rates have fallen to levels close to 20 percent.[2] The end of forced saving, declining income, higher expected future income, and stock adjustment of consumer durables are among the possible explanations behind lower saving during systemic transition. However,

[2] Seven Eastern European countries (Bulgaria, Czech Republic, Hungary, Poland, Romania, Slovakia, and Slovenia) and nine other FSU countries (Belarus, Estonia, Kazakhstan, Kyrgyzstan, Latvia, Lithuania, Turkmenistan, Ukraine, and Uzbekistan) are included in the unweighted regional averages depicted in Figure 2.4. The data are from the World Bank.

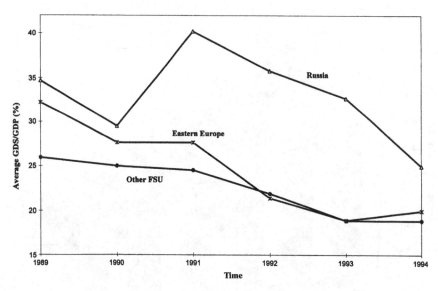

Figure 2.6. Saving rates in transition economies (gross domestic saving rate, unweighted averages, 1989–94).

the saving rates observed in 1993–94 in these countries appear remarkably high in comparison to the depressed saving ratios often observed in developing market economies undergoing deep recessions.

Long-Term Saving Rates and Income Levels Are
Positively Correlated across Countries

Let us now turn to the empirical association between the saving ratio and other key macroeconomic variables. We start with the relationship between saving and the level of development – as measured by real per capita GNP. A scatter plot for 1965–94 averages of these two variables and for three country groups (takeoff developing countries, other developing countries, OECD countries) is shown in Figure 2.7.[3] In the figure, countries appear clustered in rough correspondence to their development level, with the noted exception of the takeoff countries.

Saving rates tend to rise with per capita income: the correlation coefficient between the two variables for the nontransition world at large is .51 (significantly different from zero at the 5 percent level) and is somewhat lower in developing and in OECD countries separately (Table 2.1).

[3] Using per capita income at the initial year of the sample instead of its average value yields a very similar picture.

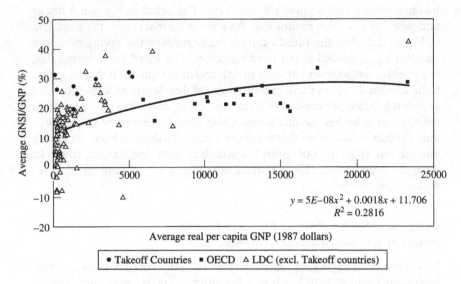

Figure 2.7. Long-term world saving and income levels (gross national saving rates including net current transfers and real per capita GNP, 1965–94 averages by countries).

Table 2.1. *Cross-country Correlation between Long-term Saving Rates and Other Variables (1965–94 Country Averages)*

Correlation Coefficient between the Gross National Saving Rate and the Following Variables:	World	OECD Countries	Developing Countries
Per capita real GNP level	0.51	0.41	0.47
Per capita real GNP growth rate	0.47	0.33	0.45
Gross domestic investment/GNP	0.42	0.55	0.40
Foreign aid/GNP[a]	—	—	−0.64

Note: The standard errors of the correlations (except that with foreign aid) are 0.09 for the world sample, 0.21 for the OECD subsample, and 0.10 for the developing country subsample. In the case of foreign aid, the standard error is 0.11.
[a] Calculated using 1970–93 averages.
Source: Calculations using World Bank data.

A number of multivariate cross-country studies of saving (e.g., Collins, 1991; Schmidt-Hebbel, Webb, and Corsetti, 1992; Carroll and Weil, 1994; Edwards, 1996; Masson, Bayoumi, and Samiei, 1995) have found a similar association.

However, Figure 2.7 also suggests that at high levels of per capita income, saving ratios appear to level off. The relationship is not linear and possibly not even monotonic. As a more formal check, the solid line in Figure 2.7 plots the fitted values from regressing the saving rate on a quadratic polynomial in per capita income.[4] The fitted curve shows that the positive association between saving and development indeed appears to be confined to lower and middle stages of development, ceases to hold at about $17,000 per capita GNP (in 1987 US$), and turns into a negative association at higher income levels. Cross-country empirical studies provide further evidence on this nonmonotonic relationship between saving and income (e.g., Sahota, 1993; Masson, Bayoumi, and Samiei, 1995). In Chapter 6 we revisit this empirical association in the context of time-series cross-section data.

Long-Term Saving Rates and Growth Rates Are
Positively Correlated across Countries

Low long-term saving and growth rates in many countries coexist with high saving and growth levels in a few others. The three country groups depicted in Figure 2.8 reflect distinct patterns. The takeoff countries exhibited relatively high saving and growth rates during 1965–94, while OECD economies showed comparable long-term saving rates but much lower growth rates. The remaining developing countries displayed a wide dispersion, but their average saving and growth record is much worse than that of the two preceding country groups. In summary, across market economies, long-term saving and growth rates are positively related. As Table 2.1 shows, their correlation coefficient is .47 (significantly different from zero at the 5 percent level) for the world at large, and somewhat higher in developing than in OECD countries.

The strong positive association between saving ratios and real per capita growth has been amply documented in cross-country empirical studies (see, e.g., Modigliani, 1970; Maddison, 1992; Bosworth, 1993; Carroll and Weil, 1994; Edwards, 1996; Masson, Bayoumi, and Samiei, 1995), and Chapter 6, this volume, contributes some additional evidence on the robustness of this link. However, its structural interpretation remains controversial, as it has been viewed both as proof that growth drives saving (e.g., Modigliani, 1970; Carroll and Weil, 1994) and that saving drives growth through the saving–investment link (e.g., Levine and Renelt, 1992; Mankiw, Romer, and Weil, 1992).

---

[4] The simple bivariate regressions reported here and in the next two figures are intended only for representing the cross-country association between saving and the corresponding variable and not for testing any causal relationship. The estimated regression coefficients (reported in the figures) are statistically significant at conventional levels.

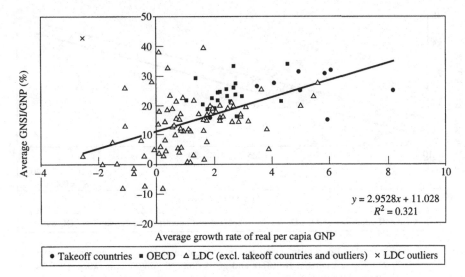

Figure 2.8. Long-term world saving and growth rates (gross national saving rates including net current transfers and real per capita GNP growth rates, 1965–94 averages by countries).

Long-Term Saving and Investment Ratios Are Strongly Positively Correlated across Countries

The robust association between long-term national saving rates and gross domestic investment is well known and also present in our data. In Figure 2.9, which plots these two variables, OECD and takeoff countries are clustered closely together, and in most cases located above the 45 degree line on the graph (along which average national saving and domestic investment rates are equal), reflecting the fact that they typically export capital to other LDCs – most of the latter are located below the 45 degree line. The correlation coefficient between the long-term national saving ratio and the gross domestic investment ratio is .42 for the (nontransition) world at large – in this case, larger in OECD countries than in LDCs (Table 2.1).

The saving–investment association was initially reported by Feldstein and Horioka (1980) and updated later by Feldstein and Baccheta (1991); using a sample of industrial countries, both studies find a saving–investment correlation coefficient close to .9. Other studies find a similarly strong (although somewhat smaller in magnitude) correlation for developing countries (e.g., Dooley, Frankel, and Mathieson, 1987; Summers, 1988). There has been considerable debate about whether this result is evidence of capital immobility. One view holds that even though barriers

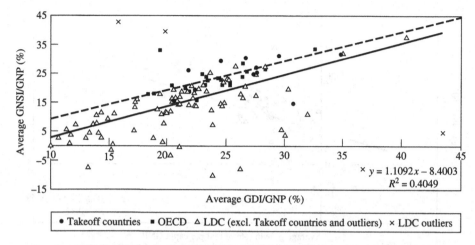

Figure 2.9. Long-term saving and investment rates (gross national saving rates including net current transfers and gross domestic investment ratios, 1965–94 averages by countries).

to capital mobility are low, asset owners keep capital at home because of political and currency risk (Feldstein, 1994) or, more generally, display home bias in their portfolio preferences (Tesar and Werner, 1992; Mussa and Goldstein, 1993). An alternative view is that the observed correlation between saving and investment says little about international capital mobility and is mainly the result of third factors that cause saving and investment to move jointly over the long term (for a recent overview, see Obstfeld, 1994). Obviously, the Feldstein-Horioka result is relevant also for the interpretation of the saving–growth correlation observed in the data: if (as seems plausible) investment is a major growth determinant, and saving and investment move closely together, then the saving–growth correlation could be mostly an indirect reflection of the covariation between investment and growth across countries.

Long-Term Saving and Foreign Aid Flows Are Negatively Correlated across Aid-Receiving Countries

The relationship between national saving and foreign resource inflows in general, and foreign aid in particular, has attracted considerable attention. Many empirical studies, starting with Chenery and Strout (1966), have attempted to establish whether foreign saving crowds national saving in or out, but no consensus has emerged. One major problem faced by this literature is of course the simultaneity between the two variables

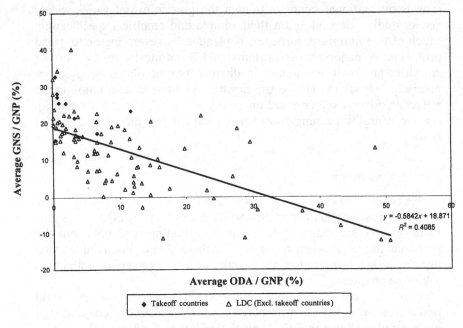

Figure 2.10. Long-term world saving rates and foreign aid (gross national saving rates including net current transfers and OECD ODA as percent age of GNP, 1970–93 averages).

under study, which can be ruled out only if domestic savers face binding borrowing constraints in world financial markets.

A related question is the association between national saving (defined as inclusive of foreign grants) and foreign aid (defined as grants plus concessional loans). Figure 2.10 plots saving rates against average foreign aid inflows, measured by the OECD's official development assistance, relative to GNP, for 99 aid-receiving developing countries. The averages are constructed for the years 1970–93, for which the aid data are available. The figure reveals an unambiguous negative association between both variables: the high-saving takeoff countries cluster at the upper left corner, and in general countries receiving higher aid inflows possess lower saving rates. The solid line in Figure 2.10 plots the fitted values from regressing the saving rate on foreign aid, confirming the negative relation between both variables. As Table 2.1 shows, the correlation between the two variables is $-.64$, significantly different from zero at the 5 percent level.

The saving–aid relation has also been examined by a number of empirical studies, starting with Griffin (1970). Most conclude that aid crowds out national saving, although the precise extent varies widely across studies, depending on their sample and empirical specification. Much of this literature, however, is plagued by severe methodological problems. A major one is causality: aid flows mostly to the poorest countries and/or to economies in distress, one of whose symptoms is precisely low saving. Hence the negative saving–aid association could reflect an adverse effect of aid on saving (as claimed by the aid critics), reverse causality running from low saving (or low income) to aid, or both.

Conclusions

In this chapter we have reviewed world patterns of national saving rates and their cross-country correlation with a number of key macroeconomic variables. We summarize briefly our main findings and point out the problems that arise when trying to give these simple empirical associations a causal interpretation, an issue that will be taken up in depth in the following chapters.

A negative correlation between the world saving rate and the world real interest rate has been observed since the 1970s. The conventional interpretation of this empirical association is that it reflects a contraction in world saving that exceeded a simultaneous contraction in desired investment levels. However, this correlation does not settle the ongoing controversy about the interest sensitivity of saving. The empirical literature tends not only to show that saving rates do not respond much to real interest rates, but also that intertemporal consumption substitution reacts little to interest rates. Chapter 4 examines the reasons behind these results and reviews at length the broader issue of the effects of financial and tax incentives on saving.

Saving rates show diverging patterns across world regions during the past 30 years, a feature that also characterizes two variables closely correlated with saving rates: investment and growth rates. While saving rates have fallen in many OECD and developing countries since 1974, the average OECD saving rate is still twice as large as the average saving rate in non-takeoff developing countries. Only 11 high-performing take-off developing countries – 8 of them located in East Asia – have been able to start and sustain a virtuous circle of high saving, investment, and growth levels.

A positive cross-country correlation is found between national saving rates and per capita income levels – but this association tends to level off at high income levels. Likewise, a strong positive association is observed between saving rates and per capita income growth rates. The literature offers contradictory causal interpretations of this correlation between saving and income growth. Chapter 3 reviews in detail the evidence and the theories that underlie this unsettled discussion on saving–growth links.

Saving and investment rates show a very robust positive correlation across countries. While various causal explanations are provided by the literature – ranging from low capital mobility to underlying common factors – the controversy is still far from being solved.

Finally, there is evidence of a strong negative association between foreign aid and national saving rates: countries that receive higher official development assistance tend to save significantly less. Here also a major issue is causality: the negative association could reflect either an adverse effect of aid on saving or the fact that poor and low-saving countries attract more aid, or both. Chapter 5 surveys the literature on this topic and analyzes the impact of foreign aid and, more generally, foreign resource inflows on saving and growth.

Methodological Appendix: Saving Data Bases, Their Shortcomings, and Improvements

> The distinction between current consumption and saving, or putting aside for the future, has been with us for ages. It was the basis for Joseph's solution to the seven lean years he foresaw (Gen. 41: 34–36) and for Aesop's fable of the ant and the grasshopper. Yet we still do not seem to have got it right, conceptually or empirically. (Lipsey and Tice, 1989, p. 1)

This appendix describes briefly the main existing international databases on saving and saving-related variables, summarizes their shortcomings, and proposes a method to adjust conventional saving measures for capital gains and losses that arise from inflation and real exchange rate devaluation.

A. *Brief Survey of Main Databases*

System-of-National-Accounts (SNA) data from national sources are maintained at various databases of international organizations. Four SNA databases are accessible through the World Bank's BESD database – those of the United Nations, IMF, OECD, and the World Bank itself, which differ in coverage (the UN's is the most detailed database) and reported values. Across countries there are major differences in the quality and coverage of data. In addition, accounting practices reflected in the historical databases differ from the revised standards set by the Inter-Secretariat Working Group on National Accounts (1993).

Government flow data at aggregate level are reported as part of the SNA data of the databases mentioned above. More disaggregate government data are reported in "Government Financial Statistics" (GFS) published by the IMF. The latter source publishes data for the central (and, in some cases, also general) government, relying on country sources that vary widely in accounting practices and data quality. Public investment levels are typically underestimated here and in the SNA data because much of investment by public corporations is excluded. Alternative databases that report corrected public-sector investment (as well as private investment) data are Pfeffermann and Madarassy (1993) and Easterly and Rebelo (1993), but they cover a smaller number of countries.

As an alternative to the limited public-sector coverage of the standard national-accounts and GFS data – limited to the central or general government – a recent research project at the World Bank has started to compile a data base for the consolidated nonfinancial public-sector deficit. Using data from country sources, these data consolidate general-government deficit measures with those of the nonfinancial public-enterprise sector for 58 developing and OECD countries during the 1970–90 period (Easterly and Schmidt-Hebbel, 1994, Table A1).

External debt, disaggregated by public and private, are put together by the World Bank's annual "World Debt Tables." For public domestic debt stocks there is no systematic database for developing countries, but time series exist for individual countries in specialized country publications.

Time-series data on various rates of interest (bank deposit and loan rates, discount rates, money market rates, treasury bill rates, and government bond yields, by maturities) are compiled in the IMF's "International Financial Statistics." The International Finance Corporation (IFC) compiles a database of stock market price indices and yields for a sample of emerging markets.

Other data on standard saving or consumption determinants – including variables on demography, income distribution, financial-sector structure – are gathered and/or published by the UN, the World Bank, and the Bank of International Settlements (BIS).

B. *Inadequacies of Existing Aggregate Data and Their Use in Empirical Studies*

Existing data and their use in applied research are affected by a host of inadequacies. As a result, the data used by applied researchers suffer from inadequacies, inconsistencies, and biases that undoubtedly have affected the quality of existing empirical work. Many of these problems have been identified in the sections on data discussion in Visaria (1980), Berry (1985), Fry (1988), Gersovitz (1988), Deaton (1989), Srinivasan (1993, 1994), OECD (1994), Schmidt-Hebbel, Servén, and Solimano

(1996), and in the NBER volume on the measurement of saving, investment, and wealth edited by Lipsey and Tice (1989).

We next summarize 18 major problems that affect income, consumption, saving, and related flow variables, and 3 problems that affect rates of interest and return. Some of these difficulties reflect conceptual shortcomings (because of the gap between theoretical concepts and their empirical counterparts), others are due to inadequate measurement efforts, and a few reflect inadequate use of existing data by applied researchers.

Problems of Income, Investment, and Consumption Data

(i) Income Exclusion. Much of income and production is excluded from SNA data, in particular that of informal and illegal sectors, (subsistence) agriculture, and households. The omission of noncash (more generally, nonrecorded) components from both income and consumption overstates saving and investment ratios but not their levels, while the omission of noncash investment from income understates both saving and investment ratios but not their levels.

(ii) Unrecorded Capital Flight. This particular form of income exclusion (involving underreporting of net exports) implies an overestimation of external saving. It implies either an underestimation of gross domestic saving or an overestimation of gross domestic investment.

(iii) International Comparability of Income Levels (As Corrected by Summers and Heston). Due to the lack of an international currency, income and consumption measures are only comparable across time within any given country. Summers and Heston (1990) denominated income and several expenditure categories in a common set of prices in a common currency, using the purchasing-power-adjusted conversion factors. The publicly available Summers and Heston database makes possible the comparison of income levels across countries and over time. However, it is also believed that the uniform valuation of national accounts ignores the systematic differences in the price structures of economies at different development stages, therefore narrowing excessively the income distances between richer and poorer countries. The purchasing-power-adjusted conversion factors are believed to include observed prices without adjustments for the large differences in product quality across countries. The gaps in the Summers-Heston coverage, quality, and timeliness of the basic survey data used in the calculation of conversion factors are also a major concern.

(iv) Misclassification of Consumer Durables. Saving and investment are undermeasured because purchases of consumer durables are

misrecorded as consumption instead of investment. Theory suggests that a more adequate consumption measure should be based on the flow of services of currently owned consumer durables and, possibly, part of the services rendered by human capital. Reclassifying private consumer durable spending as investment could raise saving ratios by 2–8 percentage points of GDP in OECD countries (OECD, 1994).

(v) Misclassification of Spending on Human Capital. Saving and investment are undermeasured because expenditure on human-capital formation (education, health, training) is misrecorded as consumption or intermediate production instead of investment. For instance, reclassification of all education expenditures would raise saving ratios in OECD countries by 4–5 percentage points of GDP (OECD, 1994). However, the difficulty in making this adjustment – and similar adjustments for health and training spending – is to identify the true investment and consumption shares of each of these spending categories.

(vi) Misclassification of Spending on Research and Development (R&D). Saving and investment are undermeasured because expenditure on R&D is misrecorded as intermediate production instead of investment. For instance, reclassification of all R&D expenditure as investment would raise saving ratios in OECD countries by 1–2 percentage points of GDP (OECD, 1994).

Problems of Investment Data

(vii) Estimation of Aggregate and Sector Investment. Gross domestic investment (GDI) is often obtained as the additions to overall capital by capital categories: machinery and equipment, construction, and inventories. Gross investment in the public and private corporate sectors are independently estimated based on their reported accounts. However, public investment is typically underestimated by excluding all or significant parts of investment undertaken by decentralized public corporations, in particular those projects not financed with central or general government funds. Gross investment of the rest of the economy (households and unincorporated business) is a residual between GDI and corporate-sector investment.

(viii) Measurement of Depreciation of Physical Assets. Depreciation of physical capital is subtracted from gross investment (and gross saving) to obtain net investment (and net saving). The world-wide average depreciation ratio is roughly 10 percent of GDP but shows significant country variation. Unfortunately, part of country differences are due to varying depreciation methods. Depreciation measures based on account-

ing principles (that vary across countries) often bear little resemblance to economic depreciation concepts. In addition, the distinction between inputs and capital goods in production sectors is often arbitrary.

(ix) Misrecording of Maintenance Expenditures on Public Capital. Maintenance of public-sector capital is typically misrecorded as recurrent expenditure, that is, government consumption. In the United States both public recurrent maintenance and public investment expenditures are misclassified as current spending.

(x) Measurement of Environmental Resources and Misclassification of Gross Output. Conventional national-accounts measures do not account for the depletion of environmental capital and hence overestimate true investment and output and income measures. While comprehensive SNA methods are being started in many OECD and some developing countries, no historical corrected time series are available for most developing countries.

(xi) Capital Heterogeneity. Intertemporal comparison of investment data is difficult because it involves comparing capital goods of different vintages and quality. This applies also to consumption, particularly durables (Berndt and Triplett, 1990). In the spatial dimension it is difficult to compare and aggregate investment from different sectors of origin because of capital heterogeneity.

Problems of Consumption Data

(xii) Varying Methods in Computing Private Consumption. SNA estimates of public consumption of central and local governments are obtained from government sources. SNA estimates of private final consumption are based on three methods: (a) the expenditure method is based on direct information from household budget or expenditure surveys, (b) the commodity-flow method is based on direct information for prices and quantities of consumer goods, and (c) the residual approach obtains private consumption as the residual balancing item of the income–expenditure identity.

A combination of the first and second approaches is the most satisfactory as it is based on direct household information, supplemented by production and foreign-trade information to allow for consistency checks. The third approach is the least satisfactory because private consumption reflects the measurement errors and biases in estimating output and all other expenditure variables.

Countries are divided in applying the three methods to compute private consumption expenditure in their SNA data as compiled by the

UN. OECD countries typically rely on a combination of the first and second methods, while the residual method is applied by a large number of African and Latin American countries.

Problems of Saving Data

(xiii) Computation of Saving as a Residual: Inconsistencies between Current and Capital-Account Saving Measures. When private consumption is not obtained as a residual (i.e., not based on method (c) above), private (and national) saving is still measured as the residual difference between private (and national) income and consumption. Then saving reflects the measurement errors and biases of income and all expenditure variables. In addition, this current-account measure of saving is conceptually different from the capital-account measure of saving. The latter computes saving as the change in net wealth derived from flow-of-funds accounts (FFA) of each sector. Consumption theory is based on income and saving measures being consistent with net wealth changes, that is, saving consistent with FFAs. Changes in net wealth differ conceptually from current-account saving by both net capital gains on asset and liability holdings resulting from revaluations (see point (xv) below) and capital transfers. Statistical differences between current- and capital-account saving measures are due to net capital gains and measurement errors in both current and capital accounts. Empirical differences between the saving measures derived from the two accounts are often large and sometimes huge, even in OECD countries (Lipsey and Tice, 1989).

The conceptual consolidation of current-account and capital-account (or FFA) measures of saving is straightforward (see, e.g., Host-Madsen, 1979; Holloway, 1989; Lipsey and Tice, 1989; Wilson et al., 1989; Inter-Secretariat Working Group, 1993). FFA measures of saving and their integration into national accounts are pursued in many OECD countries. For the United States in particular, there is a long literature on saving measures from both methods and their differences (see, e.g., Boskin, Robinson, and Huber, 1989; Hendershott and Peek, 1989; Holloway, 1989; and Wilson et al., 1989).

Few developing countries have pursued comparison and reconciliation of saving measures from the two methods, due to the absence of systematically constructed FFAs and their integration into national accounts. FFAs impose significant data requirements and costs, including detailed information on balance sheets of households, nonfinancial corporations, financial corporations, general government, and the rest of the world (the five sectors considered by the SNA). Reynolds and Camard (1989) compare saving measures from both methods for 5 Latin American countries, concluding that current-account measures typically underestimate FFA measures of saving. Unfortunately only 1 of the 5 countries – Colombia – continues to integrate its FFA into its national-accounts estimates (at both aggregate and sector levels, including households and corporations), and hence is the only Latin American country with continuous integrated saving measures from 1970 to date. A paper by Honohan and Attiyas (1989) presents saving data for 20 developing countries based on FFAs, but the data on both the capital and financial accounts was available for only 8 countries (for additional discussion, see the appendix of chapter 4 in this volume).

(xiv) Computation of Saving as a Double Residual from the Current Account. When private consumption is obtained as a residual (method (c) in point (xii)), private (and national) saving is the ultimate, double residual and reflects all inaccuracies incurred in estimating income and expenditure.

(xv) Exclusion of Net Capital Gains from Current-Account Saving. As noted in point (xii), one of the differences between current- and capital-account estimates of saving is due to the omission of revaluations from the former. Below we derive a simple reconciliation of current- and capital-account saving measures by focusing on one important conceptual difference: net capital gains from revaluations of assets and liabilities due to inflation and changes in the real exchange rate. Other sources of capital gains – such as changes in relative prices of equity and housing – are not considered in the analysis because of the lack of systematic data to engage in these corrections.

(xvi) Exclusion of Changes in Contingent and Implicit Sector Liabilities from Saving Measures. Current-account measures of sector saving typically exclude – as FFA measures of sector saving often do – changes in implicit and in contingent sector liabilities, including pension rights issued by the government to households (through state-managed and typically pay-as-you-go pension systems) and government guarantees issued by the government to private institutions (such as loan guarantees and deposit insurance). Within the OECD, only for the United States are there consistent time series of sector saving and net worth levels that include household pension wealth (see Hendershott and Peek, 1989; Holloway, 1989; McDermed, Clark, and Allen, 1989; Wilson et al., 1989). For developing countries no time series for private net worth and saving are available that comprise contingent and implicit public liabilities such as pension rights.

(xvii) Mismeasurement of Sector Income and Saving Data Due to Inadequate Public Sector Coverage. Public and private saving and disposable income measures are distorted when they are based on a too narrow coverage of the public sector. The bias stemming from using

general government (or, worse, central government) data is particularly significant in countries where large amounts of current- and capital-account transactions occur between nonfinancial and financial public enterprises (including the central bank), on the one hand, and the domestic private or external sectors, on the other. Examples of such transactions include loans by private domestic or foreign banks to public enterprises and subsidies to and bailouts of domestic private firms and households by the central bank.

(xviii) Inadequate Use of Income and Saving Data. A large number of empirical saving studies are based on inadequate saving data. They rely on aggregate measures of saving – ranging from gross domestic to national to private-sector saving – when the relevant decision unit is the household or the individual. The problem of using a too aggregated saving measure is that it assumes that households offset exactly any (permanent) change in government and/or corporate saving by a change in household saving in the opposite direction and the same magnitude. However, such a perfect offsetting can only occur in a world of perfect Ricardian equivalence (for public-household saving offsets) and perfect household piercing of the corporate veil (for corporate-household offsets), which requires empirically implausible assumptions regarding capital-market efficiency and interdependence of current and future generations. Hence, a wider use of more disaggregate saving data, particularly for households, would be much more adequate.

Problems of Data on Rates of Interest and Return

Most consumption and saving studies rely on interest rates paid on short-term deposits in banking institutions as the rate of return relevant for saving decisions. Exclusive reliance on these rates is inappropriate due to the following reasons.

(i) Official Deposit Rates Are Not Relevant under Financial Repression. When interest rates are fixed by governments – a feature that was widespread in developing countries during much of the historical 1960–94 period – they are almost irrelevant as a measure of the alternative cost of consumption. Better proxies for the latter include (typically unrecorded) interest rates charged in unofficial financial markets, (typically unrecorded) rates of return on investment, or the rates on foreign deposits corrected for the expected rate of exchange rate depreciation.

(ii) Deposit Rates Are Not Relevant for Marginal Saving Decisions. When consumers face an array of financial savings alterna-

tives, deposits are only one of the choices. Hence, rates of return on alternative instruments – including government and private bonds, onshore or offshore foreign-currency deposits, and stock market returns – or a weighted average of the relevant returns are better measures of the intertemporal cost of consumption.

(iii) Gross Rates of Return Are Not Relevant for Marginal Saving Decisions. Few studies use net rates of return (gross rates minus relevant marginal capital income taxes). But changes in marginal tax rates – due to changes in legislation or enforcement of tax compliance – are frequent and hence the use of gross rates introduces a potentially serious measurement bias when estimating marginal saving decisions.

C. *Correction of Saving Measures for Capital Gains and Losses for Inflation and Real Exchange Rate Devaluation*

Revaluation of private (and household) net assets is one of the conceptual differences between flow-of-funds accounts and current-account measures of saving (see points (xiii) and (xv)). The simple accounting framework developed next identifies three major categories of financial assets (domestic currency, domestic public debt held by the private sector, and net foreign debt issued by both public and private sectors). As shown below, adjusted private saving (and adjusted private disposable income) levels can be derived as the sum of conventional saving (and conventional disposable income) from the current account and net capital gains from inflation and real exchange rate depreciation (equations (7) and (9)). Similar expressions can be derived for adjusted public and external saving levels.

Starting from the basic income–expenditure equation in current prices, the sum of private, public, and foreign gross saving (in parentheses) is equal to the sum of private and public gross domestic investment:

$$
\left(Y_p - C_p\right) + \left(TA - TR - iB_{-1} - E\,i^*\,F^*_{g,-1}\right)
$$
$$
+ \left(-NX - E\,TR^* + E\,i^*\,F^*_{p,-1} + E\,i^*\,F^*_{g,-1} + E\,ONFP^*\right) = I_p + I_g,
$$

$$(1)$$

where Y_p is private disposable income, C_p is private disposable income, TA is taxes paid by the private sector, TR is net transfers received by the private from the public sector, i is the nominal interest rate paid on public domestic debt B held by the private sector, E is the nominal exchange rate, i^* is the foreign interest rate paid on foreign debt, F^* is the net foreign debt of the public sector, NX is net exports, TR^* is net transfers from the foreign to the domestic private sector, $ONFP$ is other (noninterest) factor payments from the private to the foreign sector, and I is gross investment. Superscript * denotes foreign-currency values, and subscripts $_p$, $_g$, and $_{-1}$ denote the private sector, the public sector, and the preceding period, respectively. All stocks refer to the end of the corresponding period. Price variables, however, are average-period variables consistent with flow variables.[5]

Consistent with equation (1), private disposable income is defined as:

$$Y_p = Y + iB_{-1} + TR + E\,TR^* - TA - E\,i^*\,F^*_{p,-1} - E\,ONFP^*, \qquad (2)$$

where Y is GDP.

Gross private saving is equal to the net (cash) accumulation of private assets, and the latter is equal to the increase in private-sector wealth minus net capital gains:

$$S_p \equiv Y_p - C_p = (B - B_{-1}) - E(F^*_p - F^*_{p,-1}) + (H - H_{-1})$$
$$\equiv P\,\Delta w_p - P\,ncg_p, \qquad (3)$$

where H is domestic base money held by the private sector, P is the private consumption deflator, w_p is real net private wealth, and ncg_p is real net capital gains of the private sector. Symbol Δ denotes the change per period of a stock variable.

Real net private wealth – the ratio of current-price net private wealth and the private consumption deflator – is defined by its components as:

$$w_p \equiv b - f^*_p + h \qquad (4)$$

Real net capital gains of the private sector – the ratio of current-price net capital gains of the private sector and the private consumption deflator – is defined as:

$$-ncg_p \equiv \left(\frac{\pi}{1+\pi}\right)b_{-1} - \left(\frac{\pi^* - \varepsilon}{1+\pi^*}\right)f^*_{p,-1} + \left(\frac{\pi}{1+\pi}\right)h_{-1}, \qquad (5)$$

where lowercase letters denote constant-price flows or stocks in domestic currency units (e.g., $f_{-1} \equiv (E_{-1}/P_{-1})\,F^*_{-1}$), and Greek letters denote rate of change of prices as follows: π is $(P - P_{-1})/P_{-1}$, π^* is $(P^* - P^*_{-1})/P^*_{-1}$, and ε is $(EP^*/P - E_{-1}\,P^*_{-1}/P_{-1})/(E_{-1}P^*_{-1}/P_{-1})$.

Note that similar equations for saving, wealth, and net capital gains can be derived for the public and foreign sectors.

Substituting Fisher equations for domestic and foreign interest rates and after simple transformation, substitution of equation (2) into (3) yields the following equation for private gross saving:

---

[5] A more complete derivation would distinguish between average-period price variables for flow variables and end-of-period price variables relevant for stock variables, as in Khadr and Schmidt-Hebbel (1989).

$$S_p \equiv P_y\, y + TR + E\, TR^* - TA - E\, ONFP^* - P\, c_p$$

$$+ P\left[r + \frac{\pi}{1+\pi}\right]b_{-1} - P\left[r^* + \frac{\pi}{1+\pi^*}\right](1+\varepsilon)f^*_{p,-1}$$

$$= P(b - b_{-1}) - P(f^*_p - f^*_{p,-1}) + P(h - h_{-1})$$

$$+ P\left(\frac{\pi}{1+\pi}\right)b_{-1} - P\left(\frac{\pi^* - \varepsilon}{1+\pi^*}\right)f^*_{p,-1} + P\left(\frac{\pi}{1+\pi}\right)h_{-1}, \qquad (6)$$

where P_y is the GDP deflator and y is real GDP. Dividing equation (5) by P allows obtaining "real" gross private saving defined as current-price gross private saving deflated by the private consumption deflator.

Adding private net capital gains (equation (5)) to private saving (equation (6)) yields adjusted gross saving, that is, a measure of saving that is consistent with wealth accumulation of the private sector:

$$S^A_p \equiv P_y\, y + TR + E\, TR^* - TA - E\, ONFP^* - P\, c_p$$

$$+ P\, r\, b_{-1} - P\left[r^*(1+\varepsilon) + \varepsilon\right]f^*_{p,-1} - P\left(\frac{\pi}{1+\pi}\right)h_{-1}$$

$$= P(b - b_{-1}) - P(f^*_p - f^*_{p,-1}) + P(h - h_{-1}), \qquad (7)$$

where superscript ^{A} denotes adjusted flows.

Similarly, adding net capital gains to private disposable income yields Y^A_p, the adjusted measure of Y_p.

Summarizing:

$$S^A_p - S_p \equiv Y^A_p - Y_p \equiv NCG_p \qquad (8)$$

A constant-price measure of adjusted private disposable income is:

$$y^A_p \equiv \frac{P_y}{P}\, y + \frac{TR}{P} + \frac{E}{P}\, TR^* - \frac{TA}{P} - \frac{E}{P}\, ONFP^*$$

$$+ r\, b_{-1} - \left[r^*(1+\varepsilon) + \varepsilon\right]f^*_{p,-1} - \left(\frac{\pi}{1+\pi}\right)h_{-1} \qquad (9)$$

Similar expressions can be derived for adjusted saving and adjusted disposable income (in constant and current prices) for the public and external sectors.

References

Berndt, E., and J. Triplett (eds.) 1990. Fifty Years of Economic Measurement: The Jubilee of the Conference on Research in Income and Wealth. *National Bureau of Economic Research Studies in Income and Wealth*, vol. 54, Chicago: University of Chicago Press.

Berry, A. 1985. "On Trends in the Gap between Rich and Poor in Less Devel-

30   Klaus Schmidt-Hebbel and Luis Servén

oped Countries: Why We Know So Little," *Review of Income and Wealth* 31: 337–54.

Boskin, M. J., M. S. Robinson, and A. M. Huber. 1989. "Government Saving, Capital Formation, and Wealth in the United States, 1947–85," in R. E. Lipsey and H. S. Tice: op.cit.

Bosworth, B. 1993. *Saving and Investment in a Global Economy.* The Brookings Institution. Washington, D.C.

Carroll, C., and D. Weil. 1994. "Saving and Growth: A Reinterpretation," *Carnegie-Rochester Conference Series on Public Policy* 40: 133–92, North Holland.

Chenery, H., and A. Strout. 1966. "Foreign Assistance and Economic Development," *American Economic Review* 56: 679–733.

Collins, S. M. 1991. "Saving Behavior in Ten Developing Countries," in B. D. Douglas and J. B. Shoven (eds.): *National Saving and Economic Performance*, National Bureau of Economic Research and University of Chicago Press.

Corbo, V., and K. Schmidt-Hebbel. 1991. "Public Policies and Saving in Developing Countries," *Journal of Development Economics* 36: 89–115.

Deaton, A. 1989. "Saving in Developing Countries: Theory and Review," *Proceedings of the World Bank Annual Conference on Development Economics* 1: 61–96.

Deaton, A. 1992. *Understanding Consumption*, Oxford: Clarendon Press.

Dooley, M., J. Frankel, and D. J. Mathieson. 1987. "International Capital Mobility: What Do Saving–Investment Correlations Tell Us?" *IMF Staff Papers* 34: 503–30.

Easterly, W., and S. Rebelo. 1993. "Fiscal Policy and Economic Growth: An Empirical Investigation," *Journal of Monetary Economics* 32: 417–58.

Easterly, W., and K. Schmidt-Hebbel. 1994. Statistical Appendix, in W. Easterly, C. A. Rodríguez, and K. Schmidt-Hebbel (eds.): *Public Sector Deficits and Macroeconomic Performance*, Oxford University Press.

Edwards, S. 1995. "Why Are Latin America's Saving Rates So Low? An International Comparative Analysis," *Journal of Development Economics* 51(1): 5–44.

Feldstein, M. 1994. "Tax Policy and International Capital Flows," *NBER Working Paper* No. 4851.

Feldstein, M., and P. Bacchetta. 1991. "National Saving and International Investment," in B. Douglas Bernheim and J. Shoven (eds.): *National Saving and Economic Performance.* University of Chicago Press.

Feldstein, M., and C. Horioka. 1980. "Domestic Savings and International Capital Flows," *Economic Journal* 90: 314–29.

Fry, M. 1988. *Money, Interest, and Banking in Economic Development.* Johns Hopkins University, Baltimore, Maryland.

Gersovitz, M. 1988. "Saving and Development," in H. Chenery and T. N. Srinivasan (eds.): *Handbook of Development Economics*, North Holland.

Giovannini, A. 1983. "The Interest Elasticity of Savings in Developing Countries: The Existing Evidence." *World Development* 11(7): 601–7.

Giovannini, A. 1985. "Saving and the Rate of Interest in LDCs," *Journal of Development Economics* 18: 197–217.

Griffin, K. 1970. "Foreign Capital, Domestic Savings, and Economic Development," *Bulletin of the Institute of Economics and Statistics (Oxford University)* 32: 99–112.

Group of Ten. 1995. "Saving, Investment, and Real Interest Rates," Group of Deputies, October 1995.

Hendershott, P. H., and J. Peek. 1989. "Aggregate U.S. Private Saving: Conceptual Measures," in R. E. Lipsey and H. S. Tice: op.cit.

Holloway, T. M. 1989. "Present NIPA Saving Measures: Their Characteristics and Limitations," in R. E. Lipsey and H. S. Tice: op.cit.

Honohan, P., and I. Attiyas. 1989. "Intersectoral Financial Flows in Developing Countries." Policy Research Working Paper 164. The World Bank.

Host-Madsen, P. 1979. "Macroeconomic Accounts: An Overview," *IMF Pamphlet Series* No. 29, Washington, D.C.

IMF. 1995. *World Economic Outlook 1995.* International Monetary Fund. Washington, D.C.

Inter-Secretariat Working Group on National Accounts. 1993. *System of National Accounts 1993.* Brussels.

Khadr, A., and K. Schmidt-Hebbel. 1989. "A Method for Macroeconomic Consistency in Current and Constant Prices," *PRD Working Paper* No. 306. The World Bank, Washington, DC.

Levine, R., and D. Renelt. 1992. "A Sensitivity Analysis of Cross-Country Growth Regressions," *American Economic Review* 82: 942–63.

Lipsey, R. E., and H. S. Tice (eds.). 1989. *The Measurement of Saving, Investment, and Wealth,* NBER Studies in Income and Wealth, vol. 52. NBER, Washington, DC.

Maddison, A. 1992. "A Long-Run Perspective on Saving," *Scandinavian Journal of Economics* 94: 181–96.

Mankiw, N. G., D. Romer, and D. N. Weil. 1992. "A Contribution to the Empirics of Economic Growth," *Quarterly Journal of Economics* 107: 407–37.

Masson, P., T. Bayoumi, and H. Samiei. 1995. "Saving Behavior in Industrial and Developing Countries," in *Staff Studies for the World Economic Outlook,* Washington, D.C.

McDermed, A., R. L. Clark, and S. G. Allen. 1989. "Pension Wealth, Age-Wealth Profiles and the Distribution of Net Worth," in R. E. Lipsey and H. S. Tice: op.cit.

Modigliani, F. 1970. "The Life-Cycle Hypothesis of Saving and Intercountry Differences in the Saving Ratio," in W. A. Eltis, M. F. G. Scott, and J. N. Wolfe, (eds.): *Induction, Trade, and Growth: Essays in Honour of Sir Roy Harrod,* Oxford: Clarendon Press, 197–225.

Mussa, M., and M. Goldstein. 1993. "The Integration of World Capital Markets," International Monetary Fund Working Paper No. 93/95. International Monetary Fund, Washington, DC.

Obstfeld, M. 1994. "International Capital Mobility in the 1990s," in *Understanding Independence: The Macroeconomics of the Open Economy,* Princeton Unversity Press.

OECD. 1994. "Taxation and Household Savings." Paris: Organization for Economic Cooperation and Development.

Pfeffermann, G., and A. Madarassy. 1993. "Trends in Private Investment in Developing Countries," *IFC Discussion Papers* No. 16, Washington, DC.

Reynolds, C. W., and W. Camard. 1989. "Flow-of-Funds and National Income and Product Account Savings Estimates in Latin America," in R. E. Lipsey and H. S. Tice: op.cit.

Sahota, G. 1993. "Saving and Distribution," in J. H. Gapinski (ed.): *The Economics of Saving.* Boston: Kluwer Academic Publishers, 193–231.

Schmidt-Hebbel, K., L. Servén, and A. Solimano. 1996. "Saving and Investment: Paradigms, Puzzles, Policies," *World Bank Research Observer* 11(1): 87–117.

32   **Klaus Schmidt-Hebbel and Luis Servén**

Schmidt-Hebbel, K., S. B. Webb, and G. Corsetti. 1992. "Household Saving in Developing Countries: First Cross-Country Evidence," *The World Bank Economic Review* 6: 529–47.

Srinivasan, T. N. 1993. "Saving in the Development Process," in J. H. Gapinski (ed.): *The Economics of Saving*, Kluwer Academic Publishers, Boston.

Srinivasan, T. N. 1994. "Data Base for Development Analysis: An Overview," *Journal of Development Economics* 44: 3–27.

Summers, L. 1988. "Tax Policy and International Competitiveness," in J. Frenkel (ed.): *International Aspects of Fiscal Policies*, Chicago: University of Chicago Press.

Summers, R., and A. Heston. 1991. "The Penn World Table (Mark 5): An Expanded Set of International Comparisons, 1950–1988," *Quarterly Journal of Economics* 106(2): 327–68.

Tesar, L., and I. Werner. 1992. "Home Bias and the Globalization of Securities Market." *NBER* Working Paper 4218. National Bureau of Economic Research, Cambridge, MA.

Visaria, P. 1980. "Poverty and Living Standards in Asia: An Overview of the Main Results and Lessons of Selected Household Surveys," *Living Standards Measurement Study Working Paper* 2, The World Bank.

Wilson, J. F., J. L. Freund, F. O. Yohn, and W. Lederer. 1989. "Measuring Household Saving: Recent Experience from the Flow-of-Funds Perspective," in R. E. Lipsey and H. S. Tice: op.cit.

CHAPTER 3

Saving and Growth

Angus Deaton

Introduction

Few economists would attribute the differences in growth rates between Asia and Africa to the optimal workings of the invisible hand, and most would favor policies that would raise African growth rates. Even in the absence of distortionary policies and even abstracting from skepticism that consumers make adequate intertemporal decisions, most governments and policy makers appear to regard growth as a good thing per se. A necessary (but certainly not sufficient) condition for growth is investment, in machines, in people, or in both. In a closed economy, these investments can come only from postponing consumption, that is from saving. In an international economy, investment in one country can be supported by saving elsewhere in the world, but as a matter of fact, there is a very high correlation between national investment and national saving at least when both are defined to exclude education (for recent assessments, see Feldstein and Horioka, 1980; Feldstein and Bacchetta, 1991; and Bosworth, 1993). Indeed, Feldstein and Bacchetta (1991) conclude that "an increase in national saving has a substantial effect on the level of investment" (p. 218). If so, it is a short step to the conclusion that saving drives growth, and that the appropriate policies for growth are those that promote saving.

That such a conclusion is logically coherent must be checked using a formal growth model, but as we shall see in the next section, the task is readily accomplished. Furthermore, the empirical evidence using cross-country regressions based on the Penn World Table (and other international data) show a significant positive and robust relationship across countries between saving rates and growth, whether interpreted as the effects of investment on growth (e.g., Levine and Renelt, 1992; and Mankiw, Romer, and Weil, 1992) or as growth driving saving (many studies since Modigliani, 1970). Of course, neither these studies nor the investment to growth argument have any bearing on whether it is saving that causes growth, growth that causes saving, or both simultaneously, the last itself an attractive option since it suggests the possibility of multiple growth – saving equilibria. The causation is important, not just for understanding the process, but for the design of policy. If saving is merely the passive adjunct to growth or investment, then policies for growth should presumably be directed at investment (in people, plant, or equipment) or at the efficiency of such investment, with saving allowed to look after itself. But if saving is the prime mover, the focus would shift to the effects of saving incentives, such as tax breaks or special instruments like IRAs, compulsory saving in (fully funded) employee provident funds, as in Malaysia, Singapore, and Chile, to the design of social security systems, or to the role of financial intermediation in general, improvements in which are variously argued both to increase and to decrease saving.

This chapter reviews the evidence on growth and saving, considering various models in turn and summarizing the extent to which they appear to be consistent with the facts. These reviews are necessarily brief, and apart from the first two sections, I focus on models of household behavior that still have the most promise for helping us understand the process of saving and growth. The first section is a brief review of how we might interpret the world in terms of a saving to growth story. The second covers "plain vanilla" versions of the life-cycle and permanent income hypotheses, their implications for the relationship between saving and growth, and the evidence that shows they are not very useful for thinking about the saving and growth process in economic development. I then go on to discuss various modifications of these models, all consistent with intertemporal choice in general, but emphasizing various features that are given short shrift in the standard models. I also give brief attention to "classical," or post-Keynesian, models of saving and development. I then discuss in turn precautionary and liquidity constraint models, how such models can generate "two classes" of consumers (nonsavers and accumulators), and how restrictions on loans for house purchase might affect saving, bequests, and habits. I believe that all of these topics show promise for future research, and in a concluding section I summarize research directions for the future. In particular, I argue that attention should also be given to international comparisons of *micro*economic data on consumption and income. In many cases, the latter are more readily available, especially for the high-saving Asian countries. Recent research has shown that such data can yield important insight into intertemporal behavior in a way that does not require accurate measurement of saving, something that has been the stumbling block for many previous studies of saving in developing countries. Such data are sometimes better than time-series data for distinguishing various hypotheses, and they avoid many of the econometric difficulties that beset international comparisons using aggregate time-series data, such as the Penn World Tables.

From Saving to Growth: Growth Models

The relationship between saving and growth is often taken as axiomatic in the development literature, essentially for the reasons given in the opening paragraph of the introduction. If the capital–output ratio v is fixed, the rate of growth of output g is equal to the rate of growth of capital, so that as a matter of accounting, the rate of growth is equal to the ratio of the share of investment in output to the capital–output ratio, or $g = s/v$, where s is the saving rate, taken to be equal to the share of investment in output, as must be the case in a closed economy. Higher saving means higher growth, at least if there are no constraints in the labor market. Or perhaps better, higher *investment* leads to higher growth, with the saving rate automatically equilibrating to investment as in simple Keynesian models. The early Harrod-Domar growth models ran along these lines, and have never been entirely supplanted in the development literature, much less in the minds of practitioners and policy makers.

In Solow's (1956) neoclassical growth model, output comes from a linear homogeneous and concave production function of capital and labor, and the growth rate of the latter is given by an exogenous rate of population growth n. The share of saving in output, s, is also fixed. The system then satisfies two equations: the production function making output per head y a concave function of capital per head k,

$$y = f(k), \tag{1}$$

and the saving–investment identity, which takes the form

$$\dot{k} = sy - (n + \delta)k, \tag{2}$$

where δ is the rate at which the capital stock physically depreciates. Equations (1) and (2) have a unique (and stable) equilibrium solution for output per head and capital per head, y_0 and k_0, say. The steady state growth rate of total output is given, essentially by assumption, at the rate of population growth n, and the capital–output ratio v adjusts to equal the ratio $s/(n + \delta)$. Increases in the saving rate increase the capital–output ratio, raise output and capital per head, but cannot change the steady state rate of growth.

Output per head in this model increases only through technical progress, most simply modeled as Harrod-neutral or labor augmenting, by which the labor force grows in efficiency units at a rate $n + \gamma$, permitting output per *actual* unit of labor to increase at rate γ. Although

Solow's model takes the saving rate as fixed, in apparent contradistinction to the models of saving behavior with which I am going to deal below, it is readily converted into an optimal growth model. See Cass (1965) and Koopmans (1965), in which the forces of thrift are captured, not by an assumed exogenous saving rate, but by the rate of time preference and the intertemporal elasticity of substitution.

One interpretation of the Solow model is that saving does *not* cause growth, at least not in long-run equilibrium. Indeed, the understanding of this fact, and the associated dismissal of the simplistic saving to growth argument as a vulgar fallacy, was for many years a good test of a properly educated economist (although the test would have been failed by many successful finance ministers). However, it was also recognized that an increase in the saving rate would increase the rate of growth *temporarily* as output per head moved from the old equilibrium to the new higher one, and that the transition could be a very long one (for some early calculations, see Atkinson, 1969). One way of making the point and of leading into the recent work is to examine the dynamics by linearization around the equilibrium. If we approximate equation (2) around the equilibrium capital stock k_0, we reach

$$\dot{k} = -(n+\delta)(1-\alpha)(k-k_0), \tag{3}$$

where α is the elasticity of output per head with respect to capital per head at k_0, a quantity that is the (constant) exponent of capital if the production function is Cobb–Douglas. The solution to equation (3) is that k approaches k_0 exponentially, so that

$$k = k_0 + \theta\exp[-(1-\alpha)(n+\delta)t], \tag{4}$$

where θ reflects initial conditions. Output per head will approach its equilibrium in the same way (see also Mankiw, Romer, and Weil, 1992).

According to equations (3) and (4), the speed at which the system regains its equilibrium is inversely related to the elasticity of output with respect to capital, or to the share of capital in output if production is Cobb–Douglas. When α is large – or when population growth and the rate of depreciation are small, so that the effects of disequilibria in capital per head take a long time to wear off – adjustment will be slow. As a result, if economies share the same technology, but differ in their initial endowments of capital per head and in their preferences – here represented by the saving rate – they will "conditionally" converge, that is, converge to their respective different equilibrium levels of output per head, but slowly. As α approaches one, in which case the technology takes the "AK" form $Y = AK$ for (total) output and (total) capital Y and K, there is no tendency to return to equilibrium, and an increase in saving can permanently increase growth. The AK model is one of the standard models in the "increasing returns" growth literature, and thinking about the Solow model with α close to unity provides a useful bridge between the old and new literatures (or, perhaps as accurately, back to the Harrod-Domar literatures).

Recent work has not only been concerned with explaining the rate of technical progress in the Solow model, but also refocused attention on whether the unmodified Solow model can explain divergences in growth rates across countries. If transitions are short, so that the data come from countries that are more or less in equilibrium, the Solow model is an unpromising candidate for explaining what we see, since, in equilibrium, all countries that have access to international technology but have different tastes, that is, different saving ratios, should have approximately the same rate of per capita economic growth. But if transitions take many years, there is scope for attributing international differences in growth rates to international differences in saving rates. Research on the rate of convergence by Barro and his collaborators (Barro, 1991; and Barro and Sala-i-Martin, 1992) suggests slow transitions, and the paper by Mankiw, Romer, and Weil (1992) has shown that a Solow model, albeit augmented for human capital and in which saving rates are treated as exogenous (i.e., as given by tastes), is capable of explaining a large fraction of the international variation in growth rates. Hence, even without abandoning the Solow model, it is possible to revive much of the standard view that higher rates of saving engender higher economic growth.

The other strand in the modern literature is concerned with modeling technical progress and, in particular, the incorporation of knowledge and human capital into the production function and the process of growth. Although such models were quite well developed in the earlier literature, particularly by Arrow (1962), Uzawa (1965), and Kaldor and Mirrlees (1962), their modern incarnation starts with Lucas (1988) and Romer (1986, 1990). Romer eloquently argues that a production function containing knowledge, capital, and labor must exhibit greater than constant returns to scale; doubling labor and capital with existing technology should double output, so that the doubling of all three must more than do so. Lucas and Romer develop models containing human capital or stocks of knowledge in addition to capital and labor, and demonstrate how growth rates can be permanently increased in societies that are prepared to postpone consumption, not just to increase capital formation, but to increase simultaneously both capital and knowledge (or human capital). Such an expansion overcomes the diminishing returns to capital in the Solow model and can conveniently be thought of in terms of the simple AK model discussed above, provided that capital K is defined as a broad aggregate including human as well as physical capital.

There is also a good deal of empirical evidence, including once again

Barro (1991) and Mankiw, Romer, and Weil (1992), that shows that various measures of education add significantly to the explanation of growth offered by saving rates alone. (Of course, such regressions are subject to exactly the same causality issues as are the regressions that relate growth to saving; indeed, there is an older literature that interpreted the regression of education on output in terms of the elasticity of demand for education.) In the context of this chapter, these models take me away from my main purpose. The effects of education on growth are of the greatest importance, and it is hard to disagree with the proposition that knowledge and its production are an integral part of the growth process. But I am interpreting my topic as the relationship between growth and saving as conventionally defined, not as the relationship between growth and a broader aggregate of saving and educational expenditures. Note however the possibility that in the presence of liquidity constraints, parents may have to save up for their children's education, generating another link between growth, education, and saving. This effect is similar to saving up for housing, which will be dealt with later in this chapter.

From this brief account of the matter, it seems that as a matter of theory, it is hard to deny that higher saving should engender higher growth. The empirical evidence is consistent with the theory, although almost all of the empirical evidence is interpretative, in the sense that it shows that the configuration of growth rates, saving rates, and education across countries is consistent with what would be expected from Solow models or Solow models augmented to include measures of human capital. Of course, such evidence offers no explanation of what determines saving rates (or the amount of education that societies choose to provide their children), and they clearly have no power to detect the reverse causality that saving (and/or education) is caused by income or the growth of income.

Carroll and Weil (1994) address the causality issue explicitly and find some evidence against the proposition that growth comes from saving using Granger causality tests. Using pooled five-year averages of saving and growth for both the OECD and a wider sample of countries, they find that lagged saving lacks explanatory power for growth conditional on lagged growth, whereas the reverse is not true, so that lagged growth predicts saving conditional on its own lags. It is not entirely clear what to make of these results. Growth has to come from somewhere, and it is hard to think of growth rates as a pure time-series process, unaffected by previous levels of investment (= saving). At the same time, there are econometric difficulties with these sort of vector auto-regressions (VARs) in panel data in the presence of both fixed effects and lagged dependent variables (for discussion and possible remedies, see Holtz-

Eakin, Newey, and Rosen, 1988; Arellano and Bond, 1991; and Arellano and Bover, 1995).

From Growth to Saving: Standard Models of Saving

In this section, I consider two standard models of intertemporal choice, the permanent income hypothesis and the life-cycle hypothesis, focusing on their implications for the relationship between growth and saving. I conclude with a brief review of some classical and neo-Keynesian models of growth and saving.

The Permanent Income Hypothesis

The permanent income hypothesis (PIH) is most often used for studying macroeconomic fluctuations and the short-run dynamic relationship between consumption, saving, and income. However, it also has implications for the long-run relationship between saving and growth. Although there are almost as many versions of the PIH as there are chapters in Friedman (1957), the version that is the basis for modern work sets consumption equal to the annuity value of the sum of assets and the discounted present value of expected future labor income (Flavin, 1981). Such a model can be formally derived from the maximization under uncertainty of a quadratic intertemporally additive utility function under the assumption that the real rate of interest and the rate of time preference are constant and equal to one another (see Deaton, 1992, Ch. 3 for an elementary exposition). The horizon is usually taken to be infinite – partly for algebraic convenience, and partly because we are usually concerned with a representative agent – in which case Flavin's version of the PIH takes the form

$$c_t = \frac{r}{1+r}\left(A_t + \sum_0^\infty \frac{E_t y_{t+k}}{(1+r)^k}\right), \tag{5}$$

where r is the constant real rate of interest, c_t is real consumption in period t, y_{t+k} is real *labor* income (earnings) in year $t + k$ whose expectation conditional on information available at time t is $E_t y_{t+k}$, and A_t is the real value of the single asset whose return is r.

For current purposes, equation (5) is best rewritten in an equivalent form suggested by Campbell (1987). He defines *disposable* income as the sum of earnings and asset income, here $y_t + rA_t/(1 + r)$, and then shows that saving s_t, defined as the difference between disposable income and consumption, satisfies the "rainy day equation"

$$s_t = -\sum_1^\infty E_t \frac{\Delta y_{t+k}}{(1+r)^k},\tag{6}$$

so that saving is the discounted present value of expected future *falls* in earnings. (Deriving equation (6) from (5) takes a little practice, but the point to note is that the two formulations of the PIH are precisely equivalent; each can be derived from the other.) The rainy day equation comes directly from the assumption underlying the PIH that optimal consumption is flat over time. Hence, if earnings are also flat, there is no need to save; if earnings are growing, the consumer should borrow and repay later; and if earnings are expected to fall in the future, most notably because of retirement in a finite-life model, the consumer should save to hold consumption constant over that anticipated drop.

Equation (6) also shows why the PIH is not a very good candidate to explain a positive correlation between saving and growth (see also Carroll and Summers, 1991). Provided that growth is anticipated, saving should be *negative*, so that the PIH is consistent with high household saving in Thailand, Indonesia, Japan, Korea, Hong Kong, and Taiwan only if the citizens of those countries continue to be surprised by the growth in their incomes, even after a (more or less) continuous quarter century of growth. If they know what is coming, they should be borrowing en masse so as not to have to wait for higher incomes to materialize. Even if consumption is only *proportional* to permanent income, rather than equal to it, saving still ought to be lower the higher is the expected future increase in labor income, which once again violates the facts. Again as pointed out by Carroll and Summers (1991) and also by Viard (1993), the productivity slowdown of the early 1970s, which generated well-publicized declines in the rate of growth of future earnings, should also have generated higher saving (or less dissaving) if consumers were planning on smoothing their consumption over the rest of their lives. Once again this is the opposite of what happened; in *all* the OECD countries, saving declined with growth rates decade by decade, from the 1960s to the 1970s to the 1980s (see Modigliani, 1993).

I have been playing fast and loose with finite and infinite lives, but all of the conclusions can be restated correctly at the price of a little more algebra (for a finite-life version of equation (6), see Deaton and Paxson, 1994a). In finite-life models, retirement causes an anticipated drop in earnings and so provides a motive for saving. Hence, retirement can explain why people save even when they expect their earnings to grow in every year up to retirement. Even so, an increase in the expected rate of increase of labor income will still warrant an increase in consumption, although by an amount that is much larger for young consumers than for consumers nearing retirement. Similarly, the productivity slowdown should have increased saving by more for younger workers, yet as far as we can tell, saving rates fell for all age groups (for the United States, see Bosworth, Burtless, and Sabelhaus, 1991; for Britain, see Attanasio, Guiso, Jappelli, and Weber, 1992).

The Life-Cycle Hypothesis

Unlike the PIH, the life-cycle model is closely associated with the relationship between saving and growth, and its creator, Modigliani (1986), has argued the positive relationship between growth and saving as the central and most important prediction of his model. But as we have seen, the PIH with finite life, which is a simple form of the life-cycle model, predicts that increases in growth will *reduce* saving. That the life-cycle hypothesis (LCH) does the opposite is a consequence, not of its assumptions about behavior, but of its assumptions about how growth works, assumptions that are in principle testable. Growth in earnings is assumed to take place across generations (or cohorts) but not within them, so that when the growth rate of earnings shifts up, no individuals expect additional growth over their lifetime, only that their successors will have higher lifetime earnings profiles. There is a larger gap between the lifetime earnings profiles of successive cohorts, but no change in their slope. As a result, no individual wishes to decrease saving according to equation (6).

What happens instead is illustrated in Figure 3.1, which shows a lifetime profile of earnings and consumption that, although schematic, is a good deal more realistic than the simple "stripped-down" model used in the textbooks, in which consumption is taken to be constant throughout life, and earnings constant until retirement. The hump in consumption reflects the changing demographic composition of the household as children are born, grow expensive, and leave, and the hump in earnings reflects the standard age–earnings profile. I assume that consumption drops at retirement, not because of the fall in earnings, but because, when people no longer go to work, they no longer have to bear many of the expenses associated with work – transportation, working clothes, meals – that are counted as part of consumption during the working life. (Such expenses are immediately apparent in U.S. and British data if we compare consumption patterns of one- and two-earner households, and although some of these expenses are likely to be less important in poorer countries, this is not so for all, transport being the most obvious example.)

As shown in Figure 3.1, household members want to borrow at the beginning of their career, save in the middle, and run down the accumulated assets after retirement. If we measure the average age of each dollar saved and each dollar borrowed or dissaved, then as illustrated, the average age of the saved dollars is less than the average age of

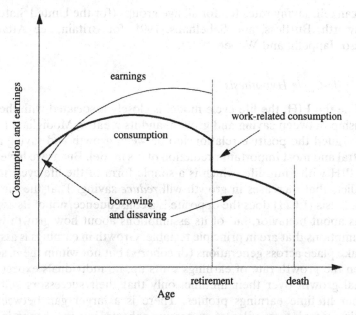

Figure 3.1. Schematic life-cycle profiles of earnings and consumption.

the dissaved dollars. In consequence, if there is economic growth across cohorts, with younger generations richer than older generations, but without any tipping of individual age–earnings profiles, saving will increase because the average age of savings is less than the average age of dissaving, and growth redistributes resources toward younger cohorts.

Figure 3.2 illustrates the effects on cross-sectional profiles of saving. The line for zero growth, $g = 0$, shows the lifetime profile of saving – here earnings less consumption, because the interest rate is taken to be zero – corresponding to the earnings and consumption paths in Figure 3.1. Because the growth rate is zero, the cross section over households at any instant replicates the lifetime profile for any and all of them. For positive growth rates, cross sections diverge from lifetime profiles, because younger households are on higher trajectories. The lines for growth of 2, 4, and 6 percent in Figure 3.2 come from the zero growth profile by scaling up the latter by the factor $(1 + g)^{T-a}$, where T is the date of death and a is age, and show the cross-sectional age profiles of saving in economies in long-term equilibrium at growth rate g. The total area under the zero growth line is zero; saving during the prime age years just finances borrowing in youth and retirement. At higher growth rates, there is net saving, since the midlife saving of the younger generations is greater than the retirement dissaving of their elders. At very high growth

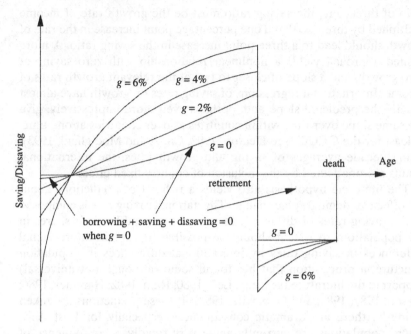

Figure 3.2. Cross-sectional profiles of saving as a function of the growth of earnings corresponding to Figure 3.1.

rates – higher than those shown here – the dissaving by the youngest households will eventually predominate, the age of dissaving will fall below the age of saving, and the direction of the growth effect on saving will flip. However, this may be a remote possibility in practice, and we can follow Modigliani in ruling it out by assuming – quite reasonably in my view – that the youngest households cannot borrow for consumption. This restriction then guarantees that the age of saving is less than the age of dissaving and, together with the assumption about the way in which growth affects the earning process, guarantees that higher growth will produce more saving.

This model has had many impressive successes to its credit. A crude version of Figure 3.1, in which consumption is constant over life, predicts a wealth to income ratio of three to four, which is close to the actual figure in the United States and other developed economies. (As we shall see below, the more realistic Figure 3.1 does less well.) The crude model also predicts a relationship between saving rates and growth rates that is close to that shown by the cross-country evidence. Although the ratio of wealth to income in these models is not independent of growth rate, a reasonably accurate first approximation to the effect of growth on saving comes from assuming a fixed ratio. Thus, to maintain a wealth to income ratio of three, say, the saving ratio must be the growth rate of income multiplied by three, so that a one percentage point increase in the rate of growth should lead to a three point increase in the saving ratio. A more refined approach yields a nonlinear relationship with zero saving at zero growth, and a slope of closer to two at the relevant growth rates of income. International regressions of saving rates on growth have almost exactly the predicted slope and, perhaps even more impressively, give the same slope over time within countries as over countries at one time, at least for the OECD (see Deaton, 1992, Ch. 2; and Modigliani, 1993). Using decade averages of saving and growth rates, the international results are unaffected by the inclusion of country fixed effects.

The life-cycle hypothesis also yields a rich set of predictions about the effects of demographic change. The national saving rate is composed of the saving rates of different age groups weighted by their shares in the population, so that it should be possible to explain international differences in saving rates by international differences in population structure, a proposition that has found some (although not universal) support in the literature (see, e.g., Leff, 1980; Ram, 1982; Hammer, 1986; Mason, 1987, 1988; and Gersovitz, 1988). If these predictions are taken seriously, there are dramatic consequences, especially for East Asia, where populations are currently aging very rapidly, a consequence of post-war baby booms, increases in life expectancy, and later declines in fertility. For example, Horioka (1989) predicts that Japan's saving rate will become negative early in the next century. The life-cycle hypothesis has also proved a fertile vehicle for analyzing the effects of social security on private saving (for some of the early international evidence that points to social security as a cause of lower saving, see Feldstein, 1980; as well as the recent symposium edited by Arrau and Schmidt-Hebbel, 1994).

That such a simple model should yield accurate predictions is re-markable. It is also impressive that in contrast to much modern work on saving, no use is made of representative agents; indeed the growth and saving results do not hold for individual agents, but are explicit aggrega-tion effects, one of the few examples in empirical macroeconomics where aggregation is used positively, not shrugged off as a nuisance. It is thus unfortunate that the closer scrutiny to which the model has been put in recent years should have revealed irreparable difficulties.

First, examination of age profiles of consumption and incomes, al-though admittedly beset by measurement error, usually yields shapes that are much more like Figure 3.1 than they are like the standard, stripped-down model in which consumption is flat throughout life. In consequence, there is not enough hump saving in the data to account for aggregate wealth in the economy, with the implication that a substan-

tial amount of national wealth (perhaps a half or more) must be attributed to bequests (see Kotlikoff, 1988; Kotlikoff and Summers, 1981;
and Modigliani, 1988). Similar results seem to hold for other developed
countries, while in developing countries the survey data often show
little, no, or even negative saving. While this is almost certainly a consequence of the gross difficulties in measuring income and saving in survey
data, there is no direct survey evidence from poor countries that household saving for retirement plays any role in accounting for national
wealth.

Second, if life-cycle wealth is a smaller fraction of national wealth,
and therefore a relatively small multiple of national income, then the
effects of growth on saving are correspondingly smaller and are also no
longer consistent with the cross-country relationship. This conclusion
is supported by other evidence. According to the life-cycle model, the
declines in the saving rates in the OECD countries are attributable to
declines in growth and the resulting reallocation of real income away
from younger savers and toward older dissavers. But in the United States
and the United Kingdom, where it is possible using survey data to give
some account of who is doing the saving, the decline does not appear
to be a compositional phenomenon; instead, and as I have already
noted, saving fell for all groups (for the United States, see Bosworth,
Burtless, and Sabelhaus, 1991; for the United Kingdom, see Attanasio
et al., 1992).

There is also evidence from cross-sectional age profiles of consumption. As noted by Carroll and Summers (1991), age profiles of consumption in a single cross section are not the age profiles of any one individual,
but are distorted by cohort effects. In rapidly growing economies, young
cohorts are much wealthier over their lifetimes than old cohorts, and
since consumption is proportional to lifetime resources, the consumption
of the young will rise more relative to that of the old the faster is the rate
of growth of real earnings. If different countries have the same tastes for
the distribution of consumption over the lifetime, an assumption that
is required to give the life-cycle model empirical content for an international cross section, then the age profiles of consumption in any given
cross section must be tipped more toward the young in the faster-
growing countries. But Carroll and Summers show that the profiles are
roughly similar for a number of developed economies, including the
United States and Japan, with the tipping if anything going in reverse,
and Deaton (1991, 1992) shows that the same is true for a number of
developing countries. The cross-sectional age profiles of consumption
in the rapidly growing economies of Indonesia, Taiwan, and Korea are
tipped toward older households, while in slow-growing Côte d'Ivoire,
the profile favors the young. In all of these examples, the cross-sectional

profile of consumption is much better explained by the cross-sectional profile of earnings, not the cross-sectional profile of lifetime resources. That this is also true for cohorts of households tracked over time is confirmed using 15 cross-sectional household surveys for Taiwan by Deaton and Paxson (1994b).

Given the appropriate data, it is possible to estimate life-cycle models for individual countries and to use the results to calculate the effects of growth on saving. This requires either panel data or a time series of cross sections, so that cohorts of households can be tracked over time and the age profiles of saving calculated. This has been done for Britain, Taiwan, Thailand, and the United States by Paxson (1996), who finds that the increases in the rate of growth of income will generate little or no saving in any of these countries, because there is too little saving in general, and because what there is is not sufficiently negatively correlated with age. Yet these countries lie along the line linking growth and saving in international comparisons, so that, whatever the cause of the link, it is not the life-cycle hypothesis. Paxson's results are consistent with those of Carroll and Summers (1991), but provide a much more direct refutation of the life-cycle growth to saving mechanism.

It is surely no real surprise that saving for retirement is an unpromising candidate for explaining patterns of national saving in developing countries. Even in Western Europe, the cohort born in the mid-1920s is the first in history to have an uninterrupted 40-year work history over which they might have hoped to accumulate enough to fund their retirement. The lifetimes of earlier cohorts were punctuated by wars, not to mention inflations and political turmoil – events that still occur in much of the developing world. It is hard to see that ordinary people would have much hope of saving for retirement in such an environment, where there is little chance of securing the fruits of 40 years of saving, even if the sacrifice of consumption were itself possible. Nor do most people in the world have a need for this sort of protection. In most societies and for most people, the family provides better insurance than the market against the inability to work in an extended old age, in itself a relatively rare event in agricultural societies with relatively low life expectancy. For whatever reason, such arrangements seem to break down with economic development, as well as with decreases in mortality and fertility, so that more years of parental old age have to be covered by fewer children. Although this breakdown may turn some people into life-cycle savers, I suspect that a more common response is a political demand for old age social security, at least to the extent of eliminating a growing problem of poverty among the elderly. Although there are many different ways in which this demand can be satisfied, all require the state to accept at least some of the responsibility for financial security in old age.

Classical Explanations of Saving and Growth

For lack of anywhere better to discuss them, I want to note here the existence of older theories of saving that are much more explicitly focused toward development, and that also yield an explanation in which growth drives saving. These are the classical saving models associated with Lewis (1954) and (his teacher) Kaldor (1957). In both Lewis's and Kaldor's models, there are two classes of people, savers and non-savers, or workers and capitalists. In the simplest formulation, workers spend what they earn and capitalists, whose sole purpose is accumulation, save their incomes, although it is also possible to give different saving propensities to the two groups. In the Lewis model, the activities of the capitalists in the modern sector increase the share of the latter as the economy grows, and thus increases the share of saving in national income. The more rapid the accumulation, the faster the distribution of income tips toward profits, and the higher is the saving rate. In Kaldor's model, which is more focused on short-run dynamics and which has a more Keynesian flavor, investment is set by the "animal spirits" of the capitalists – though there is no reason why this could not be given a more modern flavor – and the income distribution adjusts between workers and capitalists so as to satisfy the identity between saving and investment. More investment brings more growth, a tip in income distribution toward the capitalists, and a higher saving rate. In the extreme case where workers save nothing and capitalists everything, investment is self-financing; workers "spend what they get" and capitalists "get what they spend" – the widow's cruse.

These models deserve more serious empirical attention than they have received to date, although it is not clear that there have been major changes in either the personal or functional distributions of income associated with increases in saving rates – for example, in Taiwan and Korea. Of course, the Lewis and Kaldor models are highly schematic and require filling out before we know what to look for. Even so, the idea that there are two classes of savers is something that appears in a number of guises, and I will return to it below. For the moment, note that any such specification will forge a link between income distribution and national saving, an old topic that will be pursued in depth in Chapter 6, and one that was seen as central and obvious in the first consumption functions estimated in the 1930s and 1940s, but that has not been the focus of much recent research. It is more difficult to specify what we are talking about when we talk about "capitalists" and "workers," so that we know where to look, both for high saving rates and for changes in the distribution of income. Lewis had in mind enclaves or nascent modern sectors, "not one island of expanding capitalist employment, surrounded by a vast sea of subsistence workers, but rather a number of such tiny islands," objects that are not obviously well reflected in surveys or in national accounts. Kaldor thought of his capitalists as the directors of corporations deciding on how much to retain and how much to distribute, so that the distribution of income would be the functional not the personal distribution. Other possibilities are the small-business sector, but it is not clear that this would apply everywhere; for example, it is surely a better story for Taiwan than for Korea. Kaldor's focus on profits versus earnings is surely one that is worth following up, at least in those countries where it is possible to disaggregate private saving into its personal and corporate components. In industrialized countries, saving by firms is often the major source of finance for business investment, and it would be useful to investigate the extent to which the same is true in developing countries.

Precautionary Saving, Buffer Stock Models, Saving, and Growth

By far the most active area of recent research in saving has been the move away from the PIH and life-cycle models toward a richer class of models, still within the general framework of intertemporal choice under uncertainty, but with a number of distinct predictions of their own. One line of work has been to relax the certainty equivalent utility function that underlies the PIH, so that the marginal utility of consumption is assumed to be nonlinear, typically convex. Such convexity generates precautionary motives for saving. A second line has been to consider the effects of borrowing constraints. I consider each topic in turn, again with a focus on saving and growth. A more detailed treatment is given in Deaton (1992, Ch. 6); see also Browning and Lusardi (1996) for an update.

Precautionary Saving

The usual vehicle for intertemporal choice under uncertainty is one in which the consumer maximizes expected utility given by

$$EU = E_t \sum_0^{T-1} (1+\delta)^{-k} \upsilon(c_{t+k}), \qquad (7)$$

where δ is the rate of time preference, and $\upsilon(c)$ is the instantaneous (sub)utility function. In the simplest case, expected utility is maximized subject to the intertemporal budget constraint

$$A_{t+1} = (1+r)(A_t + y_t - c_t), \qquad (8)$$

where A_t is the real value of a single asset and r is the constant real interest rate. As before, it is important to emphasize that y_t is earnings, or labor income, not total income. The PIH (equation (5)) is the solution to this problem in the special case when $r = \delta$ and when the subutility functions are quadratic. But linear marginal utility supposes that the value of consumption is increased by a fall in consumption by the same amount that an increase in consumption decreases marginal utility, which many people find implausible. Quadratic utility also implies decreasing absolute risk aversion, which is implausible to even more people. A more attractive assumption is that marginal utility of consumption $\lambda(c)$ is strictly convex, where

$$\lambda(c) \equiv v(c_t). \tag{9}$$

While consumer theory carries no general supposition that marginal utility be convex, the assumption has a number of interesting consequences. Increased uncertainty about future consumption, next period or any period in the future, causes current consumption to decrease so that saving increases. The same effect tilts lifetime consumption profiles away from early consumption and toward late consumption. Until people know more about their lifetime prospects, it is prudent not to consume too much and to limit borrowing, an effect that will be stronger the greater the uncertainty about *lifetime* income. Transfers of funds that leave present values unaffected can affect behavior. Higher taxes now with lower taxes later will cause consumption to decrease if people have to rebuild precautionary balances and if they cannot borrow against their future tax breaks. In extreme cases, if people are very cautious and there is a great deal of uncertainty, consumption can be quite closely tied to income over all but the shortest time span, so that the aggregate economy behaves as if there were a close Keynesian link between consumption and income. The marginal propensity to consume out of earnings is higher when assets are low, so that transfers between consumers will also affect saving; income distribution matters.

Perhaps the main relevance of precautionary saving for saving and growth is a negative one. We now know, particularly from the work of Carroll (1992, 1997), that it is possible to construct plausible models of optimal intertemporal choice over the life cycle in which the path of consumption is closely related to the path of earnings, so that the growth to saving implications of the standard LCH are annulled. That higher growth should increase saving is an implication of the special assumptions that underlie the life-cycle model; it is not a general implication of optimal intertemporal choice. That said, we are still at the level of logical implications; the importance of precautionary saving in the data is far from fully established. The implications listed above all seem to have some support in the data, and it is possible to rig up precautionary models to tell very interesting stories about consumption tracking earnings (Carroll, 1997) and about the effects of social security and spend-down rules on saving (Hubbard, Skinner, and Zeldes, 1992). It is also true that with different preference parameters and different assumptions about earnings, very different results can be obtained; indeed, as the precautionary motive becomes small, we can return to the PIH. Nor is it clear that all the predictions of precautionary models are correct. For example, Dynan (1993) finds no relation between consumption growth and future consumption uncertainty in the microdata; while such isolated findings can be explained away, much more work needs to be done before precautionary saving can be regarded as an established phenomenon.

Liquidity Constraints: Buffer Stock Models

Another way of complicating the standard model – and perhaps of making it more realistic – is to allow for the possibility that consumers may not be able to borrow, or at least that they cannot borrow more than some given limit. Although credit markets clearly exist in developing countries, it may in some circumstances make more sense to examine the consequences of prohibiting borrowing altogether than to allow the possibly large borrowing for consumption that can result from life-cycle, PIH, or precautionary models.

Liquidity constraints and their consequences for saving will be covered at length in Chapter 4; here we focus mainly on their implications for the saving–growth link. The basic model is as in equations (7) and (8) with the addition of the borrowing constraint

$$A_t \geq 0, \tag{10}$$

which can be trivially extended to allow for any fixed borrowing limit. As with precautionary saving and in contrast to the LCH and PIH, there is no explicit solution, but intertemporal behavior can be characterized by an Euler equation and solved numerically for any given utility function and set of parameters. The results depend on a number of factors, most importantly (i) the nature of the stochastic process driving earnings y_t, particularly its trend rate of growth and level of variability, (ii) preferences, particularly the rate of time preference δ and the curvature of the functions $v(c)$, the latter controlling the intertemporal elasticity of substitution, and (iii) the real rate of interest r. The configuration of these factors determines whether an individual is likely to be affected by the borrowing constraint, and if so, what behavior will look like. If the individual is patient, or if growth is low or negative, or if future incomes are uncertain, or if interest rates are high, all of which provide incentives to postpone consumption and to accelerate the rate of growth of consumption by accumulating first and decumulating later, and if the consumer has a high elasticity of intertemporal substitution so that he or she responds to these incentives, then borrowing constraints are unlikely to bind, and consumption and saving will be much the same as if there had been no constraints. When the factors stack up the other way, so that an unconstrained consumer would borrow early in life in order to finance a level of consumption that is higher than earnings, then behavior will be changed by the constraints. To take the simplest example where earnings follow an i.i.d. stationary process, individuals will accumulate if $\delta < r$ and will be "trapped" by the borrowing constraints if $\delta > r$. Relatively patient consumers get richer with time, but it is optimal for the relatively impatient to stay poor – never accumulating, spending something close to their earnings, and using assets (if at all) only to smooth out short-term fluctuations in earnings.

Such models divide consumers into two groups, only one of which saves. The distinction depends on preferences, but even if preferences are continuously distributed over the population, the borrowing constraints themselves will divide consumers into two groups; it is not necessary to postulate two distinct types of people or preferences. Note also that the division into savers and nonsavers depends not only on preferences, but also on the rate of growth of earnings – with higher expected rates of growth generating *fewer* savers – the variability of earnings, and interest rates, so that there is no fixed division between savers and nonsavers, and there is potential scope for policy to shift individuals from one group to the other. The nonsavers are not too poor to save, as in vicious-circle or subsistence models; indeed, being close to subsistence would seem to make people more sensitive to intertemporal issues, not the reverse. Instead, the poor are voluntarily poor because they do not save, and they would be worse off if they were forced to accumulate assets and become rich. Their lack of assets comes from their impatience, not from any structural inability to save.

The dynamics of borrowing-constrained consumers or buffer-stock savers has been worked out in papers by Schechtman (1976), Bewley (1977), Schechtman and Escudero (1977), and Deaton (1991, 1992). Under the relevant assumptions about earnings processes, consumers use assets only to buffer consumption, accumulating them when times are good and running them down to protect consumption when earnings are low. Over horizons of only a few years, consumption will be closely matched to earnings, and assets are regularly drawn down to zero when times are bad enough, and the last unit of assets is worth more as current consumption than it is as a precautionary balance. Assets are important for these consumers, not as a mode of accumulation, but as a protection against poor earnings and, in particular, against poor earnings coupled with the inability to borrow.

The relationship between saving and growth in these models is presently unclear and, as with precautionary saving, is likely to depend on the precise configuration of preferences and earnings processes. In the stationary stochastic equilibrium, there is a constant average assets to earnings ratio, in very much the same way as the standard life-cycle model produces a stationary assets to earnings ratio. However, the ratio in the latter is from two to four depending on the importance of bequests, whereas simulations of the buffer-stock models – which is really all that we currently have – suggest that the ratio is a good deal less than one, perhaps as low as 10 percent. If so, growth will increase saving as buffer stocks are restored, but the effect will be small; if buffer stocks are even a half of income, a one point increase in growth will increase the saving ratio by half a point, not the two to three points predicted by the crude life-cycle model and confirmed by the international and long time-series evidence. But the fixed-ratio view is itself too simple. Higher growth should decrease the numbers of savers relative to the nonsavers, because growth will make more people want to borrow, and anticipated growth will change the buffer-stock equilibrium for the nonsavers. For example, if the expected growth of earnings is high enough relative to the variance of earnings, it is easy to produce the simple "rule-of-thumb" consumers who simply spend their earnings, in which case there will be no saving at all for the group; for further discussion and some results, see Deaton (1991) and Carroll (1997).

As with the precautionary model, research into the buffer-stock model has enriched our understanding of saving behavior. It has also provided a formal justification for phenomena that seem to be present in the data – many households accumulating nothing in the long run and possessing few if any financial assets, but still using cash and other liquid assets to separate consumption and income at high frequencies, if not at low. Like the precautionary models, it is also far from having been fully estimated and tested on the data. As for the link between saving and growth, it is possibly consistent with a link from higher growth to higher saving, but the effects are surely small. It is worth also noting that, in many respects, liquidity constraints and precautionary motives have similar effects. The inability to borrow when the consumer is in trouble induces a precautionary motive even where none would otherwise exist. Correspondingly, consumers who are extremely cautious may voluntarily abstain from borrowing in bad times because they are fearful of having to repay when things are even worse. In consequence, buffer-stock saving can be generated by either precautionary saving or liquidity constraints, and it is unclear that many new insights would be gained by constructing models with both liquidity constraints and precautionary motives.

Liquidity Constraints: Housing

Rather different effects of liquidity constraints are associated with housing; these have received some attention in recent years, and probably deserve a good deal more, since there is evidence that housing finance is somehow implicated in the saving story. Houses are the largest and most expensive assets that most people ever own. In many countries, markets for the consumption of the services of these assets are distorted in various ways. Rental markets can be eliminated or restricted by rent control policies, and tax policies typically favor home ownership over rental and over the possession of alternative assets. There are typically no taxes on the return from the ownership – the implicit rental value – and low or zero taxes on capital gains from home sales. But the purchase of housing is also made difficult in many countries by restrictions on the amount that can be borrowed for house purchase, so that consumers have to accumulate saving before they make a purchase; the same may be true for other large durables and for educational expenditures. In many countries, there are also restrictions on the extent to which home owners can borrow against home equity, although these have been relaxed in a number of countries in recent years, and the relaxation may have contributed to declining saving ratios (Miles, 1992), as well as (perhaps) allowing the old to behave more like life-cycle dissavers. What determines these borrowing restrictions is something of a puzzle; they are much more severe in some European countries (e.g., Germany and Italy) than others, and in some East Asian countries, such as Korea and Taiwan, the lack of development of financial intermediation for households seems to have been a conscious pro-saving policy. Yet in Singapore and Malaysia (but not in the reformed pension schemes of Latin America), which have explicit saving policies in the form of mandatory saving for retirement schemes, accumulations may be used for house purchase.

Saving up for house purchase is analogous to saving up for retirement, although the timing in the life cycle is different. Such saving can be added on to a standard life-cycle model or it can be taken alone, which we might want to do if we believe that people save for housing, but not for retirement above and beyond what is provided by social security and employment related schemes. The fact that the saving takes place *before* the dissaving, although irrelevant in a stationary economy, means that saving up for house purchase will elicit positive saving in an economy with growth in *total* GNP, which is exactly as in the life-cycle model. If the housing equity can be effectively run down during retirement – for example, through reverse annuity mortgages – housing and life-cycle saving can substitute for one another. In practice, there is very limited evidence of the elderly behaving in this way, although even if they did, the housing motive is likely to decrease the age at which saving begins. Since the effect of real income growth on saving depends on the difference between the average age of saving and the average age of dissaving, saving for house purchase will lower the average age of saving and thus increase the effects of growth on saving (for a demonstration, see Jappelli and Pagano, 1994).

These results suggest a possible route from policy to saving; if governments deliberately restrict mortgage availability – for example, by setting minimum down payment ratios – saving will increase, and the sensitivity of saving to growth will increase. If saving drives growth, through the transitional dynamics of a Solow model or through an AK model, such financial restrictions can set up a virtuous circle of growth and saving, moving the economy from low-saving/low-growth to a high-saving/high-growth equilibrium, what might be called the Korean model. Note that this is exactly the opposite of the financial repression view, in which financial liberalization generates more saving, capital deepening, and growth for a recent statement (see McKinnon, 1991; for a skeptical analysis in the Korean and Taiwanese contexts, see Park, 1993).

The documentation of such effects is the purpose of Jappelli and Pagano's (1994) paper. They find that, even allowing for the standard variables in international saving regressions – mainly the growth and level of GDP and dependency ratios – the higher the minimum down payment ratio, the higher the saving rate. In a typical regression, an increase in the minimum down payment from 20 to 50 percent will raise the saving rate by 6 percentage points, holding constant the rate of growth. They also estimate Barro type regressions in which the down payment ratios increase growth itself. Of course, these regressions suffer from all of the same problems as the standard cross-country regressions in which saving is regressed on growth. Quite apart from causality issues, the cross-country evidence lacks the conviction that comes from a demonstration that the estimated effects are the size that we would expect from the within-country evidence. Indeed, in the one study that has attempted to simulate the effects, Hayashi, Ito, and Slemrod (1988), the contribution to the Japanese saving ratio of differences in credit arrangements between the United States and Japan is modest and accounts for only a small fraction of the difference between the U.S. and Japanese saving rates. Even so, this study is based on a large number of assumptions about behavior and institutions, and it is unclear how robust the findings are to alternative assumptions. Certainly, a good deal more work needs to be done along these lines.

There are some other reasons why housing is worth a good deal more attention. Informal conversations in Taiwan or Korea about saving nearly always lead quickly to housing. The young say that they are saving 30 or 40 percent of their incomes in order to buy a house, while their elders claim that they are saving even in retirement so that they can buy houses for their children; whether and under what circumstances these reports can be reconciled is itself an interesting topic for research. The cost of housing is also frequently mentioned, and apartments in Taipei appear to cost as much as apartments in New York, in spite of the differences in real incomes. These sorts of conversations tend to (a) support the saving for house purchase story, (b) suggest again that bequests are important, and (c) point out that land prices are part of the story, especially in relatively small economies. I shall turn to bequests in the next section, which leaves the question of land prices and saving. This certainly needs investigation, and it is surely worth attempting to find out about land prices, as well as to link house prices to saving in more formal analyses. But while it is straightforward to see why the relative price of land ought to be high and to rise quickly in rapidly growing economies, it is harder to see why this should drive increases in saving rates.

Starting with land prices themselves, suppose that there is a fixed supply of land for housing A and that land does not depreciate, so that if the real interest rate is r, the cost of holding one unit of land for one period – the user cost – is $rp_t - \dot{p}_t$, the rental cost less capital appreciation. Hence, if we assume Cobb-Douglas preferences and equate demand to supply,

$$A = \frac{\alpha y_t}{rp_t - \dot{p}_t}. \tag{11}$$

If total national income is growing at rate $n + g$, the sum of the rates of population growth and per capita income, the solution to (11) is given by

$$(p_t/y_t) = \alpha/A(r - g - n), \tag{12}$$

so that land prices grow at the same rate as national income. (This result requires that $r > n + g$, and the equilibrium price to income ratio equation (12) can be reached only if the initial price to income ratio is higher than the equilibrium.) Prices can be very high relative to national income if the cost of holding land is low, which will be the case if real interest rates are not much higher than the rate of growth. According to even this simple story, and given a common world interest rate, the ratio of the value of land to national income will be highest in the most rapidly growing economies. We can also relax the Cobb-Douglas assumption that the income and (absolute) price elasticities of land are unity; if the former is η and the latter is $(-)\upsilon$, then the price of land rises at the rate of growth of output multiplied by the ratio η/υ. Although the demand for housing is presumably price inelastic since structures can be substituted for land, so that η/υ might be greater than 1, but the possibility remains that the value of land could rise more rapidly than does national income.

At first blush, the land price story seems to add to the attractiveness of the saving for house purchase account of saving. If there are restrictions on borrowing for housing, the amount required for a deposit is increased the higher are house prices, so that the effect of growth on saving would be further enhanced. But it is hard to tell this story in any convincing way. The problem is that, unlike housing, land does not depreciate, so that, although it is true that first-time buyers are faced with higher prices when land prices rise, they are also the beneficiaries of the increase in land prices, if not directly, at least through eventual bequests by their parents or whoever currently owns the land. In the simplest PIH or LCH, where consumption is driven by present values, the increase in the price of land that requires more saving for one person also generates a capital gain for someone else, a capital gain that can be used for consumption and dissaving. As with any form of bequest, the saving of the donor provides a motive for dissaving for the recipient. It is possible that precautionary motives or other effects may introduce enough asymmetry so that there is a positive effect on saving, but there is no simple story that immediately comes to mind.

Bequests

There is some direct evidence for bequest motives, such as that in Bernheim (1991), who finds that people increase their life insurance and reduce annuities (i.e., increase bequeathable wealth) in response to the involuntary annuitization of social security. But much of the evidence for the importance of bequests is indirect, in the sense that it is often difficult to reconcile the evidence with anything other than a bequest motive. Even so, there are sometimes quite plausible alternative explanations. I have already discussed the Kotlikoff and Summers work, that it is difficult to find enough life-cycle saving in the microdata to explain the level of national wealth. Because the microeconomic data are so difficult to use to measure life-cycle saving, such calculations are subject to a wide band of error, although there has certainly been an upward revaluation in the profession's assessment of the importance of bequests in accounting for national wealth.

There is also a great deal of evidence that old people save, or at least do not dissave, as required by the simple life-cycle model without bequests. Such evidence goes back at least as far as Mirer (1979) and is continuously being updated as new data sets become available. In many household surveys from around the world, rates of saving among elderly households are as high or higher than among younger households, who are supposed to be saving for their retirement. (Note however that household surveys rarely have adequate data on private pensions and other annuities; an elderly couple living on a pension from an ex-employer is running down the value of an annuity, but if their consumption is less than their income – here the annual yield from the annuity –

they will be reported as saving.) Such saving among the elderly is observed in the United States, Japan, the United Kingdom, Germany, Italy, and Taiwan (see Attanasio, 1991; Börsch-Supan, 1992; Deaton and Paxson, 1994b; Banks and Blundell, 1995; and the papers collected in Poterba, 1995). Such results are certainly consistent with bequests, and in some cases, particularly Taiwan, casual conversations and (largely unsupported) statements in the literature tend to emphasize bequests. There is also a very large small business sector in Taiwan, investment in which is not usually thought of as retirement saving. But there are other explanations and some contrary evidence. Elderly people – or very rich people – may have a low or zero marginal utility of consumption, so that once their needs are met, additional income is saved faute de mieux; see Börsch-Supan and Stahl (1991), who focus on the German case, where the elderly receive extraordinarily generous state pensions.

There are also difficult selectivity problems in trying to study the elderly using household survey data, problems that are particularly severe in developing countries. Household surveys, by construction, survey households, not individuals, and even though the surveys yield a great deal of information about individuals within each household, they cannot collect information on saving by individuals, if only because consumption can be measured only at the household level. As a result, evidence that saving rates are high among elderly households usually means that saving rates are high among households headed by an elderly person, or are high among households containing only elderly people. But household formation and dissolution depends on economic factors, health, and age, so that, even if we had panel data, such as the American Retirement History Survey (RHS) or the new Health and Retirement Survey (HRS), the households and individuals that survive to old age are not randomly selected. In particular, since wealthier (i.e., lifetime high savers) have a lower risk of death as individuals, and presumably as household heads, there will be a progressive selection toward high savers over time (see Shorrocks, 1975). In industrialized countries, most elderly people live in independent households, so that the selection is probably less severe than is the case in developing countries, where living with children is the norm. Selection seems intractable in transitional economies such as Taiwan, where living arrangements are rapidly changing (Hermalin, Ofstedal, and Li, 1991; and Lo, 1989). The option of living alone is one that is increasingly available to wealthier Taiwanese – though it is also increasing as a result of increased life expectancy and decreased fertility – so that it is plausible that parents move in with their children when they no longer have the resources to live by themselves.

The contrary evidence on bequests comes from Hurd (1992), who uses data from the RHS to argue that the elderly in the United States do indeed dissave, though these data are hard to use, much depends on the treatment of housing, and there is a good deal of scope for alternative interpretations. Hurd (1987, 1989) also shows that in the RHS, older people with children have no more assets than people without children, an implausible finding if bequests are important. Of course, the RHS, like all household surveys, has difficulty generating good measures of assets. But the new HRS in the United States appears to have been much more successful than previous surveys in collecting wealth data; respondents who at first refuse are faced with a series of bracketing questions, which most are prepared to answer. These "new" respondents are much richer on average than those who respond to the first, direct question, so that the estimates of total assets from the HRS are much higher than those from comparable surveys, though there is still a core group who refuse to cooperate and who presumably have the highest wealth of all. These results, reported in Juster and Smith (1994), are important for further research because they show constructively, at least in one context, that it is possible to get much better wealth data than was previously thought. These techniques are well worth extending to developing countries.

Some evidence on bequests can also be gleaned from the literature on the permanent income hypothesis and from international comparisons. In the standard life-cycle model with no bequests, the present value of lifetime consumption is equal to the present value of lifetime resources. If a fixed share of lifetime resources is set aside as bequests, then consumption will be proportional to lifetime resources, but the elasticity of consumption to permanent income will still be unity. However, it is possible that bequests are a luxury good, so that the elasticity of consumption with respect to lifetime or permanent income is less than unity. If bequests are a luxury, saving rates will be higher for lifetime richer consumers, and saving rates will be higher in richer countries, so that there will be a relationship between saving rates and the level (not the rate of growth) of national income.

There is some evidence in favor of these predictions. The older literature on the permanent income hypothesis, from Friedman (1957) up to Hall (1978), usually found elasticities of consumption to permanent income that were substantially less than unity, both on time-series and cross-sectional data. This evidence also holds good in developing countries, where cross-sectional regressions of consumption on income rarely give unit elasticities, even when measures of long-term income and assets are used as instruments; see Bhalla (1979, 1980) and Wolpin (1982) for India, Musgrove (1978, 1979) for Latin America, and Paxson (1992) for Thailand. Even more explicit is the evidence from Taiwan in Deaton and Paxson (1994b), who use 15 successive cross-sectional surveys to decompose consumption and income into cohort and age effects, the former representing the lifetime components of consumption and income. But these cohort effects show steadily decreasing ratios of consumption to income for the more recent and lifetime wealthier generations.

The international cross-sectional evidence on growth and saving (e.g., Modigliani, 1993) shows that in the OECD countries the level of national income does *not* increase the saving rate once the rate of growth of income is taken into account. However, there is a positive effect among developing countries, a result supported for private saving in 10 Asian countries in Collins (1991) and for household saving in 10 Asian and Latin American countries in Schmidt-Hebbel, Webb, and Corsetti (1992). According to this evidence, bequests could be a luxury good at low or medium levels of income, but stop being so in rich countries. Indeed, some such relationship is necessary if the ratio of bequests to national income is not to increase indefinitely. Starting with Leff (1969), there is also a controversial literature on dependency effects, in which saving rates are regressed on the proportion of the population that is old and on the proportion of the population that is young, sometimes separately and sometimes summed. Careful reviews, such as Gersovitz (1988), conclude that these effects are not robust across studies, and that there are good theoretical reasons to expect such a result. Nevertheless, there is perhaps a preponderance of studies showing that the fraction of elderly decreases saving, as would be predicted by the standard LCH, and even the absence of a positive effect is in stark contrast to the survey evidence showing that saving rates are high among the elderly. But Weil (1994) has argued that both sets of results are consistent with an important bequest motive if the recipients of bequests (or expected bequests) reduce their consumption. He finds that data from the American Panel Study on Income Dynamics support such an effect.

Where does all this leave us, and what are the implications for the relationship between saving and growth? I suspect that, like housing, bequests are worthy of a good deal more study, that it would be a good idea to use the new techniques to collect more wealth data in LDCs, and that we should explore techniques of explicitly getting at the question of bequests. Dynastic accumulation – for example, through the founding of small businesses and the turning of small businesses into large businesses – is surely an important aspect of development in many countries. The development of a bequest motive may increase the saving rate as income begins to increase and contribute toward an acceleration of the growth rate.

Habits

The standard theoretical models of intertemporal choice make the assumption that preferences are intertemporally separable, so that the marginal rate of substitution of consumption between any two periods is independent of what happens in any other period. A simple way of recognizing intertemporal dependencies is through habit formation, according to which the subutility in any period depends positively on consumption in that period, but negatively on consumption in earlier periods. Such models are quite rich and can be used to give a number of interesting and nontrivial predictions. Perhaps the simplest model is one in which subutility is written in the form

$$u_t = \upsilon(\alpha c_t - \beta S_t), \tag{13}$$

where S_t is a stock of habits, defined (for example) as a distributed lag on past levels of consumption. A simple special case of equation (13) arises when the stock is proportional to the preceding period's consumption, so that

$$u_t = \upsilon(c_t - \gamma c_{t-1}). \tag{14}$$

According to equations (13) and (14), current consumption is good, but as the consumer gets used to that level of consumption, he or she needs more in order to attain the same level of utility. Given these specifications, consumers can be modeled as myopic, in which case they ignore the influence of their current decisions on the future stock, or as nonmyopic, in which case they take the future bad effects into account when considering how much to consume today. The former is sometimes justified in representative agent models by treating the state variable S as other people's consumption, which each agent takes as given (Abel, 1990; Campbell and Cochrane, 1994).

In these sort of models, the presence of habits acts as a drag on consumption, so that in some contexts, the effects are similar to simply assuming that it is costly to adjust consumption, or that it is only possible to do so over time. When consumers are not myopic, the habit effects will make them less likely to consume when they are young, because habits (like a wife and children) are hostages to fortune, so that there is an effect similar to that of precautionary saving, or indeed liquidity constraints if earnings are low in early life. But the effect is associated not only with uncertainty; consumption is costlier for young consumers, because the habit it induces has to be fed for the rest of life, and cheaper for old consumers, who do not have long to live. These sort of habits tip consumption profiles away from the young and toward the old. Consumers with habits also respond differently to surprises in earnings. For example, in the standard PIH, consumption follows a martingale process, so that the change in consumption from one period to the next is simply the change in the expectation of the discounted present value of earnings, a quantity that is not predictable by previously known information. In the equation (13), it is $\alpha c_t + \beta S_t$ that follows a martingale process (see

Deaton, 1992, pp. 29–34), so that although changes in $\alpha c_t + \beta S_t$ are unpredictable, changes in *consumption* can be predicted, as we find in the data. In the "moving-average" case, equation (14), the change in consumption follows an autoregression

$$\Delta C_{t+1} = \gamma \Delta C_t + \eta_{t+1}, \tag{15}$$

where η_{t+1} is a surprise determined by the innovation in current and future earnings. Equation (15) shows how the drag works and that in any given period, consumption responds only partially to new information.

These habit models are useful in a number of different contexts. They are consistent with the "excess sensitivity" literature in that they imply that the change in consumption is predictable by previously known information. They have also been used in the asset-pricing literature (see Constantinides, 1990; Singleton, 1990; and Campbell and Cochrane, 1994). The presence of habits heightens risk aversion by effectively making consumers much poorer than their total consumption would suggest. Habits therefore help explain what might appear to be excessive risk premia, though they have a much harder time explaining the correlation between asset returns and the rate of growth of consumption. There is also a large literature on the time-series consumption function showing that consumption is well described by an error-correction process in which consumption adjusts slowly to some long-run fixed ratio with disposable income (see almost any large macroeconometric model and, in particular, Davidson, Hendry, Srba, and Yeo, 1978).

Habit models are also consistent with a link between saving and growth. At its crudest, consumption takes time to catch up to higher income levels, and the faster income grows, the further behind consumption lags and the higher the saving rate increases. Consumption is not attached to income by an inflexible link, but is dragged behind it on an elastic cord. To make this work, there has to be an element of surprise in income growth. By itself, the tipping toward the young that is induced by habits will make consumption more like earnings and so reduce both savings and the sensitivity of the saving rate to changes in the rate of growth. But it is at the least arguable whether the high-saving citizens of Japan, Korea, Taiwan, or Indonesia continue to be surprised by their rates of growth. If so, these saving rates are ultimately transitory phenomena, albeit long-lived ones. Nevertheless, habits remain one of the more plausible of the growth to savings explanations for the international correlations, and there is also the previously cited evidence of Carroll and Weil (1994), who interpret their Granger causality tests in favor of the habit-based story. Even so, the leads are not exactly obvious in their time-series plots, nor are those presented by Collins (1991). Some only partially confirmatory evidence comes from Deaton and

Paxson's (1994b) work on Taiwan; they find that birth cohorts that experienced the highest rates of earnings growth were those with the highest saving ratios, as would be expected if consumption habits are important. But the effects are not very large, and certainly not large enough to explain the slope of the international correlation between growth and saving.

Directions for Research

This final section draws on the previous ones to outline what seem the most promising directions for future research. We need to know more about national income data on saving and its relationship to survey data, we need to collect better survey data on wealth and on bequests, we need to assemble internationally comparable time-series data, and we need to pull together international panels of household survey data.

The central question concerns disentangling the paths of influence between growth and saving, whether one causes the other, whether there is mutual dependence, or whether both are affected by some third common factor. This nexus has been investigated for many years, without a great deal of progress, so it makes sense to approach it from different angles, using a range of tools and data from several different sources. What gives a reasonable hope of progress now is that there are more data available now than ever before, especially from the rapidly growing and high-saving economies of the East. One possible way forward is to take as a working hypothesis that the relationship between growth and saving results from investment driving growth; the reverse mechanism from growth to saving is at best relatively unimportant. If this hypothesis is true, policies that promote saving will enhance growth, provided of course that the efficiency of investment is being properly maintained.

Because there are so many different strands to the growth–saving relationship, the working hypothesis can usefully be broken down into a number of implications that need to be examined individually. First, I suspect that nowhere in the world is there a long-term, low-frequency detachment of consumption from earnings/income, at least for the vast majority of people. Consumption growth is rapid when earnings growth is rapid, both for different groups within countries and for the same groups across countries. In consequence, there is no common taste-determined, lifetime profile of consumption, but lifetime profiles of consumption are determined by lifetime profiles of earnings and income. In consequence, there is no tendency for higher growth to generate higher saving through the age compositional effects of the life-cycle hypothesis. The international correlation between growth and saving rates comes from the response of growth to investment, as predicted by a variety of growth models. Saving responds passively to investment through mechanisms that are at present not well understood. A likely candidate is the saving behavior of firms or small entrepreneurs, who retain profits in order to finance investment. In any case, such saving is done, not by the mass of households, who play little part in the process of aggregate accumulation, but by a few relatively well-off people or by firms.

Second, bequest and dynastic motives are more important in explaining national saving than are life-cycle retirement motives. Life-cycle retirement saving implies that increases in growth rates will increase saving rates through age compositional effects. There is no such necessary implication in the case of bequest motives, although if bequests are a luxury good, richer economies – not more rapidly growing economies – will have higher saving rates. It is also possible that bequests are luxury goods only in the early stages of economic growth.

Third, because most households are not saving for retirement, changes in the rate of population growth will not reduce private saving rates. There is no reason to expect that the "graying" of East Asia will reduce its saving rates over the next two decades, or that population aging will threaten economic growth by limiting the supply of saving to finance investment.

Fourth, because most households are not saving for retirement, the substitution of (unfunded) social security will not much reduce private saving, so that the introduction of such social security systems cannot be held responsible for reductions in private savings rates and the associated reductions in growth, at least not through the direct mechanism of a reduction in private retirement saving.

Fifth, house prices and the arrangements for house purchase are *not* a major determinant of international differences in saving behavior. While we can expect land prices to be high and to rise rapidly in small, rapidly growing economies, the associated high price of housing does not generate additional saving, even in the absence of markets for home mortgages.

Sixth, consumption is subject to habit formation, but the effects are too small to explain the correlations between saving and growth in the international data.

I do not know if these implications are true, though in all cases, except possibly the fifth, I would bet (modestly) on the propositions as stated rather than on their opposites. If true, they put a heavy weight on (a) firm behavior and (b) bequest – or accumulation – motives as an explanation of the international differences in saving rates.

It is much easier to state hypotheses about saving than it is to propose data on which they might usefully be tested. The inadequacy of data, especially but not exclusively household survey data, has been a major stumbling block in designing research on saving. Saving measured from household surveys is typically very different (much less or even negative) than saving measured in national accounts estimates, which is itself derived as a residual or, worse, as the difference between two large residuals. Even in the United States and the United Kingdom, saving data from the Consumer Expenditure Surveys (U.S.) and the Family Expenditure Surveys (U.K.) behave differently than do the national aggregates that they might be thought to mirror, and in both countries coherence between the two data sources seems to be getting worse over time. In the United States, it is hard to track the recent decline in the saving rate through to the microdata, so that we cannot be sure whether the decline is a compositional effect – as would be the case if the LCH were true and the productivity slowdown were driving down the saving rate – or whether, as Bosworth et al. (1991) argue, the decline is more uniform across groups. Nor has there been any real progress in resolving the question of whether IRA saving incentives actually increase saving; they appear to do so in the microdata, but not in the aggregate.

It is therefore no accident that many of the most important papers over the past 15 years either have been theoretical or have come from thinking about intertemporal issues in a way that does not require good data on saving. A large fraction of the U.S. literature on the microeconomics of intertemporal choice has used the Panel Study of Income Dynamics (PSID), which collects data on only a fraction of consumption, so that it is (perhaps conveniently) impossible to calculate saving totals. The RHS, as well as the new HRS, do not attempt to collect consumption data. Important insights have come from thinking about what the various hypotheses mean for the behavior of consumption or for its growth rate, stochastic behavior, and profile over the life cycle. I think that the best work from individual researchers is likely to come from continuing to think this way. However, there are international institutions, such as the World Bank, that have an interest in saving, that do not have to take the quality and quantity of data as given, and that can play a role in improving the quality of saving data.

As a matter of urgency, a few selected countries should attempt a reconciliation between survey data and national accounts. This should entail the investigation of both types of data, with a full explication of how saving and income data are *actually* put together in the national accounts. At the survey level, there should be some small-scale experimental surveys that track cash flows and asset formation. Attention will also have to be given to a better separation of private saving into its household and firm components; while this is close to impossible for small business within the household sector, it should not be so for large corporations. This exercise should be done in countries where there are several years (not necessarily consecutive) of household income and expenditure surveys. Trends in survey saving rates can then be compared with trends in the national encome accounts, the accounting procedures in each systematically compared, and the effect of various adjustments tested. The statistical output would be (a) a better understanding of the sources of discrepancy in the selected countries and (b) general recommendations about national accounts and survey practice in general. The latter should not exclude the possible general recommendation that surveys do not attempt to collect saving data, a position to which the LSMS (Living Standards Measurement Study) surveys are coming close. Much of the survey data we currently have suggests that saving is done by relatively few households. A well-based comparison with the national accounts can help us decide whether this finding is correct or simply reflects measurement error. The disaggregation of macroeconomic saving totals is also a prerequisite for resolving the growth–saving puzzle, as in the U.S. example cited above. It is not possible to make much progress in interpreting changes in national saving without some idea of who is responsible for those changes.

There should also be more attempts to collect data on wealth in household surveys. Although it may be difficult to collect the accurate income information that would be required to compute saving flows, there is a better chance of obtaining data on the asset stocks, at least if the questions are asked in the right way. In particular, the bracketing techniques for collecting wealth that have been pioneered in the HRS in the United States should be applied to developing countries, perhaps as part of the natural evolution of the World Bank's LSMS surveys. The collection of data on bequests and on bequest intentions and expectations is also a priority. If it can be established that bequests are important, we have further evidence that growth does not drive saving through life-cycle considerations, and if we say something about the relationship between bequests and lifetime wealth, we can calibrate the likely effect of growth on saving through the bequest motive. In addition, if saving for bequests is important among the elderly, the aging of Asia may actually increase saving rates, not decrease them, while higher economic growth may actually dampen saving through a reverse life-cycle effect. If it is the old who save, the redistribution of relative income to the young with higher growth will redistribute income from high to low savers. If this effect looks real, it is yet more evidence that the saving–growth correlation is coming from somewhere else, most likely from the relationship between investment and growth.

References

Abel, Andrew B. 1990. "Asset Prices under Habit Formation and Catching Up with the Joneses," *American Economic Review*, Papers and Proceedings, 80: 38–42.

Arellano, Manuel, and S. R. Bond. 1991. "Some Tests of Specification for Panel Data: Monte Carlo Evidence and an Application to Employment Equations," *Review of Economic Studies* 58: 277–97.

Arellano, Manuel, and Olympia Bover. 1995. "Another Look at the Instrumental Variable Estimation of Error-Components Models," *Journal of Econometrics* 68: 29–51.

Arrau, Patricio, and Klaus Schmidt-Hebbel. 1994. "Pension Systems and Reform in Developing Countries," Special Issue of *Revista de Análisis Economico* 9: (June).

Arrow, Kenneth J. 1962. "The Economic Implications of Learning by Doing," *Review of Economic Studies* 29: 155–73.

Atkinson, Anthony B. 1969. "On the Timescale of Economic Models: How Long Is The Long Run?" *Review of Economic Studies* 36: 137–52.

Attanasio, Orazio P. 1991. "A Cohort Analysis of Saving Behavior by US Households," Stanford University (Sept.), mimeo.

Attanasio, Orazio P., Luigi Guiso, Tullio Jappelli, and Gugielmo Weber. 1992. "The Consumption Boom in the UK and Italy in the Late 1980s," Stanford University, Bank of Italy, Universita di Napoli, and University College London (May), mimeo.

Banks, James, and Richard Blundell. 1995. "Household Saving Behaviour in the UK," in Poterba (1995).

Barro, Robert J. 1991. "Economic Growth in a Cross-Section of Countries," *Quarterly Journal of Economics* 106: 407–43.

Barro, Robert J., and Xavier Sala-i-Martin. 1992. "Convergence," *Journal of Political Economy* 100: 223–51.

Bernheim, B. Douglas. 1991. "How Strong Are Bequest Motives? Evidence Based on Estimates of the Demand for Life Insurance and Annuities," *Journal of Political Economy* 99: 899–927.

Bewley, Truman. 1977. "The Permanent Income Hypothesis: A Theoretical Formulation," *Journal of Economic Theory* 16: 252–92.

Bhalla, Surjit S. 1979. "Measurement Errors and the Permanent Income Hypothesis: Evidence from Rural India," *American Economic Review* 69: 295–307.

        1980. "The Measurement of Permanent Income and Its Application to Saving Behavior," *Journal of Political Economy* 88: 722–43.

Börsch-Supan, Axel. 1992. "Saving and Consumption Patterns among the Elderly: The German Case, *Journal of Population Economics* 5: 289–303.

Börsch-Supan, Axel, and Konrad Stahl. 1991. "Life Cycle Savings and Consumption Constraints: Theory, Empirical Evidence, and Fiscal Implications," *Journal of Population Economics* 4: 233–55.

Bosworth, Barry P. 1993. *Saving and Investment in a Global Economy*, Washington, D.C., The Brookings Institution.

Bosworth, B. P., Gary Burtless, and John Sabelhaus. 1991. "The Decline in Saving: Some Microeconomic Evidence," *Brookings Papers on Economic Activity*, 183–241.

Browning, Martin J., and Annamaria Lusardi. 1996. "Household Saving: Micro Theories and Micro Facts," *Journal of Economic Literature* 34: 1797–855.

Campbell, John Y. 1987. "Does Saving Anticipate Declining Labor Income? An Alternative Test of the Permanent Income Hypothesis," *Econometrica* 55: 1249–73.

Campbell, John Y., and John H. Cochrane. 1994. "By Force of Habit: A Consumption Based Explanation of Aggregate Stock Market Behavior," Harvard U. and University of Chicago, Mimeo.

Carroll, Christopher D., 1992. "The Buffer Stock Theory of Saving: Some Macroeconomic Evidence," *Brookings Papers on Economic Activity*, 2: 61–156.

——— 1997. "Buffer Stock Saving and the Life Cycle/Permanent Income Hypothesis," *Quarterly Journal of Economics* 112: 1–55.

Carroll, Christopher D., and L. H. Summers. 1991. "Consumption Growth Parallels Income Growth: Some New Evidence," in B. Douglas Bernheim and John B. Shoven (eds.), *National Saving and Economic Performance*, Chicago: Chicago University Press for NBER, 305–43.

Carroll, Christopher D., and David N. Weil. 1994. "Saving and Growth: A Reinterpretation," *Carnegie-Rochester Conference Series on Public Policy*, 40: 133–92.

Cass, David. 1965. "Optimum Growth in an Aggregative Model of Capital Accumulation," *Review of Economic Studies* 32: 233–40.

Collins, Susan M. 1991. "Saving Behavior in Ten Developing Countries," in B. Douglas Bernheim and John B. Shoven, eds., *National Saving and Economic Performance*, Chicago: Chicago University Press for NBER, 349–72.

Constantinides, George M. 1990. "Habit Formation: A Resolution of the Equity Premium Puzzle," *Journal of Political Economy* 98: 519–43.

Davidson, James E. H., David F. Hendry, Frank Srba, and Stephen Yeo. 1978. "Econometric Modeling of the Aggregate Time-Series Relationship between Consumers' Expenditure and Income in the United Kingdom," *Economic Journal*, 88: 661–92.

Deaton, Angus S. 1991. "Saving and Liquidity Constraints," *Econometrica* 59: 1221–48.

——— 1992. *Understanding Consumption*, Oxford: Clarendon Press.

Deaton, Angus S., and Christina H. Paxson. 1994a. "Intertemporal Choice and Inequality," *Journal of Political Economy* 102: 437–67.

——— 1994b. "Saving, Growth, and Aging in Taiwan," in David A. Wise, ed., *Studies in the Economics of Aging*, Chicago: Chicago University Press for NBER, 331–57.

Dynan, Karen E. 1993. "How Prudent Are Consumers?" *Journal of Political Economy* 101: 1104–13.

Feldstein, Martin J. 1980. International Differences in Social Security and Saving, *Journal of Public Economics* 14: 225–44.

Feldstein, M. J., and Philippe Bacchetta. 1991. "National Saving and International Investment," in B. Douglas Bernheim and John B. Shoven, eds., *National Saving and Economic Performance*, Chicago: Chicago University Press for NBER, 201–26.

Feldstein, M. J., and Charles Y. Horioka. 1980. "Domestic Saving and International Capital Flows," *Economic Journal* 90: 314–29.

Flavin, Marjorie. 1981. "The Adjustment of Consumption to Changing Expectations about Future Income," *Journal of Political Economy* 89: 974–1009.

Friedman, Milton, 1957. *A Theory of the Consumption Function*, Princeton: Princeton University Press.

Gersovitz, Mark. 1988. "Saving and Development," in Hollis Chenery and T. N. Srinivasan, eds., *Handbook of Development Economics*, New York and Amsterdam: North Holland.

Hall, Robert E. 1978. "Stochastic Implications of the Life Cycle–Permanent Income Hypothesis: Theory and Evidence," *Journal of Political Economy* 96: 971–87.

Hammer, Jeffrey. 1986. "Population Growth and Savings in LDCs," *World Development* 14: 579–91.

Hayashi, Fumio, Takatishi Ito, and Joel Slemrod. 1988. "Housing Finance Imperfections, Taxation and Private Saving: A Comparative Simulation Analysis of the United States and Japan," *Journal of the Japanese and International Economies* 2: 215–38.

Hermalin, Albert, Mary Beth Ofstedal, and Chi Li. 1991. "The Kin Availability of the Elderly in Taiwan: Who's Available and Where Are They?" Ann Arbor: University of Michigan, Population Studies Center.

Holtz-Eakin, Doug, Whitney Newey, and Harvey Rosen. 1988. "Estimating Vector Autoregressions with Panel Data," *Econometrica* 56: 1371–95.

Horioka, Charles Y. 1989. "Why Is Japan's Private Saving Rate So High?" in Ryuzo Sato and Takashi Negishi, eds., *Developments in Japanese Economics*, San Diego: Academic Press, 145–78.

Hubbard, R. Glenn, Jonathan Skinner, and Stephen P. Zeldes. 1995. "Precautionary Saving and Social Insurance," *Journal of Political Economy*, 103: 360–99.

Hurd, Michael D. 1987. "Savings of the Elderly and Desired Bequests," *American Economic Review* 77: 298–312.

1989. "Mortality Risk and Bequests," *Econometrica*, 57: 779–813.

1992. "Wealth Depletion and Life-Cycle Consumption," in David A. Wise, ed., *Topics in the Economics of Aging*, Chicago: Chicago University Press for NBER, 135–60.

Jappelli, Tullio, and Marco Pagano. 1994. "Saving, Growth, and Liquidity Constraints," *Quarterly Journal of Economics* 109: 83–109.

Juster, F. Thomas, and James P. Smith. 1994. "Improving the Quality of Economic Data: Lessons from the HRS," Ann Arbor: Institute for Social Research, University of Michigan, and RAND.

Kaldor, N. 1957. "A Model of Economic Growth," *Economic Journal* 57.

Kaldor, Nicholas, and James A. Mirrlees. 1962. "A New Model of Economic Growth," *Review of Economic Studies* 29: 174–92.

Koopmans, Tjalling C. 1965. "On the Concept of Optimal Economic Growth," in *The Econometric Approach to Development Planning*, Amsterdam: North Holland.

Koltikoff, Lawrence J., and Lawrence H. Summers. 1981. "The Role of Intergenerational Transfers in Aggregate Capital Formation," *Journal of Political Economy* 89: 706–32.

Leff, Nathaniel. 1969. "Dependency Rates and Saving Rates," *American Economic Review* 59: 886–96.

1980. "Dependency Rates and Savings Rates: A New Look," in J. Simon and J. Da Vanza, eds., *Research in Population Economics*, Greenwich, CT: JAI Press.

Levine, Ross, and David Renelt. 1992. "A Sensitivity Analysis of Cross-Country Growth Regressions," *American Economic Review* 82: 942–63.

Lewis, A. 1954. "Economic Development with Unlimited Supplies of Labor," *Manchester School* 22: 139–91.

Lo, Joan Chi-chiung. 1989. "The Changing Patterns of Household Structure and Economic Status of the Elderly: 1976 to 1985," in *Conference on Economic Development and Social Welfare in Taiwan*, Vol. 1, Taipei: Institute of Economics, Academia Sinica.

Lucas, Robert E. 1988. "On the Mechanics of Economic Development," *Journal of Monetary Economics* 22: 3–42.

Mankiw, N. Greg, David Romer, and David Weil. 1992. "A Contribution to the Empirics of Economic Growth," *Quarterly Journal of Economics* 107: 407–37.

Mason, Andrew. 1987. "National Saving and Population Growth: A New Model and New Evidence," in D. G. Johnson and R. D. Lee, eds., *Population Growth and Economic Development: Issues and Evidence*, Madison, WI: University of Wisconsin Press.

1988. "Saving, Economic Growth, and Demographic Change," *Population and Development Review* 14: 113–44.

McKinnon, Ronald. 1991. The Order of Economic Liberalization, Financial Capital in the Transition to a Market Economy, Baltimore: Johns Hopkins University Press.

Miles, David. 1992. "Housing Markets, Consumption and Financial Liberalization in the Major Economies," *European Economic Review* 36: 1093–136.

Mirer, Thad W. 1979. "The Wealth–Age Relationship among the Aged," *American Economic Review* 69: 435–43.

Modigliani, Franco. 1970. "The Life-Cycle Hypothesis of Saving and Intercountry Differences in the Saving Ratio," in W. A. Eltis, M. F. G. Scott, and J. N. Wolfe, eds., *Induction, Trade, and Growth: Essays in Honour of Sir Roy Harrod*, Oxford: Clarendon Press, 197–225.

1986. "Life Cycle, Individual Thrift, and the Wealth of Nations," *American Economic Review* 76: 297–313.

1993. "Recent Declines in the Savings Rate: A Life Cycle Perspective," in Mario Baldassarri et al., eds., *World Saving, Prosperity, and Growth*, New York: St. Martin's Press, 249–86.

Musgrove, Philip. 1978. *Consumer Behavior in Latin America*, Washington, DC: Brookings Institution.

1979. "Permanent Household Income and Consumption in Urban South America," *American Economic Review* 69: 355–68.

Park, Yung Chul. 1993. "The Role of Finance in Economic Development in South Korea and Taiwan," in Alberto Giovannini, ed., *Finance and Development: Issues and Experiences*, Cambridge: Cambridge University Press.

Paxson, Christina H. 1992. "Using Weather Variability to Estimate the Response of Savings to Transitory Income in Thailand," *American Economic Review* 82: 15–33.

1996. "Saving and Growth: Evidence from Micro Data," *European Economic Review* 40: 255–88.

Poterba, James. 1995. *International Comparisons of Saving*, Chicago: Chicago University Press for the National Bureau of Economic Research.

Ram, Rati. 1982. "Dependency Rates and Aggregate Savings: A New International Cross-Section Study," *American Economic Review* 72: 537–44.

Romer, Paul M. 1986. "Increasing Returns and Long-Run Growth," *Journal of Political Economy* 94: 1002–37.

1990. "Endogenous Technical Change," *Journal of Political Economy* 98: S71–102.

Schechtman, Jack. 1976. "An Income Fluctuation Problem," *Journal of Economic Theory* 12: 218–41.

Schechtman, Jack, and Vera Escudero. 1977. "Some Results on 'An Income Fluctuation Problem,'" *Journal of Economic Theory* 16: 151–66.

Schmidt-Hebbel, Klaus, Steven B. Webb, and Giancarlo Corsetti. 1992. "Household Saving in Developing Countries: First Cross-Country Evidence," *World Bank Economic Review* 6: 527–49.

Shorrocks, Anthony F. 1975. "The Age–Wealth Relationship: A Cross-Section and Cohort Analysis," *Review of Economic Statistics* 57: 155–63.

Singleton, Kenneth J. 1990. "Specification and Estimation of Intertemporal Asset Pricing Models," in Benjamin M. Friedman and Frank H. Hahn eds., *Handbook of Monetary Economics*, Vol. 1, Amsterdam: North Holland, 583–626.

Solow, Robert M. 1956. "A Contribution to the Theory of Economic Growth," *Quarterly Journal of Economics* 70: 65–94.

Uzawa, Hirofumi. 1965. "Optimal Technical Change in an Aggregative Model of Economic Growth," *International Economic Review* 6: 18–31.

Viard, Alan D. 1993. "The Productivity Slowdown and the Savings Shortfall: A Challenge to the Permanent Income Hypothesis," *Economic Inquiry* 31: 549–63.

Weil, David. 1994. "The Saving of the Elderly in Micro and Macro Data," *Quarterly Journal of Economics* 109: 55–82.

Wolpin, Kenneth I. 1982. "A New Test of the Permanent Income Hypothesis: The Impact of Weather on the Income and Consumption of Farm Households in India," *International Economic Review* 23: 583–94.

CHAPTER 4

Financial Policies and Saving

Patrick Honohan

Introduction

The financial sector plays an important role in the saving process. On the one hand, use of financial instruments offers the household saver wide, albeit indirect, access to the yield on the investment opportunities available in the economy. An established literature stresses the importance of ensuring effective operation of this channel, as intermediated savings are likely to be more productive than where the household saver is limited to his or her own production and storage technologies. Of course, not all saving involves the accumulation of financial assets; furthermore, the characteristics of different financial assets likely influence the total volume of saving much less than they do the composition of the savings portfolio, a topic that is not dealt with here.

On the other hand, reliable access to borrowed funds through the financial system can reduce precautionary saving as well, turning some households into dissavers. Recently, the rapid deregulation of financial systems in many industrial countries has highlighted the fact that financial repression may have constrained some households from borrowing more than it constrained others from saving. Although financial liberalization can enhance the efficiency with which saved resources are channeled into productive use, the suspicion that it may have contributed to the sharp decline in saving ratios in many industrial countries has brought financial-sector policy to the fore in the discussion of saving.

Differences in the structure and performance of the financial sector in different parts of the world may help explain some of the empirical contrasts noted in Chapter 2 – for example, in regard to the historical average decline in savings rates and the fact that this decline has been absent in many Asian countries. Improvements in the efficiency of the international financial system may help to reduce the correlation between national saving and investment ratios. In order to be in a position to evaluate the validity of such hypotheses, we need much more information about the degree to which financial constraints and opportunities do in fact shape saving behavior in the developing countries.

Econometric research on financial aspects of saving in developing countries has not been lacking. For various reasons, including the poor quality of much of the data, robust conclusions have been hard to come by. This chapter reviews the main empirical financial-sector issues in relation to saving. The discussion focuses on the two main channels of effect: the impact of credit availability, and the role of the financial sector in providing attractive savings media.

Following this introductory section, then, the chapter begins by exploring the role of liquidity constraints and, in general, the barriers to consumption smoothing by households. First, the strengths and limitations of Euler equations and sample splitting, two main methodological devices commonly used in the empirical analysis of this area, are described, along with the evidence of liquidity constraints that they have revealed. Then the two main theoretical approaches to the modeling of optimal saving behavior in the presence of liquidity constraints are described, followed by a discussion of the likely quantitative importance of such constraints – for both precautionary and life-cycle saving – with special mention of the role of housing finance, the impact of financial liberalization, and the special features of household credit in low-income areas.

The chapter then turns to the role of asset characteristics, beginning with the rate of return, whose ambiguous impact on savings rates is well known. Institutional characteristics of savings media that may influence their use are then briefly considered. These include confidence, convenience, and habit, as well as the tax and regulatory environment facing financial intermediaries – though, as mentioned, they have more impact on portfolio composition than on total saving and as such require limited attention in the context of the present volume. The effectiveness of direct tax incentives for saving and the impact of social security and efficient annuities markets on saving are then reviewed. Finally, the question of sectoral consolidation is briefly examined: to what extent are government and business saving substitutes for household saving?

Finally, the chapter draws some general lessons regarding the use of different sources of data for assessing financial-sector influences on saving. This includes the use of financial-sector balance sheet information itself for improving the data on aggregate sectoral saving and the use and limitations in this context of panels of national data and of microdata. The need for innovative approaches for developing sources of information in the financial field is also noted. The appendix to this chapter briefly describes the use of financial accounts for the estimation of aggregate saving.

Liquidity Constraints

One of the important influences of the financial sector on saving behavior is the degree to which it allows households to borrow. The fact that households cannot borrow all they would wish – or at least not without paying interest rates that are much higher than those available to depositors – is almost too well known to require empirical proof. Indeed, it is many years since Hayashi (1987) pointed out as conclusive evidence the sizable gap between money market rates and those charged by banks for unsecured household lending even in the United States, and remarked that "future research should examine the causes not the existence of liquidity constraints" (p. 91). In addition to the causes, it is desirable to know the magnitude of the effect of liquidity constraints on saving, particularly with a view to assessing what net benefit might be obtained from policy interventions to alleviate liquidity constraints.

Models of consumption under liquidity constraints were examined in Chapter 3, and the discussion here focuses mainly on the empirical evidence and the implications for financial policy. An obvious point bears restating at the outset, namely that easing liquidity constraints is likely to reduce the domestic saving ratio. Liquidity constraints tend to reduce consumption of the constrained households, thereby increasing aggregate domestic saving at any level of aggregate disposable income. The policy case for easing liquidity constraints derives more from the static microeconomic efficiency gains that might ensue, particularly for lower-income households that are likely to be disproportionately affected.

Evidence of Liquidity Constraints: Euler Equations and Sample Splitting

Two methodological tricks underlie much of the empirical work that has tried to detect evidence of liquidity constraints. They apply across a variety of underlying theoretical models. These are (i) the use of Euler equations predicting a relationship between optimally chosen consumption in successive periods, and (ii) (in cross-section data) the selection of a subsample of households considered unlikely to be liquidity constrained.

Euler Equations. The enormous focus on liquidity constraints in saving studies over the past 15 years has largely resulted from the empirical failure of simple Euler equation models of consumption growth. As long as the household can freely transfer resources between periods, household borrowing and lending will (according to any of a variety of simple intertemporal optimization models) be used to smooth out the consumption path relative to predictable income fluctuation. In particular, such models predict a simple dynamic structure linking consumption in successive periods, with expected change in consumption depending primarily on the rate of interest at which resources can be transferred between the periods.

If there is no uncertainty, and no gap between borrowing and lending rates, the optimal growth rate of consumption is a simple function of the rate of interest. A noteworthy feature of this theoretical relationship (known as a Euler equation because of the mathematical technique used to derive its optimality) is that it does not depend on current disposable income, essentially because the impact of fluctuations in income has been smoothed by the optimization. However, when disposable income is included in empirical regressions based on such Euler equations and using aggregate data, it is generally found to be statistically significant (Deaton, 1992, is a valuable reference to this extensive literature). The econometric rejection of the hypothesis that disposable income should not be significant suggests that current income matters more for consumption than it would were resources freely transferable between periods at the measured interest rate. This therefore provides indirect evidence that liquidity constraints may be important (though it might equally be attributable to the failure of some other of the many assumptions on which the Euler equation relies).[1]

Evidence from Developing Country Macrodata. The first extensive tests of this type of Euler equation on aggregate savings data for developing countries were carried out by Haque and Montiel (1989), who confirm the results of many others for industrial countries. They estimate separate equations explaining aggregate private saving for each of 16 developing countries over the period 1960–85, paying particular attention to the issue of residual correlation. The theoretical framework underlying their estimates allows households that have no liquidity constraints to optimize over a possibly finite lifetime. By distinguishing between the evolution of human and nonhuman wealth for these unconstrained households, and by assuming that liquidity-constrained households simply consume current income, they are able to test separately the hypotheses of infinite household life and absence of liquidity constraints. They accept the first, but reject the second decisively. Indeed, for most of the 16 countries their estimate of the fraction of disposable income accounted for by the constrained group is a good deal

---

[1] A more elaborate approach distinguishes between intertemporal substitution and risk aversion as motives for saving (see Attanasio and Weber, 1989; Farmer, 1990; Weil, 1990; Epstein and Zin, 1991).

higher than estimates obtained for industrial countries, suggesting that liquidity constraints are more important in the developing world.[2]

Raut and Virmani (1989) also found current income to be highly significant in a Euler equation estimated for a panel of developing countries. However, their results proved highly sensitive to the inclusion of interest rates, real or nominal. If interest rates are included in the equation, current income is no longer significant. Their data (which is for expenditure, rather than consumption) covers 23 countries for all or some of the period 1973–82. A drawback of their approach is that, although much of the data variation is between countries, the authors chose not to include fixed effects (country dummies). Accordingly, between-country differences in the mean rate of consumption growth are left to be explained by levels of per capita consumption and income, as well as by the interest and inflation rates. It seems unlikely that omitted country-specific factors would be uncorrelated with the included variables; therefore, the estimated coefficients are likely to be biased. Furthermore, the central bank discount rates that were used are unlikely to correspond closely to private-sector opportunity costs over the period studied because of rationing of central bank funds at those rates.

Sample Splitting in Micro–Data Sets. In microeconomic data sets, there is the possibility of identifying households that are more likely to be subject to liquidity constraints. If we know that the households in a certain subset are not liquidity constrained, then we can estimate the parameters of unconstrained behavior. Assuming that these parameters are common to the constrained households also, inferences can be drawn from a comparison of the complementary subset.

The most prominent example here is where explicit questions on liquidity or borrowing constraints were used in the questionnaire. The respondents to some surveys were asked whether they had been refused credit or whether they had not sought credit because they anticipated refusal. Apart from providing a direct estimate of the number of households who are constrained, this allows a very precise cut of the sample, from which the quantitative impact of the liquidity constraints may be estimated.

The 1983 U.S. Survey of Consumer Finances (SCF) was the first such survey.[3] Since then the Banca d'Italia has also asked similar questions

---

[2] In this context it is worth noting the assessment made by Browning and Lusardi (1996), in their lucid review of the U.S. literature, that the evidence in favor of liquidity constraints in the United States is probably not sufficient to outweigh strong prior beliefs to the contrary.

[3] Browning and Lusardi (1996) provide a convenient review of some of the saving-relevant results from these U.S. surveys.

(see Guiso and Jappelli, 1991). The questions asked in the SCF were "In the past few years has a particular lender or creditor turned down any request you (and your husband/wife) made for credit or have you been unable to get as much credit as you applied for?" and "Was there any time in the past few years that you (or your husband/wife) thought of applying for credit at a particular place but changed your mind because you thought you might be turned down?" Using the answers to these questions, it is possible to deduce that about one-in-five respondents reported themselves to be liquidity constrained (Jappelli, 1990).

More indirectly, one can separate (as unlikely to be liquidity constrained) those households that are currently saving from those who are not, or those that currently have liquid assets, or those whose members are currently in employment. In practice, however, the indirect approach selects rather different subsets of ostensibly liquidity-constrained households than do the explicit SCF questions (Hayashi, 1985, 1987; Alessie, Kapteyn, and Melenberg 1989; Zeldes, 1989; Jappelli, 1990; Runkle, 1991). An early application of this kind of approach was to Indian data (Bhalla, 1979), where a subsistence level of consumption was defined, and households with income below this were assumed not necessarily to obey the permanent income hypothesis.

The fitted values of a saving function estimated for the unconstrained households can be applied to the remainder of the sample, and the scale of the consumption shortfall attributable to the liquidity constraints can be deduced. Alternatively, sample splitting can be applied to the Euler equation. Many studies (an exception is Runkle, 1991) have found that the Euler equation restrictions are more nearly satisfied by the subsample not thought to be liquidity constrained, thereby providing more focused evidence than can be obtained from aggregate data that liquidity constraints may be the source of the problem.

Limitations of the Euler Equation Approach. A drawback of analysis based on the Euler equation is that, because of its focus on the rate of *change* of consumption, it often yields little information about the determinants of the *level* of consumption or the saving rate. This is partly because obtaining explicit solutions to models of optimal behavior is usually more difficult than deriving these Euler equations (and may be impossible) and partly because the focus of the research is on testing a precise hypothesis. What may be regarded as nuisance parameters from the point of view of a test of the permanent income hypothesis are often exactly the parameters of interest in a more general study.[4]

---

[4] In his discussion of Poterba (1987), Hall goes so far as to suggest that measurement of income, and therefore of savings, raises so many conceptual problems as to make its avoidance highly desirable in empirical work. Nevertheless, measuring income seems unavoidable for many of the questions of interest in the present context.

Optimal Household Behavior under Liquidity Constraints

There are two main approaches to the analysis of optimal household behavior under conditions of liquidity constraint, namely the approach that posits a wedge between borrowing and lending rates, and that which proposes instead an exogenous borrowing limit.[5] (The former may be regarded as a special case of the latter with borrowing rates at infinity.)

Wedge between Borrowing and Lending Rates. Naturally, the analysis is more tractable if uncertainty is neglected. In this case, if the household does have borrowing possibilities, but only at a much higher interest rate than for household lending (deposits), there will be a range of income over which households will not choose to borrow, but will instead consume exactly their current income (Flemming, 1973; Pissarides, 1978). Only an exceptionally low income will trigger some borrowing. It follows that the size of the wedge between borrowing and lending rates will influence the level of saving and the marginal propensity to consume out of disposable income.

If data on the average wedge in an economy is available, it may plausibly be modeled as a function of macroeconomic conditions (e.g., rate and trend of unemployment) as has been done by King (1986).[6] He found that fluctuations in the wedge were negatively associated with aggregate consumption in the United Kingdom.

So far as developing countries are concerned, the availability of short-term loans from money lenders in all societies would seem to argue for the wedge theory as opposed to an absolute borrowing limit. However, in order to test the theory, one needs to have some indication of the size and variability of the wedge. Time-series or cross-section data on the interest rate wedge, or on the cost of borrowing from moneylenders is rarely available.[7] Fitted values of an equation that is estimated for some

---

[5] A third approach, which makes the household's borrowing limit a function of its current earnings, has also been proposed (Alessie, Kapteym, and Melenberg, 1989) and should be distinguished from the other two in view of its rather different implications. If they can adjust their household labor supply, such households may be able to ensure that, despite the borrowing constraint, they are not at a corner solution. In their application, Alessie et al. suggest that all employed persons should be assumed to be in this position.

[6] The emergence of such a wedge may reflect an equilibrium in the financial market considering the probability of default (even in the absence of the kinds of asymmetric information and adverse selection discussed by Stiglitz and Weiss, 1981). King (1986) describes such a situation within a two-period partial equilibrium framework where neither the bank nor the household knows in advance whether it will be in a high-earning or low-earning condition in the second period.

[7] Though Aleem (1990) has an interesting account of the determination of the wedge in an

other country and that relates the wedge to macroeconomic conditions could conceivably be used as a proxy for the wedge in situations where explicit wedge data are not available.

A Fixed Borrowing Ceiling. The alternative assumption of a fixed ceiling on household borrowing (possibly zero) is sufficiently simple to allow rigorous analysis of household responses to uncertain income flows. In the framework proposed by Deaton (1991a, 1991b), the household is in receipt of a stochastic income flow and may hold a liquid asset that yields a given rate of return: no borrowing is possible. If the household optimizes the discounted present value of expected utility (with a constant discount rate and a time-invariant felicity function), then its optimal consumption decision rule is a function only of the cash resources in hand – current income plus liquid assets. If these are low, all current resources are consumed, but beyond a certain threshold (which will depend on interest rates and the parameters of the utility function), liquid assets are held over into the next period. They represent a kind of precautionary balance against the risk of high-frequency income fluctuations. Thus, consumption is a kinked function of the cash in hand: a 45 degree line up to the threshold and a shallower curve thereafter.

Deaton (1991b) has shown that the shallow curve can be well approximated by a straight line, thereby offering a very simple rule-of-thumb approach: "If you have any cash left after reaching the threshold consumption, save about 30 percent of that remainder" (p. 257). The 30 percent figure is not perturbed much by alternative plausible assumptions about utility function parameters, but the model is clearly applicable primarily to low-income households and where bequest motives are not very important.[8]

Both of these theoretical approaches to liquidity constraints provide a rationale for why year-to-year fluctuations in household consumption may track household income more closely than would be implied by the permanent income hypothesis. An alternative framework, which does not rely on ad hoc restrictions on borrowing, has been advanced by Carroll (1992). Carroll's households would prefer to borrow were there no uncertainty, but because of the possibility of catastrophic and permanent loss of income, they do hold precautionary savings. (Note that Carroll's framework does not take account of the possibility of households defaulting on their borrowings, and thus of shifting some of the longer-term income risk to lenders.)

---

environment of monopolistic competition in the informal household credit market in Pakistan.

[8] Past accumulations of household debt can also affect behavior in important ways, potentially acting as a destabilizing factor (King, 1994), but such problems seem unlikely to be important in the experience of developing countries up to now.

How Big an Effect on Saving?

Whether they are accumulated because of liquidity constraints or because of the curvature of the utility function, the size of precautionary liquid balances is not necessarily very high. Simulation of a variety of calibrated theoretical models suggests that precautionary balances should be low (see Aiyagari, 1994), though other models imply the opposite (see Hubbard, Skinner, and Zeldes, 1994). Survey evidence was reported in Guiso, Jappelli, and Terlizzese (1992). Focusing on risk aversion rather than liquidity constraints, and drawing on Italian survey data of self-reported income uncertainty, they found a very small effect on consumption. They estimated that this kind of precautionary saving reduces consumption by less than 0.2 percent of permanent household income.

However, just because precautionary liquid balances (held to smooth high-frequency income fluctuations) may not be large does not at all imply that saving is little affected by the existence of liquidity constraints. Indeed, the main effect would be present even in the absence of uncertainty and would come from the impact of borrowing constraints over the life cycle (see Hubbard and Judd, 1986). Plenty of evidence indicates that young households do not dissave as much as would be predicted by intertemporal optimization at money market interest rates. Instead life-cycle consumption patterns track the hump-shaped life-cycle income patterns fairly closely. Attempts can be made to explain this away, for example by pointing out that the felicity functions themselves may be life cycle dependent, with greater expenditure being required by large families to equalize the marginal felicity with that attained when young.[9] But the favored explanation of many for much of this hump is the existence of borrowing constraints, restraining consumption below desired levels on a long-term basis and even when income flows are nonstochastic or substantially predictable.

The evidence reported by Hayashi (1985) is relevant here. He estimated the unconstrained consumption level for the households in his (1963 US-SCF) sample, on the basis of the equation estimated for unconstrained households. He arrived at a shortfall of 2.7 percent of household consumption, which has sometimes been described as a rather small figure – but by 1991, net household saving was so low that an addition of 2.7 percent to consumption would have lowered net private saving by over one-third.

Housing Finance. A particular medium-term issue for the savings of many households is the accumulation of resources for house purchase or

---

[9] As W. M. Gorman's schoolteacher put it: "A penny bun costs threepence when you have a wife and a baby."

house construction. Where well-developed mortgage finance institutions exist, newly formed households can promptly acquire or build a house commensurate with their lifetime income. The related saving by such a household will typically be smoothed over the maturity of the mortgage loan as the loan is amortized. In the absence of mortgage finance institutions, the saving must precede or at least be simultaneous with the acquisition of the asset, thereby depressing other consumption. Aggregate saving in an economy without mortgage finance institutions is thus likely to be greater than in those with well-developed housing finance.

Most countries lie between these two extremes, with some availability of mortgage finance, but with a ceiling on the loan-to-value ratio, and with many households excluded from the market because of the level and variability of their incomes. Mortgage finance is also typically subject to specific tax treatment, with important tax expenditures available in many countries. Partial liberalization of the mortgage market may not necessarily result in reduced savings, especially if it brings households into a position where they want to save in order to accumulate the necessary down payment in lieu of renting throughout their lifetime. Removal of tax concessions for housing-related saving may also affect saving.

Jappelli and Pagano (1994) have examined these effects both theoretically and empirically (and their paper also looks into the general equilibrium and growth implications). The normal loan–value ratio obtainable from mortgage finance institutions in 30 countries (including 8 outside the OECD) is a highly significant explanatory variable in their regression of net national saving rates, and the point estimate implies that a 15 percentage point increase in the loan–value ratio (or reduction in the down payment ratio) reduces the national saving rate by 2.6 percentage points. It remains unclear whether this substantial effect is entirely a housing-related one, or whether the coefficient on the loan–value ratio is also capturing the effect of other omitted variables that are correlated with the loan–value ratio; but the result is suggestive of an important long-term impact.

Financial Liberalization. It is worth distinguishing between the steady-state impact on the saving ratio of a particular configuration of the financial markets with the transitional effects of financial liberalization. As well as allowing households to consume the amounts they would have chosen for their particular life-cycle position, the sudden availability of consumer credit will also lead to a revision of target precautionary balances and will allow some young households that had hitherto been constrained from life-cycle borrowing to consume at a higher rate than they would over a full unconstrained lifetime. These latter two effects suggest that, for a transitional period, aggregate household saving will fall below its steady-state level and that a surge in consumption will be observed (Muellbauer, 1994).

In addition to extensive evidence for the United Kingdom, an easing of credit market conditions facing households is widely believed to have caused a dip in saving in the 1980s in Scandinavian countries (see Lehmussaari, 1990; Koskela, Loikkanen, and Virén, 1992), and it will certainly be a relevant factor for the analysis of optimal policy phasing in developing countries. It will be worth collecting a number of case studies along these lines of liberalizing developing countries (an early example here for Uruguay is de Melo and Tybout, 1986).

Among the U.K. evidence is the paper by Miles (1992), which focuses on liberalization of the mortgage market in the United Kingdom from 1979 on, mainly through a new availability of "second mortgages" allowing owners of housing equity to dissave without moving house. Of special interest here is the variable used to measure the effects of the liberalization, namely an estimate of the total amount of home equity withdrawn in each year. The estimate is based on measures of the total value of investment in housing and of the change in mortgage debt. While the precise measure has been criticized, and while it begs the question of whether a demand or a supply shift is at work, it does have the merit of being quantitatively linked to a specific form of dissaving. Miles finds that almost 80 percent of withdrawn equity is consumed (rather than involving just a portfolio shift) and that this additional consumption accounts for essentially all of the very substantial fall in the U.K. personal savings ratio from 12 percent to less than 5 percent during the 1980s (see also Bayoumi, 1993).

Special Characteristics of Developing Countries. The relevance of these considerations for households in developing countries will differ widely from country to country and between income levels in any given country. Middle- and upper-income households will find much the same factors entering their decisions as the bulk of households in the industrial countries. Financial liberalization will not rescue all low-income households from liquidity constraints, and such households will also tend to rely more on nonfinancial mechanisms, such as coinsurance through village or extended family networks, for precautionary saving (Udry, 1990; Townsend, 1994).

In addition, the forms of debt contract and the collateral provided sometimes differ qualitatively in developing countries, particularly in rural areas. Hoff and Stiglitz (1990) point out the use of such devices as pledging the harvest from a stand of cocoa trees or giving the lender the usufruct of a parcel of land, in lieu of conventional collateral. (Indeed such innovative tailored financial contracts have had some vogue in international lending to developing countries too.) Simply using quoted wholesale financial market interest rates as a measure of the cost of borrowing is unlikely to give reliable results in such circumstances.

The use of local and idiosyncratic credit and insurance mechanisms in parts of the developing world means a major departure from the conventional picture of household savings being collected in a national pool that can be allocated to efficient uses. Instead the picture is more of a highly segmented set of credit and savings markets between which arbitrage is imperfect. Udry's (1990) finding that 97 percent of loans in rural northern Nigeria were between individuals in the same village or at least the same kinship group is illustrative here. The informational problems that localize the demand for credit are clear enough: the supply price of such funds depends partly on the opportunity cost in terms of alternative savings media. It is to the latter that we now turn.

Insurance and Intertemporal Substitution: The Financial Assets of Households

We turn to the question of financial asset holdings of households. Not all savings are held in financial form – far from it. Indeed, a larger part of household assets in many countries are in the form of housing (Miles, 1992). So far as financial assets are concerned, in few developing countries do relatively illiquid claims on pension rights constitute as large a share as they do in industrial countries (especially for middle-income households; see Wolff, 1994). Currency and bank deposits are relatively more important in developing countries. The decision as to how much financial savings to accumulate and in what form to hold them will depend in part on the availability of various types of asset, on their rate of return (taking account of taxation considerations), and on the existence of complementary assets, including government social insurance programs.

The Rate of Return

The rate of return at which resources can be transferred between different periods of a household's life cycle is the most obvious financial factor that needs to be taken into account in considering saving behavior. For households that have access to financial assets, the rates of interest on these will be the natural reference point. In optimizing models, only under special conditions will saving be insensitive to the rate of interest. On the other hand, because of the wealth and current income effects that will generally be present, there is no presumption as to the direction of the aggregate saving response to an exogenous interest rate change. Despite many studies, this remains a controversial area – partly because of a surprising shortage of reliable and comparable cross-country data on retail interest rates.

The empirical analysis of this issue has attracted partisans, as it has been linked with the debate on whether or not financial liberalization is "good." If higher interest rates could be shown to increase savings, thereby fueling productive capital investment and boosting growth, then this would seem to be a powerful argument for a financial liberalization that does increase interest rates. In fact, such a simple proposition does not have strong empirical support.

So far as developing countries are concerned, the literature has recently been reviewed again by Srinivasan (1993), who updates the study by Balassa (1990). Basically the conclusion remains that more studies have found a positive interest elasticity of saving than a negative one, but the coefficients have generally been small and often insignificant. If there are strong and consistent interest rate effects on saving, they are not evident in the data. The fragility of the evidence is illustrated by the succession of papers by Fry (1988) and Giovannini (1983, 1985).[10] Giovannini cast doubt on Fry's positive coefficients by adding or subtracting countries and years by comparison with Fry's samples. In addition, the low Durbin-Watson statistics reported by Fry in many of his panels suggests that there may be a bias from missing variables (or at least important country effects) and there may also be autocorrelation. These are only partly technical questions of econometric technique: underspecified equations cannot always be rescued by the application of robust estimation techniques.

Since the interest elasticity of saving is theoretically ambiguous, some economies may exhibit positive income elasticity and others negative. A parametrization of the interest response according to observed country characteristics (e.g., per capita income, growth rate, region) may allow a reconciliation of the diversity of results hitherto obtained (see Ogaki, Ostry, and Reinhart, 1996).

The effect of interest rates on saving could be nonlinear, perhaps involving threshold effects. At the level of the individual household, a degree of nonlinearity could be present both in the Euler equation and in the formula for the level of saving (through the nonlinear influence of the level of interest rates on household wealth).[11] From the systemic point of

---

[10] Other multicountry papers that explore the role of interest rates include Gupta (1987), Leite and Makonnen (1986), Ostry and Reinhart (1992), Rossi (1988), and Schmidt-Hebbel, Webb, and Corsetti (1992) – the latter paper looking specifically at household-sector saving. The paper by Ostry and Reinhart employs a two-good model – traded and nontraded goods – in order to identify the role of terms of trade changes. For the most part, however, it seems premature to be thinking in terms of multigood models, such as those surveyed by Blundell (1988).

[11] Another source of nonlinearity could be the kind of option consideration that can be

view, the notion that the reduced form impact of an exogenous change in the interest rate in a repressed economy might be nonlinear (with small deviations from the unrepressed equilibrium generating only a modest impact on system performance) is well established.[12] A further source of nonlinearity could lie in the consideration that very high real interest rates may reflect political uncertainty, peso effects, and the like. If so, the observed interest rate may overstate the saver's expected return. Then even if the response of saving to expected return were linear, the response to observed interest rates might become flat at high interest rates. Whatever the source, it would be worth estimating the importance of such nonlinearity in future empirical work, whether through simple power and interactive terms, or using more sophisticated techniques such as neural network approximation (see Granger, 1991).

While it is real interest rates that influence the intertemporal substitution aspects of saving in a world of certainty, inflation may have an additional role over and above that which it plays as deflator of nominal interest rates. Accelerating inflation may create confusion over relative prices, and may be associated with a generalized increase in uncertainty, in either case tending to increase saving. The separate role of inflation therefore needs to be allowed for in empirical studies, as in Lahiri (1989), who also distinguishes between anticipated and unanticipated inflation.

Far more important for aggregate saving is the availability of a variety of alternative nonfinancial assets, the return on which may not be captured by deposit interest rates. While the use of real interest rates implicitly acknowledges that goods inventories are an alternative to financial assets, it may be necessary to take explicit account of alternative investment opportunities, notably the rate of return on owner-occupied housing and other real estate investment. Many developing countries have experienced property booms, and household saving may have been very sensitive to the after-tax rate of return on investment in real estate (see, e.g., Koskela and Virén, 1994).

---

introduced by transactions costs inhibiting immediate response to reversible interest rate changes.

[12] Notably by Dornbusch and Reynoso (1989). They observe that, although measured saving has increased following major stabilization programs, there are some ready explanations that cast doubt on the reality of the increase. In particular, capital flight through misinvoicing of trade serves to conceal saving that is being hidden abroad: an apparent increase in saving may really be a reduction in capital flight. Furthermore, stabilization tends to reduce the incentive for saving in the form of durable goods purchases, which are usually counted as consumption in the data. A recent theoretical contribution that formalizes the notion of a genuine nonlinearity in the relationship between inflation and saving is Azariadis and Smith (1996).

Increasingly important too in some countries are the rates of return on quoted equities and bonds, and on foreign-currency denominated assets. The degree to which households have access to such assets for their saving, and the channels by which such savings are intermediated are quite diverse, and analysis using such data needs to be informed by country-specific institutional knowledge.

It is worth stressing that the interest elasticity of saving cannot in general be deduced from the coefficient of the interest rate in Euler equations of short-term consumption growth rates (discussed in the previous section). Even if consumption growth rates are positively correlated with interest rates, a shock to interest rates will in general alter the whole intertemporal consumption path resulting in ambiguous predictions for saving.

Intangible Institutional Aspects

Econometric work has tended to neglect a number of obviously important but somewhat intangible issues relating to expectations, psychology, and institutions in the mobilization of savings. Although especially important for the composition of savings, they can also affect its overall level.

Security and Confidence. Security is probably the single most important characteristic sought by savers in a store of value. There are many dimensions to security, and they relate not only to the risk characteristics of the contracted instrument, but to the issue of default on the part of the financial intermediary and to a variety of political risks, including the risk that the instrument could be subject to confiscation, devaluation, or unexpectedly onerous taxation, or that the use of the proceeds on maturity could be restricted (for example, through the imposition of foreign exchange controls).

Risk of default may be offset by the existence of a credible deposit insurance, but default is not confined to the private sector. In some countries, governments have incurred lengthy payments arrears in respect of such financial liabilities as the postal savings system or treasury bills. Lengthy delays without compensation amount to partial default, and such governments have difficulty in inducing further voluntary saving in similar forms.

Fear of taxation or expropriation can be a strong disincentive to placing one's savings with a domestic financial institution whose accounts may be examined by the government authorities. Recognizing this, many governments have granted bank depositors a degree of confidentiality. Where political institutions are sufficiently stable for this to be credible, it can contribute to a sense of security. But confidentiality of bank deposits facilitates illegal transactions, and there have been moves in recent years to limit the scope of such confidentiality.

In some countries, currency reforms have had the effect of expropriating savings.[13] Where this has happened, savers reasonably fear a recurrence, perhaps under a different guise. In other countries such expropriation would be considered "unthinkable" in political and administrative circles; and in those countries savers will rightly ignore that risk, even if fiscal and payments difficulties prevail. Whatever its basis, political risk encourages capital flight, where residents choose to place their savings with foreign financial intermediaries despite incurring transactions costs and settling for lower yields than apparently available at home. Conversely, it is common for special tax and exchange control privileges to be available to nonresident depositors, and this has been effective in some countries in inducing emigrants to hold substantial deposits in their home country.

Convenience. Under the heading of convenience, the physical location of bank branches comes first. Opening a branch is a sure (but often costly) way for a bank to obtain deposits. Conversely, many savers will not choose to travel long distances to obtain access to a financial intermediary, especially if information flows are so poor that the trustworthiness of that intermediary may be hard to evaluate. Fry (1986, 1988) reports regressions for six Asian countries, which suggest a large effect on the aggregate savings rate of increases in the density of rural bank branches. He estimates that increased banking density over 20 years increased the Indian saving rate by 5 percentage points.[14] While it may very well be that the push to increase rural branching in India diverted funds from the informal financial sector rather than truly increasing national saving, the effect is suggestive of the importance of institutional arrangements for attracting household savings.

Other convenience features such as queuing time in bank offices and ease of transferability of funds through checks, direct debits, and the like

---

[13] Recent examples would be the 1993 demonetization of old rubles in Russia, the 1991 forced exchange of cash for blocked deposits in Brazil, and the earlier demonetization of high-denomination banknotes in Ghana. Holders of onshore foreign currency accounts have not been exempt, as in Mexico in 1982, when foreign currency accounts were compulsorily converted to peso accounts at the overvalued official exchange rate.

[14] A fall of 10 percent in the rural population per rural branch was estimated to result in an increase in the saving rate of 0.16 percentage points. In contrast to the fragile coefficients on interest rate, which become insignificant when the Cochrane-Orcutt adjustment for serial correlation is introduced, the coefficients on branching in these studies seem robust (Fry, 1986). Alternative measures of branch density could be envisaged, such as percentage of population within a given radius of a branch or the number of branches per unit area.

are also important. Short branch opening hours, minimum deposit amounts that put bank accounts beyond the reach of a large segment of the population, and a process of interrogation as to the intended use of the funds withdrawn are familiar inconveniences in many developing countries.

For low-income households, and in remote rural areas, other types of institutions become relevant. In the poorest countries of Africa and Asia the formal financial system (licensed banks, insurance companies) has limited penetration in terms of the percentage of households using its services. Cash is universally held, but is a bad store of value where inflation is high. Saving of poor households is not then predominantly in the form of financial assets or housing, but commonly takes the form of livestock, grain, or (in some areas) precious metals.[15] A network of informal financial institutions often known as rotating savings and credit associations (ROSCAS) is also important. Despite many microstudies documenting the operation of these informal financial institutions, too little is still known about their quantitative importance. Some estimates of the amount of financial assets outstanding in ROSCAS are very high (Chandavarkar, 1986; Hoff and Stiglitz, 1990), but the basis for most of these estimates is unsure and there may be a considerable degree of double counting.

Other Institutional Aspects. What the financial system will offer to the saver in terms of yield and liquidity depends on the degree of institutional development and competition in the financial sector, and on the tax treatment – implicit and explicit – of the sector.

For banks, the real after-tax interest offered to depositors is often reduced by administrative ceilings on bank lending rates and by a variety of explicit and implicit taxes on banking, such as unremunerated reserve requirements, gross receipts taxes, and the like, all of which tend to bite severely in times of inflation. Directed lending to unprofitable sectors also limits the deposit rates that can be offered to depositors. Unless it is indexed, explicit taxation of interest income from deposits can be quite onerous in times of inflation – at least if an effective tax regime, such as a withholding tax, is in place. These taxes and regulations are typically supported by the operation of exchange controls, which, though never fully effective, give the local financial system a partially captive market. In nonbank areas such as life insurance it is also common to see onerous regulations that have the effect of greatly reducing the yield that such intermediaries can offer to savers.

The existence of well-functioning stock markets could also be a

---

[15] A notable recent study by Rosenzweig and Wolpin (1993) stresses the role of bullocks as the main store of value in Indian agriculture.

factor influencing saving. Such markets offer savers a richer menu of assets allowing an improved risk–return frontier while retaining liquidity. Again, the predicted impact on aggregate saving is theoretically ambiguous. Recent empirical evidence suggests that funds attracted to liquid stock markets in developing countries come mainly as a switch from other assets and that these markets do not actually stimulate additional saving (Levine and Zervos, 1996; see also Bonser-Neal and Dewenter, 1996). This conclusion was drawn from the insignificance of indicators of stock market development in cross-section regressions where the dependent variable was the ratio of private saving to GDP. (The share of bank lending to the private sector was also included in the regressions as a measure of banking system development, but it too was insignificant.)

Habit. Historians of finance stress the importance of bounded rationality and information costs in determining the range of savings instruments that will be considered in a society at any given time. Even though modern financial technology has reduced information costs dramatically, household savers are still creatures of bounded rationality and habit. The differing degrees to which various classes of financial institutions have succeeded in mobilizing saving in different countries may be partly attributed to this consideration. As Thaler (1994) points out, awareness that "experts" consider a savings medium to be good value is a powerful inducement to shift resources in its direction.

Among others, Thaler and Shefrin (1981) have argued for the importance of habits along a different type of dimension, namely the fact that saving is a type of activity where self-discipline comes into play. Whereas standard time-consistent preferences do not generate the sorts of issue discussed by Thaler and Shefrin, they propose a more realistic modeling of household behavior according to which the household (or individual) may find it optimal to precommit to saving so that problems of time inconsistency and lack of self-discipline will be reduced.[16] Regular contractual savings schemes that impose penalties for failure to keep to a preestablished saving profile can be attractive for households in this type of situation. It is also a possible rationale for compulsory savings schemes mandated by government, especially in regard to provision for old age.

Tax Incentives for Saving

The industrial country literature has considered the question of tax incentives for saving, both in terms of the overall tax structure (expendi-

---

[16] Thaler's (1994) suggestion, that an immediate reward to the saving has a stronger effect (for equal present value) than a high yield accruing over a long interval, can be seen as an aspect of this point too.

ture tax versus income tax) and in terms of specific tax-favored investment media. Both positive and normative issues are discussed in the
excellent survey by Boadway and Wildasin (1994; see also OECD, 1994),
but we do not consider normative issues here. The general question of
encouraging saving by a switch from income to consumption taxes is one
that may only be of modest importance in developing countries given the
leaky nature of the personal income tax system in such countries and the
likelihood that much of capital income can avoid heavy income taxation
anyway. Perhaps more interesting is the potential for targeted savings
incentives (though, as mentioned above, the tax treatment of mortgage interest can also be very important and is sensitive to the rate of
inflation).

A number of microlevel studies of the response of U.S. households
to special federal income tax concessions available to long-term
savers through so-called IRAs and other incentive schemes have not
concluded unambiguously whether or not these have led to an increase
in household savings. A recent study plausibly suggests that, while the
long-term effects of the incentives would be to increase savings, the
short-run effects are small, as savers substitute IRAs for other already
accumulated assets (Engen, Gale, and Scholz, 1994; but see Venti and
Wise, 1990, and the symposium introduced by Hubbard and Skinner,
1996).

In the process of analyzing household behavior in response to the
tax incentives, researchers have uncovered what appears to be evidence
for irrational behavior. For instance, though this is possible to rationalize
in terms of expected changes in tax rates or in terms of liquidity, there is
a very strong preference for front-loaded over back-loaded savings incentives even when they are equivalent in present value terms. Furthermore, while savers would benefit more from the tax deferral on accruals
early in the tax year, most IRA savers wait until the end of the tax year.
Such hard-to-explain behavior has strengthened the case for the existence of psychological factors and rule-of-thumb behavior discussed
above.

More generally, one of the important messages for developing
countries to come from the analysis of household response to saving
incentives is that households may differ significantly in the degree to
which they accumulate assets for retirement, and indeed in the degree to
which their asset accumulation behavior can be rationalized. Bernheim
and Scholz (1993) note significant differences in this regard between
U.S. households who are versus those who are not college educated.
Households who are less educated appear to accumulate too little
relative to their postretirement consumption needs. In addition, the
less educated respond much less vigorously to targeted tax incentives
and to employer-provided pensions. With a much lower proportion
of those who are college educated, households in many developing

countries might also be expected to exhibit systematic undersaving, whether in a life-cycle sense or in the degree to which they respond to specific saving incentives. The differential role of the social safety net in affecting the saving behavior of low-income households needs to be kept in mind.

Social Security and Annuities

Although there are dissenting voices, a plausible case can be made for the proposition that a very high proportion of bequests are accidental, in the sense that they represent wealth held for the purpose of smoothing consumption flows in old age. Because the age at death is uncertain, and in the absence of well-functioning annuities markets, it will not be possible to program one's wealth holdings so that they are just exhausted at the moment of death.

Provided it is a credible one (something that cannot be guaranteed for all developing countries for reasons such as inflation and a poor record of government payments), the establishment of a social security system that provides an annuity to retired persons can obviously reduce this precautionary saving motive, and the effect may be an important one. Although early studies both for the United States and a cross section of industrial countries suggested a sizable impact here (e.g., Feldstein, 1980), the empirical literature on this area has been very controversial (Atkinson, 1987; Davis, 1995). At a theoretical level, labor supply (through age of retirement) may also be affected by the introduction or improvement of social security benefits, and there may accordingly be an increase in life-cycle savings in anticipation of the earlier retirement, so that the net effect on savings is ambiguous. At the empirical level, results have tended to be sensitive to the measures of households' "social security wealth," both at the aggregate level and in microdata. Although Feldstein's early claims of a one-for-one substitution of social security wealth for other savings do not appear to hold up, it would be unwise to conclude that there is no effect. Atkinson (1987) counsels agnosticism.

The potential role of private annuities markets in influencing the story here should not be neglected. The presence of private intermediaries offering actuarially fair annuities would make it more likely that any effects of the introduction of a social security system will tend to be neutralized by offsetting transactions in the market for annuities. Furthermore, there is no presumption that the introduction of actuarially fair private annuities on its own will reduce private saving: an income effect of the introduction will tend to be offset by a substitution effect.[17]

---

[17] The substitution effect is absent from the typical social security system, to the extent that

Even though fair annuity pricing appears to have been absent even in the United States until recently (Friedman and Warshawski, 1990; Mitchell, Poterba, and Warshawski, 1997), these are important considerations to bear in mind in assessing the savings impact of alternative institutional designs for pension provision. For example, the much-discussed systems of Singapore and Chile have defined-contribution characteristics, unlike the defined-benefit social security system commonly analyzed in the literature, and there is no guarantee that fairly priced annuities will be purchasable at retirement (Vittas, 1993). Because of the institutional diversity, it would appear necessary to analyze such schemes on a case-by-case basis.

Whatever these theoretical issues, growing awareness of the aging population structure in many countries has put pension finance to the top of many agendas, and many commentators expect pension finance to be a growth area in the years ahead. The modest size of pension funds in all but a handful of developing countries to date indicates that the potential for growth is significant. Of course, of itself the aging process tends to reduce the size of pension funds as a share of GDP compared with a population structure that has already stabilized. Nevertheless, the emergence of doubts about the ability or willingness of the public sector to fund generous pensions in the coming decades is beginning to lead to a growing interest in privately funded pensions, whether funded by employers or by individuals.

The semiautomatic and often quasi-involuntary nature of the pension fund contribution probably accounts for the considerable share of pension funds in many industrial economies today, as it does in such developing country models as the Singapore provident fund and the Chilean retirement savings scheme. But it must not be forgotten that the very long-term nature of the pension contract means that political uncertainty assumes an important role. Despite the success of mandatory schemes for pension saving managed by private intermediaries in Chile and elsewhere (Corsetti and Schmidt-Hebbel, 1997), it remains unlikely that any society without a modicum of political and economic stability will enjoy a significant growth in voluntary saving in onshore pension funds.

Sectoral Consolidation

As households are the ultimate owners of private corporations, and to the extent that government debt must ultimately be serviced out of taxation, it is unlikely that household saving behavior is entirely unaf-

it does not allow for choice over the amount of savings to be held in the form of social security (see Abel, 1985).

fected by the saving of corporations and of the government. Indeed, going further, if the household sector acted as if it had fully consolidated its claims on corporate savings and all future tax liabilities, then (ceteris paribus) all changes in corporate and government saving would be fully offset by changes in household saving. Clearly, this extreme consolidation hypothesis implicitly assumed a considerable degree of financial market efficiency, as the household sector is assumed to be able, for example, to offset fully temporary tax increases with borrowing, and that such borrowing would be at the same interest rate as is available to government. These conditions prevail in few developing countries (as confirmed by the cross-country panel study of Corbo and Schmidt-Hebbel, 1991, which regresses private consumption on government saving for 13 developing countries),[18] but it may be increasingly approximated as financial liberalization progresses. The changing degree of private-sector–public-sector consolidation (i.e., the degree to which "Ricardian equivalence" prevails) is of the utmost importance in assessing the potential role of public policy in influencing aggregate national saving. If the Ricardian proposition were true, it would overturn the traditional view in development economics that the government's deficit is the most powerful instrument for influencing national saving.

It is important to bear in mind that Ricardian equivalence would not deny a potential impact of changing marginal tax rates or changing levels of government expenditure on private saving. Such changes do alter marginal conditions and would in general lead to a behavioral response. In a 30-country study, Karras (1994) looked specifically at the issue of whether government spending may be complementary to private consumption and finds this to be the case.

The integration of corporate and household decisions is implicit in the specification of private-sector savings as the dependent variable in many developing country studies. However, researchers often acknowledge that this practice is driven more by data availability than by a firm belief

---

[18] The Corbo and Schmidt-Hebbel study is careful to distinguish (as far as possible) between consumption expenditure and capital formation, and between "permanent" and "current" concepts. They also include fixed country effects in their panel estimates, normalize most variables by expressing them as a proportion of current disposable income, and use two-stage least squares estimators. Thus, their approach is free of the most pervasive econometric problems in this area. Eight of the 13 countries in the sample are in Latin America. The balance of payments deficit on current account is included as an explanatory variable and has a strong and significant effect. In contrast, interest rate, inflation, and the liquidity ratio do not contribute significantly. The estimated impact of a $100 increase in government saving on private saving is a reduction of between $16 and $50 if the saving results from a decline in government spending and between $48 and $65 if the saving is from increased taxation.

in the transparency of the corporate veil for savings. It is true that liquidity constraints are unlikely to bind for many corporate share-holders, as they are almost exclusively drawn from the higher wealth quantiles, so one of the major a priori arguments against Ricardian equivalence does not apply to consolidation of corporate saving. The relative tax treatment of distributed and retained earnings is obviously an important factor influencing the quantity of corporate savings, but it is not the only one, and indeed it is hard to explain why corporations in economies where the full imputation tax system[19] does not apply still pay substantial dividends – the so-called dividend puzzle. Some of the pro-posed resolutions of this puzzle rely on the fact that managers are but imperfect agents for shareholders, so that retained earnings may not have the same value to shareholders as cash in hand.[20] If so, there will not be full consolidation.

Any attempt to estimate the degree to which increases in corporate savings influence household savings at the aggregate level is liable to fall foul of the econometric problem of simultaneity, as most of the factors influencing corporate saving are liable to influence household saving also. Poterba (1987, 1991) suggests the use of changes in the relative tax treatment of distributed and retained earnings as an instrument in the estimation: such changes are likely to be independent of household savings behavior. Substantial cash payments to shareholders as a by-product of mergers or corporatization of mutual enterprises also have the potential to generate quasi-experimental data and have been of occasional macroeconomic importance in some countries.

Contrasting Approaches to Empirical Analysis

It will be evident from the above discussion that the key limiting factor in assessing the role of the financial sector in influencing saving has been the difficulty of obtaining suitable data that can allow precise inferences. A great diversity of approaches has been adopted in the literature to try to overcome this problem. This section looks at some lessons that have been learned.

---

[19] With a full imputation system, all corporate tax paid is credited against individual income tax on dividends received by shareholders. Many countries do not have a full imputation system, but allow either a partial credit or no credit at all. Without full imputation, there may be a tax disincentive to the payment of dividends.

[20] Among the resolutions of the dividend puzzle that do not rely on agency problems is the "trapped equity" argument, according to which the company may not have sufficient profitable investment opportunities to absorb cash flow from existing operations. If so, the extra dividend taxes will have to be paid sooner or later and there remains no real tax advantage to retention.

Financial Sector Balance Sheets as a Source of Saving Data

All aggregate saving research needs to face up to the fact that saving is very imperfectly measured. The major concepts have long been defined in the System of National Accounts, SNA (recently revised; see Inter-Secretariat Working Group, 1993). In particular, despite well-known difficulties, the SNA does provide a usable definition of saving. However, the precision with which saving is measured is not high. All surveys of saving behavior in developing countries stress this point, but it is also true for industrial countries as witness the very large revisions in the U.K. saving ratio documented by Muellbauer (1994). For the most part, national private and household saving concepts are measured as a residual in a commodity balance framework. (For a detailed discussion of data problems see the appendix in Chapter 2 of this book.)

It is perhaps surprising against this background that, in practice, national-accounts statisticians rarely take account of an important alternative data source, namely the balance sheets of financial institutions. Yet by constructing the so-called accumulation accounts of the flow of funds using balance sheet information, it is possible to obtain a useful independent check on the accuracy of the commodity balance equations. After all, saving results in the accumulation of assets, whether physical or financial, and to neglect available data on the accumulation of financial assets is clearly an important omission. Flow-of-funds accounts distinguishing[21] between the household and business sector do exist, at least on a partial basis, for about 20 developing countries (Honohan and Atiyas, 1993). Of course, this is not a perfect data source either and is not necessarily a more reliable approach to estimating national saving aggregates. For example, capital flight does not show up directly in the balance sheets of national financial intermediaries (although some further development of the international bank deposit statistics could help). These issues are described in more detail in the appendix of this chapter.

Panel Studies of Countries

Even given good-quality aggregate saving data, it can be difficult in a single time series to distinguish the role of changing financial factors from many other nuisance variables. This sort of factor is the major reason for the current vogue in the increasing use of panel studies in

---

[21] Though it has to be acknowledged that the distinction between corporate and personal- or household-sector saving becomes increasingly blurred in low income countries where the business and household finances of the self-employed and owners of unincorporated enterprises are hard to disentangle.

developing countries. Of course, there are countervailing limitations. Although the developing countries can be seen as an additional source of data variation on which standard theories may be tested, the usefulness of this perspective depends on the degree to which saving behavior is homogeneous across countries and regions, and also on the quality of the data. If countries differ widely in unobserved dimensions such as the distribution of household rates of time preference or of risk aversion, or in other unmodeled structural features, then a cross-country study that neglects such differences risks exaggerating the role of measured variables (such as financial market depth) through omitted variables bias.[22] Furthermore, data deficiencies in most of the developing countries means that adding them to the sample may introduce more noise than precision to the estimation of hypotheses about saving. For the same reason, studies of aggregate behavior from a panel of developing countries are more credible if they err on the side of including a large number of fixed individual, regional, and structural effects, both as to intercept and as to slope. Underspecified panel studies risk serious biases. For the same reason, broad-brush modeling strategies that are sure to help in summarizing the data variation seem more convincing than complex theoretical models relying on hard-to-identify or subtle effects.

Microdata Versus Macrodata

Analysis based on microdata (cross-section or panel) allows a greater degree of flexibility in estimating national or regional preference parameters (though identifying assumptions of homogeneity are still required). Indeed, it could be argued that micro–data sets are indispensable if we are to obtain precise estimates of the parameters specified in many microeconomic theories. Even in simple situations, heroic assumptions are required to permit such parameters to be recovered from aggregate regressions. In addition, aggregate data often display little or no variability on the elements of concern or, if an available aggregate data series does vary, the variation is often in a dimension that is not correlated with the underlying concept of interest.[23] On the other hand, microdata are subject to a variety of errors, including sampling error and response bias, which may well be larger than the errors associated with aggregate or

[22] Carroll, Rhee, and Rhee (1994) find no evidence that immigrants to Canada from different parts of the world differ in their saving behavior, suggesting an absence of cultural differences. However, international heterogeneity remains an issue, even within OECD countries (see Kessler, Perelman, and Pestieau, 1993).

[23] Compare, for example, two approaches to measuring the influence of credit rationing on household saving: (a) by use of aggregate time series on household saving and the measured average wedge between borrowing and lending rates; and (b) by use of a survey in which each household reports whether it has been credit constrained.

economy-wide data. Some questions – such as sectoral consolidation – may be better analyzed by aggregate data. Furthermore, the costs of collecting microdata are considerable. So one should proceed with a judicious balance between improving macrodata sources and collecting new microsamples.

The huge economies of scale in data collection means that collection of micro–panel data is contemplated only for the larger countries. It is rarely also practical to integrate panel analysis fully across countries, so that methodological differences arise, meaning that the information cannot be pooled without subtle meta-analytical work.

Nevertheless, microdata that focus directly on the issue of financial-sector impacts on saving provides the most convincing evidence. A good example is the explicit questions on the U.S. Survey of Consumer Finances concerning whether the household has been liquidity constrained. These questions have led to much persuasive modeling.[24] The Banca d'Italia also asks relatively detailed questions focused on relevant issues such as liquidity constraints and subjective income risk.

However, an important caveat must be considered here about the quality of the data obtained from household surveys on portfolio composition. The two major U.S. surveys, carried out for the Federal Reserve Board in 1963 and 1983, captured little more than one-half of the total financial assets expected from independent information. Even when augmented by a special nonrandom sample of high-income households, the 1983 FRB survey identified less than three-quarters of the total, and still captured only 40 percent of the holdings of U.S. savings bonds, for example.[25] Despite these known deficiencies, there has been a tendency

---

[24] An interesting use of this data by Jappelli, Pischke, and Souleles (1995) illustrates the potential of combining information from different data sources. By modeling the probability of reporting oneself as credit constrained to the SCF as a function of other observable household characteristics (using a probit model), the authors obtain a method for generating predicted probabilities of constraint for a (different) panel sample of households (the PSID), thereby widening the scope and usefulness of the information obtained.

[25] U.S. studies (Ferber, 1965; Ferber, Forsythe, Guthrie, and Maynes, 1969a and b) suggest a definite pattern of underreporting of wealth in U.S. surveys. Based on a sample of households for whom asset information was known from bank records, they find that failure to report ownership of an asset is by far the most important source of error on average. For savings accounts, for example, 1 in 3 asset holders reported no holdings to the U.S. survey. On the other hand, the average amounts reported by those who acknowledged holdings were almost exactly equal to the true average holdings, with overstatement of small accounts being offset by understatement of large. The second most important source of error was the fact that nonrespondents were much more likely to have substantial savings account balances than respondents: those with savings balances greater than $5,000 (in 1963) were twice as likely to refuse to respond as those with less than $1,000.

for econometricians to employ these data as if they represented unbiased information.

Ad Hoc Data Sources and Spotting Ingenious Uses for Existing Data

Although the sophistication of theoretical models has greatly evolved over the years, it could be said that (to some extent at least) the early literature was theory driven, while the more recent literature has been driven by data availability. After all, the rapid development of national income accounting was strongly influenced by Keynes's model of aggregate income determination, at the center of which was the Keynesian consumption function. More recently, attempts to understand the consumption behavior of households and how it differs over time and across countries has often been dominated by pragmatic use of available data that has not been assembled primarily to investigate these matters. Examples of this arise both for macrodata and for microdata.

An important example among the micro–data sets comes from the widely used U.S. Panel Survey of Income Distribution (PSID). Although this survey measures only the household's purchases of food, these data have been widely used as a proxy for total household consumption. A further difficulty applies at the level of attempting to proxy permanent income, and there have been a number of quite ingenious studies for developing countries that have cast around for plausible instruments.[26] When it comes to modeling financial-sector influences, the available data series are most imperfect – even ignoring serious measurement error. For instance, data on household asset holdings at the beginning and end of year from a single cross section have been differenced to infer saving, an invalid procedure in the presence of capital value changes. Household samples have been truncated at high levels of income or of liquid assets, with a view to excluding those who may have been faced with credit rationing. Modeling the likely impact of fiscal measures on the budget constraints or opportunity sets of individual households often requires considerable ingenuity in coaxing plausible information from micro–data sets.

In macroeconomic analyses, the use of data proxies has also become

---

[26] For example, Wolpin (1982) used average weather conditions as an indicator of permanent income for a study of farm households in India. Ramanathan (1968) computed normal income in Indian household data by averaging over certain group variables (occupation, age, etc.), with a modification for the expected growth in income. Again working on Indian data, Bhalla (1980) used as permanent income the fitted value from an earnings function estimated from a panel of households. Betancourt (1971) explored the permanent income hypothesis by grouping Chilean household data and testing Friedman's idea that the marginal propensity to consume between groups will be significantly higher than the average of the within-group propensities.

widespread. Although some of these can be described as farfetched and are easily criticized, the basic strategy is a constructive one and should be refined rather than dismissed.

Among the proxy measures of the prevalence of credit constraints are: expert assessments of the "normal" maximum mortgage ratio (minimum down payment ratio) in different countries, the percentage of home owners in certain age groups, and the interest rate wedge on consumer and mortgage loans (Jappelli and Pagano, 1989); and the value of consumer credit and the rate of consumer credit delinquencies (Carroll, 1992). Admittedly, albeit suggestive of the magnitude of credit constraints, these series are much further conceptually from the ideal data than are the aggregate saving data from their ideal.

The interest rate wedge (between borrowing and lending rates for households), whether for mortgage lending or for unsecured consumption loans, is closer to a theoretical concept of credit market imperfections, but in this case as in others the data is collected on a basis that is not harmonized across countries even to the limited extent that is achieved for industrial countries in the SNA.

International comparability is also an issue for measures of density of the rural branch network of the formal banking system (Fry, 1988), which represents an attempt to measure access of households to the banking system. The various measures of the evolution of financial liberalization that have been proposed for industrial countries would also need to be adapted for use in other countries on a case-by-case basis. Despite the obvious difficulties, there is much to be said for continued efforts to improve, refine, and expand the scope of such ad hoc variables.

Concluding Remarks

The speed and scale of change in the financial system in recent years has focused attention on the likely impact on aggregate savings. Partial though it is, the evidence from developing countries does suggest that liquidity constraints have been an important influence on saving in developing countries, resulting in higher aggregate saving than would otherwise have occurred. As liberalization of financial sectors in these countries is consolidated, it may well be that a fall in saving ratios will result, though increased efficiency in the use of loanable funds may outweigh any such reduction in the overall effect on growth.

Higher interest rates and improvements in asset quality will influence the allocation of saving portfolios, but it is less clear that they have much impact on aggregate saving. Compulsory pension saving may have a more reliable effect on aggregate saving; as with other forms of public saving, they do not appear to be fully offset by private responses.

The pace of financial innovation and financial reform in developing countries, as elsewhere, in recent years has outstripped the econometric analysis. There is undoubtedly a need for further empirical study of the nature and scale of the effect of financial-sector change on saving behavior. While fluctuations in macroeconomic and demographic influences may be more important in explaining the evolution of aggregate household and business saving, neglect of the financial-sector dimension could seriously bias the estimated influence of nonfinancial factors, potentially leading to mistaken policy inferences.

Appendix: Using Financial Flows to Estimate Aggregate Saving

The construction by national income statisticians of aggregate saving measures is usually based primarily on a set of commodity balance identities. National private and household saving is usually treated as a residual in this set of commodity accounts. Logically, however, aggregate saving is also a key element in a set of identities involving financial and other capital assets. Basically, the point is that any sector's net saving must be reflected in the accumulation of some asset. Changes in the capital value of assets will complicate this identity, but the basic point still holds. To the extent that much of household saving is reflected in an increase in the liabilities of banks and other financial institutions, it is clear that availability of data on the balance sheet composition of these financial institutions can provide useful independent information contributing to the measurement of household saving.

The System of National Accounts (Inter-Secretariat Working Group, 1993) presents a consistent conceptual framework that reconciles these two approaches to aggregate saving. Using this methodology, the financial flows and the commodity flows are in principle reconcilable through a single figure for savings. In practice, the figure that one obtains from the commodity balance approach can differ widely from that constructed using financial flows – sometimes by a wide margin. There are obvious difficulties with the data drawn from financial flows. For example, capital flight does not show up directly in the balance sheets of national financial intermediaries (although some further development of the international bank deposit statistics could help).

But there are weaknesses in the commodity flows too, and there is no a priori basis for considering one to be invariably superior to the other. Yet in practice, national-accounts statisticians rarely take account of the financial flows. An effort to improve the assembly of the financial flows data and to use it as a cross-check on existing sources seems worthwhile.

The two main flow of funds accounts in the System of National Accounts are the accumulation accounts, namely the financial account and the capital account. Sectoral data is provided for households (including unincorporated enterprises – e.g., family farms and small artisan enterprises), nonfinancial corporations, financial corporations, general government, and the rest of the world.[27]

The financial account (formerly known as the capital finance account) presents each sector's accumulation of financial assets and liabilities of different types. The balancing item is the sector's net lending. The main financial assets identified are: currency and deposits; securities other than shares; loans; shares and other equity; and the technical reserves of insurance. Trade credit is sometimes also identified separately. These assets can all be further subdivided. Each sector's accumulation of financial assets or liabilities of each identified type is entered in the matrix. The net sum equals that sector's net lending (or net borrowing if negative).

The capital account (formerly known as the capital accumulation account) presents the accumulation of nonfinancial assets that make up the difference between a sector's net lending and its saving. The four main asset classes identified here are produced tangible and intangible fixed assets (e.g., software), nonproduced assets (such as land, uncultivated forestry, and mineral deposits), and inventories. An additional item in this table is capital taxes and transfers. For households, accumulation of housing assets is typically the main item in the capital account.

The net accumulation of these assets plus net capital transfers or taxes paid represents the difference between net lending and saving for a sector. Thus, an estimate of net lending based on financial flow data, combined with the data of the capital account, provides an independent estimate of sectoral saving.[28] Reconciling these two estimates is of course a matter of judgment: we need to decide the relative degree of reliance to place in the commodity-based saving figure, the financial-flows-based net lending figure, and the figure for accumulation of nonfinancial assets (from the capital account).[29]

---

[27] There is also the sector of nonprofit institutions serving households, including such bodies as trade unions, charities, and churches.

[28] It should be noted that a further step would be required to obtain the change in the sector's wealth, notably to take account of capital value changes. These can be crucially important in inflationary economies. The necessary adjustments may be recorded in the "other changes in assets account."

[29] One way of doing so is to add a set of adjustment factors to the main components of each of the identities leading to the estimate of saving. The adjustment factor must be such as to reconcile the two estimates. If we attach a prior estimate of the precision of each of the main data elements, then the adjustment factors can be chosen in such a way as to minimize a sum of squares (weighted by the reciprocal of the prior precision).

Flow-of-funds accounts distinguishing between the household and business sectors exist, at least on a partial basis, for about 20 developing countries (Honohan and Atiyas, 1993). However, many of these involve only the capital account and have been constructed to be consistent with the saving data from the commodity balance accounts. In other words, they were not built up from the financial account, and cannot therefore be used for the main purpose sought in the present exercise, namely an independent source of saving data.[30]

Capital flight effected through misinvoicing of trade typically results in an underestimate of saving from the commodity balances. To the extent that international data sources, such as the banking statistics, reported by the Bank of International Settlements, can be harnessed in this context, accumulation of foreign financial assets enters directly into the financial account and thus into the financial-flow-based estimate of saving.

References

Abel, A. B. 1985. "Precautionary Saving and Accidental Bequests," *American Economic Review* 75: 777–91.

Aiyagari, S. R. 1994. "Uninsured Idiosyncratic Risk and Aggregate Saving," *Quarterly Journal of Economics* 109: 659–84.

Aleem, I. 1990. "Imperfect Information, Screening, and the Costs of Informal Lending: A Study of a Rural Credit Market in Pakistan," *World Bank Economic Review* 4: 329–49.

Alessie, R., A. Kapteyn, and B. Melenberg. 1989. "The Effects of Liquidity Constraints on Consumption: Estimation from Household Panel Data,"*European Economic Review* 33: 547–55.

Alessie, R., A. Kapteyn, B. Melenberg, M. P. Devereux, and G. Weber. 1997. "Intertemporal Consumption, Durables and Liquidity Constraints: A Cohort Analysis," *European Economic Review* 41: 37–60.

Atkinson, A. B. 1987. "Income Maintenance and Social Insurance," in A. Auerbach and M. Feldstein, eds., *Handbook of Public Economics 2* (Amsterdam: North Holland), 779–908.

Attanasio, O. P., and G. Weber. 1989. "Intertemporal Substitution, Risk Aversion and the Euler Equation for Consumption," *Economic Journal* 99: Supplement, 59–73.

Azariadis, C., and B. D. Smith. 1996. "Private Information, Money and Growth:

The least squares approach derives from that suggested by Geary (1973) in a related context.

Unlike alternative financial-flows-based approaches such as that adopted for the United States by the Federal Reserve Board (see Engen, Gale, and Sctolz, 1994), this approach does lead to a saving estimate conceptually equivalent to national-accounts saving.

[30] For only seven of the countries studied by Honohan and Atiyas (1993) was the financial account available, namely Cameroon, Cote d'Ivoire, Ecuador, Korea, Portugal, Thailand, and Yugoslavia.

Indeterminacy, Fluctuations and the Mundell-Tobin Effect," *Journal of Economic Growth* 1: 309–32.

Balassa, B. 1990. "The Effects of Interest Rates on Savings in Developing Countries," *Banca Nazionale del Lavoro Quarterly Review* 172: 101–18.

Bayoumi, T. 1993. "Financial Deregulation and Household Saving," *Economic Journal* 103: 1432–43.

Bernheim, B. D., and J. K. Scholz. 1993. "Private Saving and Public Policy," in J. Poterba, ed., *Tax Policy and the Economy* 7 (Cambridge, MA.: MIT Press).

Betancourt, R. R. 1971. "The Normal Income Hypothesis in Chile," *Journal of the American Statistical Association* 66: 258–63.

Bhalla, S. S. 1979. "Measurement Errors and the Permanent Income Hypothesis," *American Economic Review* 63: 295–307.

   1980. "The Measurement of Permanent Income and Its Application to Savings Behavior," *Journal of Political Economy* 11: 123–34.

Blundell, R. 1988. "Consumer Behaviour: Theory and Empirical Evidence – A Survey," *Economic Journal* 98: 16–65.

Boadway, R., and D. Wildasin. 1994. "Taxation and Savings: A Survey," *Fiscal Studies* 15: 19–63.

Bonser-Neal, C., and K. Dewenter. 1996. "Does Financial Market Development Stimulate Savings? Evidence from Emerging Market Stock Markets," Federal Reserve Bank of Kansas City Research Working Paper 96-09.

Browning, M., and A. Lusardi. 1996. "Household Saving: Micro Theories and Micro Facts," *Journal of Economic Literature* 34: 1797–855.

Carroll, C. D. 1992. "The Buffer-Stock Theory of Saving: Some Macroeconomic Evidence," *Brookings Papers on Economic Activity*, BPEA 2, 61–135.

Carroll, C. D., B.-K. Rhee, and C. Rhee. 1994. "Are There Cultural Effects on Saving? Some Cross-Sectional Evidence," *Quarterly Journal of Economics* 109: 685–700.

Chandavarkar, A. G. 1986. "The Non-institutional Financial Sector in Developing Countries: Macro-economic Implications for Savings Policies," in United Nations, *Savings for Development* (New York: United Nations).

Corbo, V., and K. Schmidt-Hebbel. 1991. "Public Policies and Saving in Developing Countries," *Journal of Development Economics* 36: 89–115.

Corsetti, G., and K. Schmidt-Hebbel. 1997. "Pension Reform and Growth," in S. Valdès-Prieto, ed., *The Economics of Pensions, Principles, Policies and International Experience* (Cambridge University Press).

Davis, E. P. 1995. *Pension Funds: Retirement-Income Security and Capital Markets: An International Perspective* (Oxford University Press).

Deaton, A. S. 1991a. "Savings and Liquidity Constraints," *Econometrica* 59: 1221–48.

   1991b. "Household Saving in LDCs: Credit Markets, Insurance and Welfare," *Scandinavian Journal of Economics* 94(2): 253–73.

   1992. *Understanding Consumption* (Oxford: Clarendon Press).

de Melo, J., and J. Tybout. 1986. "The Effects of Financial Liberalization on Savings and Investment in Uruguay," *Economic Development and Cultural Change* 34: 561–88.

Dornbusch, R., and A. Reynoso. 1989. "Financial Factors in Economic Development," *American Economic Review*, Papers and Proceedings, 79: 204–9.

Engen, E. M., W. G. Gale, and J. K. Scholz. 1994. "Do Saving Incentives Work?" *Brookings Papers on Economic Activity* 1: 85–180 (with discussion).

Epstein, L. G., and S. E. Zin. 1991. "Substitution, Risk Aversion and the Temporal Behavior of Consumption and Asset Returns: An Empirical Analysis," *Journal of Political Economy* 99: 263–86.

Farmer, R. E. A. 1990. "RINCE Preferences," *Quarterly Journal of Economics* 105: 43–61.

Feldstein, M. S. 1980. "International Differences in Social Security and Saving," *Journal of Public Economics* 14: 225–44.

Ferber, R. 1965. "The Reliability of Consumer Surveys of Financial Holdings: Time Deposits," *Journal of the American Statistical Association* 60: 148–63.

Ferber, R., J. Forsythe, H. W. Guthrie, and E. S. Maynes. 1969a. "Validation of Consumer Financial Characteristics: Common Stock," *Journal of the American Statistical Association* 64: 415–32.

Ferber, R., J. Forsythe, H. W. Guthrie, and E. S. Maynes. 1969b. "Validation of a National Survey of Consumer Financial Characteristics: Savings Accounts," *Review of Economics and Statistics* 51: 436–44.

Flemming, J. S. 1973. "The Consumption Function When Capital Markets Are Imperfect," *Oxford Economic Papers* 25: 160–72.

Friedman, B. M., and M. J. Warshawsky. 1990. "The Cost of Annuities: Implications for Saving Behavior and Bequests," *Quarterly Journal of Economics* 105: 135–54.

Fry, M. J. 1986. "National Saving, Financial Saving and Interest Rate Policy in Asian Developing Economies," in United Nations, *Savings for Development* (New York: United Nations).

1988. *Money, Interest, and Banking in Economic Development* (Baltimore: Johns Hopkins University Press).

Geary, R. C. 1973. "A Method for Estimating the Elements of an Interindustry Matrix Knowing the Row and Column Totals," *Economic and Social Review*, 4: 477–485.

Giovannini, A. 1983. "The Interest Elasticity of Savings in Developing Countries: The Existing Evidence," *World Development* 11: 601–8.

1985. "Saving and the Real Interest Rate in LDCs," *Journal of Development Economics* 18: 197–210.

Granger, C. W. J. 1991. "Developments in the Nonlinear Analysis of Economic Series," *Scandinavian Journal of Economics* 93: 263–76.

Guiso, L., and T. Jappelli. 1991. "Intergenerational Transfers and Capital Market Imperfections: Evidence from a Cross-Section of Italian Households," *European Economic Review* 35: 103–20.

Guiso, L., T. Japelli, and D. Terlizzese. 1992. "Earnings Uncertainty and Precautionary Saving," Centre for Economic Policy Research (CEPR), London: Discussion Paper 699.

Gupta, K. L. 1987. "Aggregate Savings, Financial Intermediation and Interest Rates," *Review of Economics and Statistics* 69: 303–11.

Hall, R. 1987. "Comment," *Brookings Papers on Economic Activity* 2: 504–6.

Haque, N. U., and P. Montiel. 1989. "Consumption in Developing Countries: Tests for Liquidity Constraints and Finite Horizons," *Review of Economics and Statistics* 34: 408–15.

Hayashi, F. 1985. "The Effect of Liquidity Constraints on Consumption: A Cross-Sectional Analysis," *Quarterly Journal of Economics* 100: 183–206.

1987. "Tests for Liquidity Constraints: A Critical Survey and Some New Observations," in T. F. Bewley, ed., *Advances in Econometrics: Fifth World Congress* (Cambridge University Press), 2: 91–120.

Hoff, K., and J. E. Stiglitz. 1990. "Imperfect Information and Rural Credit Markets: Puzzles and Policy Perspectives," *World Bank Economic Review* 4: 235–50.

Honohan, P., and I. Atiyas. 1993. "Intersectoral Financial Flows in Developng Countries," *Economic Journal* 103: 666–79.

Hubbard, R. G., and K. L. Judd. 1986. "Liquidity Constraints, Fiscal Policy and Consumption," *Brookings Papers on Economic Activity*, 1: 1–50.

Hubbard R. G., K. L. Judd, and J. S. Skinner. 1996. "Assessing the Effectiveness of Saving Incentives," *Journal of Economic Perspectives*, 10(4): 73–90.

J. S. Skinner, and S. P. Zeldes. 1994. "The Importance of Precautionary Motives in Explaining Individual and Aggregate Saving," *Carnegie-Rochester Conference Series on Public Policy* 40: 59–125.

Inter-Secretariat Working Group on National Accounts. 1993. *System of National Accounts 1993* (Brussels, etc.: Commission of the European Communities, International Monetary Fund, Organization for Economic Cooperation and Development, United Nations, and The World Bank).

Jappelli, T. 1990. "Who Is Credit Constrained in the US Economy?" *Quarterly Journal of Economics* 105: 219–34.

Jappelli, T., and M. Pagano. 1989. "Consumption and Capital Market Imperfections: An International Comparison," *American Economic Review* 79: 1088–105.

1994. "Saving, Growth and Liquidity Constraints," *Quarterly Journal of Economics* 109: 83–109.

Jappelli, T., J.-S. Pischke, and N. Souleles. 1995. "Testing for Liquidity Constraints in Euler Equations with Complementary Data Sources," Centre for Economic Policy Research (London), Discussion Paper 1138.

Karras, G. 1994. "Government Spending and Private Consumption: Some International Evidence," *Journal of Money, Credit and Banking* 26: 9–22.

Kessler, D., S. Perelman, and P. Pestieau. 1993. "Savings Behavior in 17 OECD Countries," *Review of Income and Wealth* 39: 37–49.

King, M. A. 1986. "Capital Market Imperfections and the Consumption Function," *Scandinavian Journal of Economics* 88: 59–80.

1994. "Debt Deflation: Theory and Evidence," *European Economic Review* 38: 419–46.

Koskela, E., H. A. Loikkanen, and M. Virén. 1992. "House Prices, Household Savings and Financial Market Liberalization in Finland," *European Economic Review* 36: 549–58.

Koskela, E., and M. Virén. 1994. "Taxation and Household Saving in Open Economies: Evidence from the Nordic Countries," *Scandinavian Journal of Economics* 96: 425–41.

Lahiri, A. 1989. "The Dynamics of Asian Savings," *IMF Staff Papers* 36: 228–61.

Lehmussaari, O. P. 1990. "Deregulation and Consumption Saving Dynamics in the Nordic Countries," *IMF Staff Papers* 37: 71–93.

Leite, S. P., and D. Makonnen. 1986. "Saving and Interest in the BCEAO Countries: An Empirical Analysis," *Savings and Development* 3: 219–31.

Levine, R., and S. Zervos. 1996. "Stock Markets, Banks and Economic Growth," The World Bank (Washington, DC), Policy Research Working Paper 1690.

Miles, D. 1992. "Housing Markets, Consumption and Financial Liberalization in the Major Economies," *European Economic Review* 36: 1093–135 (with discussion).

Mitchell, O., J. M. Poterba, and M. Warshawsky. 1997. "New Evidence on the Money's Worth of Individual Annuities," National Bureau of Economic Research (Cambridge, MA), Working Paper 6002.

Muellbauer, J. 1994. "The Assessment: Consumer Expenditure," *Oxford Review of Economic Policy* 10: 1–39.

Ogaki, M., J. D. Ostry, and C. M. Reinhart. 1996. "Saving Behavior in Low- and

Middle-Income Developing Countries: A Comparison," *IMF Staff Papers* 43: 38–71.

Ostry, J. D., and C. M. Reinhart. 1992. "Private Saving and Terms of Trade Shocks: Evidence from Developing Countries," *IMF Staff Papers* 39: 495–517.

OECD. 1994. *Taxation and Household Saving* (Paris: Organization for Economic Cooperation and Development).

Pissarides, C. A. 1978. "Liquidity Considerations in the Theory of Consumption," *Quarterly Journal of Economics* 92: 279–96.

Poterba, J. M. 1987. "Tax Policy and Corporate Saving," *Brookings Papers on Economic Activity*, 2: 455–503.

———. 1991. "Dividends, Capital Gains and the Corporate Veil: Evidence from Britain, Canada, and the United States," in B. D. Bernheim and J. Shoven, eds., *National Saving and Economic Performance* (NBER and University of Chicago Press).

Ramanathan, R. 1968. "Estimating the Permanent Income of a Household: An Application to Indian Data," *Review of Economics and Statistics* 50: 383–8.

Raut, L., and A. Virmani. 1989. "Determinants of Consumption and Savings Behavior in Developing Countries," *World Bank Economic Review* 3: 379–93.

Rossi, N. 1988. "Government Spending, the Real Interest Rate, and the Behavior of Liquidity Constrained Consumers in Developing Countries," *IMF Staff Papers* 35: 104–40.

Rosenzweig, M. R., and K. I. Wolpin. 1993. "Credit Market Constraints, Consumption Smoothing, and the Accumulation of Durable Production Assets in Low-Income Countries: Investments in Bullocks in India," *Journal of Political Economy* 101: 223–44.

Runkle, D. E. 1991. "Liquidity Constraints and the Permanent-Income Hypothesis: Evidence from Panel Data," *Journal of Monetary Economics* 27: 73–98.

Schmidt-Hebbel, K., S. B. Webb, and G. Corsetti. 1992. "Household Saving in Developing Countries: First Cross-Country Evidence," *World Bank Economic Review* 6: 529–47.

Srinivasan, T. N. 1993. "Saving in the Development Process," in J. H. Gapinski, ed., *The Economics of Saving* (Dordrecht: Kluwer).

Stiglitz, J., and A. Weiss. 1981. "Credit Rationing in Markets with Imperfect Information," *American Economic Review* 71: 393–410.

Thaler, Richard H. 1994. "Psychology and Savings Policies," *American Economic Review Papers and Proceedings* 84: 186–92.

Thaler, Richard H., and H. M. Shefrin. 1981. "An Economic Theory of Self Control," *Journal of Political Economy* 89: 392–406.

Townsend, R. M. 1994. "Risk and Insurance in Rural India," *Econometrica*, 62(3): 539–92.

Udry, C. 1990. "Credit Markets in Northern Nigeria: Credit as Insurance in a Rural Economy," *World Bank Economic Review* 4: 251–69.

Venti, S. F., and D. A. Wise. 1990. "Have IRAs Increased U.S. Saving? Evidence from Consumer Surveys," *Quarterly Journal of Economics*, 105(3): 661–98.

Vittas, D. 1993. "Swiss Chilanpore: The Way Forward for Pension Reform?" World Bank Policy Research Working Paper 1093.

Weil, P. 1990. "Nonexpected Utility in Macroeconomics," *Quarterly Journal of Economics* 105: 29–42.

106   **Patrick Honohan**

Wolff, E. N. 1994. "International Comparisons of Personal Wealth Inequality," Presented at the International Association for Research in Income and Wealth conference, St. Andrews, NB, Canada, August.

Wolpin, K. I. 1982. "A New Test of the Permanent Income Hypothesis: The Impact of Weather on the Income and Consumption of Households in India," *International Economic Review* 23: 583–94.

Zeldes, S. P. 1989. "Consumption and Liquidity Constraints: An Empirical Investigation," *Journal of Political Economy* 97: 305–46.

CHAPTER 5

Foreign Resource Inflows, Saving, and Growth

Maurice Obstfeld

This chapter surveys aspects of the empirical and theoretical debate over the effects of foreign resource inflows on national saving, investment, and growth.[1] The debate originated in the early 1960s in attempts to assess the role of capital inflows in development. But elements of the debate go back much further. Indeed, the classical controversy over the international transfer mechanism, initiated by Keynes and Ohlin in the 1920s, revolves implicitly around the related question: does a transfer raise the recipient's saving more or less than its investment, and by what amount? For it is the resulting incipient imbalance in the current account that drives the terms-of-trade effect of the transfer (Mundell, 1968, pp. 17–21).

A salient problem in the existing literature is a failure to define clearly the question being asked. Generally researchers have sought to discover, through cross-sectional multicountry regressions, the statistical relationship between additional foreign resource availability and saving, investment, consumption, and/or the growth rate of GDP. But the resulting numerical estimates of correlation need not correspond to the effects of any well-defined economic policy. The impact of outright aid differs from that of a loan at market interest rates. Furthermore, market borrowing, an important source of developing-country finance,[2] responds endogenously to factors that simultaneously shift other macroeconomic variables. Accordingly, a cross-sectional regression of saving, say, on

I thank Matthew T. Jones for superb research assistance. The initial version of this chapter was prepared for the Macroeconomics and Growth Division of the Policy and Research Department, the World Bank. Very useful comments from Klaus Schmidt-Hebbel, Luis Servén, Heng-Fu Zou, and anonymous referees have led to improvements. I would also like to thank the National Science Foundation for its support through a grant to the National Bureau of Economic Research.

[1] For a particularly complete set of references to the literature, see the survey article by White (1992).

[2] See Montiel (1994) for a recent survey of developing-country access to world capital markets.

capital inflows, generally cannot disclose the causal impact of those inflows on saving.

The chapter suggests a methodology for systematically studying the effects of resource inflows on macroeconomic variables. The methodology, which builds on the standard optimal growth framework, constructs a medium-scale dynamic model of the economy under study, one that is quantitatively consistent with the behavior of the economy's key macrovariables.[3] Within such a model, the effects of an exogenous aid inflow, or of an exogenous relaxation in borrowing restrictions or terms, can be evaluated. The general approach also leads to a structural regression strategy for evaluating the effects of aid flows.

An objection to the approach proposed below is its assumption of a particular economic model that might not be the true model underlying the structure of the economy under study. But the interpretation of *any* statistical results for policy purposes requires a stance on the economic mechanisms generating the observed associations among macrovariables. This is the essence of econometric identification. An advantage of the approach I advocate is that it makes maintained assumptions explicit, hence refutable, and it does so within a framework sufficiently flexible to capture a wide variety of economic structures.

The chapter is organized as follows. The first section describes early approaches to evaluating resource inflows and surveys the ensuing empirical debate. In the next section, I describe the predictions of the standard optimal growth model, showing the sensitivity of results to the aid versus borrowing distinction and to the permanence of an inflow, factors not usually considered in existing empirical studies. In the following section, I illustrate how a fairly generic optimal growth model modified to allow for the presence of financially constrained consumers can be used to study the impact of an exogenous aid inflow.[4] I also explore a model with endogenous growth and discuss more briefly other possible extensions and, finally, conclude.

The theoretical models I explore below mainly assume a representative national consumer in the recipient country, and thus might be rightly regarded as being more normative than positive in nature. However, I view these models as stepping stones to more complete positive models incorporating the competition of powerful political claimants for common resources, a process likely to raise the positive effect of foreign resource inflows (especially aid) on consumption. Tornell and Lane (1998) and Svensson (1997, 1998) look at this type of model and offer

---

[3] For earlier applications of the optimal growth framework to development issues, see, for example, Bardhan (1967) and Bruno (1970).

[4] Schmidt-Hebbel and Servén (1995) have explored a related but much more detailed model. I discuss its results at several points in this chapter.

suggestive empirical support. As will become evident below, a fairly robust normative implication even of optimal-consumption models is that much if not most of extra permanent foreign resources should be consumed rather than invested. Such a response, if found empirically, may be a much greater cause for concern when political pull rather than social welfare maximization determines the uses and distribution of inflows.[5]

Previous Approaches

Starting in the 1960s, researchers began to model and to test empirically for the role of foreign resources inflows on developing-country capital accumulation and growth. In the theoretical realm, models by Chenery and a number of associates, all based on the Harrod-Domar growth model, were especially influential.[6] These models, simulated on the basis of empirically plausible parameter values, seemed to imply that aid and capital inflows would speed the transition to a targeted self-sustaining growth path and current-account balance.

Skeptics of this optimistic view countered by arguing that resource inflows augment consumption and depress saving enough to reduce, possibly to zero, any favorable impact on investment and subsequent growth. Even funds tied to specific investment projects might not be "additional": they may finance investments that governments would have carried out anyway with resources now freed for consumption purposes. The contention that foreign resource availability either directly or indirectly raises consumption inspired a large body of empirical work, by both adherents of the optimistic view and its critics.

This section critically reviews both the theoretical framework underlying the early models of resource inflows and growth and some of the leading attempts (spanning more than a quarter century) at empirical resolution of the debate those models inspired.

A Simple Growth Model along Chenery Lines

The model, which is adapted from Grinols and Bhagwati (1976), focuses on a small open economy that receives an exogenous net resource inflow $n(t)$ from foreign sources. One can think of $n(t)$ as the noninterest

---

[5] Boone (1996) empirically studies the welfare effects of aid inflows, showing that they tend to raise government size while leaving indicators of private welfare (such as child mortality) unaffected. His conclusion is that aid serves mainly to augment, not simply aggregate consumption, but the consumption of those who already are relatively well off.

[6] See, e.g., Chenery and Bruno (1962), Adelman and Chenery (1966), Chenery and Strout (1966), and Chenery and Eckstein (1970).

current-account deficit. It is taken for granted that the economies under study here face limits to international capital market access that go strictly *beyond* the standard intertemporal budget restriction of the present value (at world prices) of absorption to the present value of income. The question is how an easing of the additional constraints will affect saving, investment, and growth.

If $y(t)$ denotes GDP, $c(t)$ consumption, and $i(t)$ investment, we have the identity

$$y(t) + n(t) = c(t) + i(t). \tag{1}$$

Output depends on the capital stock, $k(t)$, alone, perhaps because of the presence of an unlimited supply of labor à la Arthur Lewis:

$$y(t) = k(t)/\pi. \tag{2}$$

Above, π is the Harrod-Domar capital–output ratio. The capital accumulation identity is

$$\dot{k}(t) = i(t),$$

which, by virtue of equation (2), can be written

$$\dot{y}(t) = i(t)/\pi. \tag{3}$$

The final ingredient of the model is a consumption function,

$$c(t) = \gamma + (1 - \rho)y(t) + \lambda n(t), \tag{4}$$

which allows for a direct "leakage," $\lambda n(t)$, of foreign resources out of saving and into consumption. This leakage could arise because, for example, additional foreign resources depress domestic interest rates or spur government consumption. Models in the vein of Chenery and Strout (1966) simply assumed that $\lambda = 0$.

Combining equations (1), (3), and (4) leads to

$$y(t) + n(t) = \gamma + (1 - \rho)y(t) + \lambda n(t) + \pi\dot{y}(t),$$

which can be rewritten as an equation in the output growth rate, $g_y(t) = \dot{y}(t)/y(t)$:

$$g_y(t) = \frac{\rho}{\pi} - \frac{\gamma}{\pi y(t)} + \frac{(1 - \lambda)n(t)/y(t)}{\pi}. \tag{5}$$

Equation (5) clarifies the potential role of foreign resources in development. In the absence of resource inflows from abroad ($n = 0$), $g_y(t)$ converges to Harrod's "warranted" growth rate, ρ/π, provided the initial capital stock, $k(0)$, is bigger than $\gamma/\rho\pi$. Positive resource flows $n > 0$ speed growth, however, and can hasten the transition to self-sustained balanced growth. Indeed, a constant ratio n/y of resource inflow to output induces a long-run growth rate above the warranted rate.

These growth-enhancing effects of foreign resources on growth presuppose that the leakage λ is incomplete: $\lambda < 1$. If, instead, *all* resource transfers are consumed, the economy's growth path is not altered. And the positive growth effect is greater the lower is λ. Hence, the importance of ascertaining the fraction of foreign resource inflows that is invested domestically.

The model also makes strong predictions concerning the dynamics of saving. Differential equation (5) implies an output level of

$$y(t) = y(0)e^{\rho t/\pi} + \frac{1}{\pi}\int_0^t e^{\rho(t-s)/\pi}[(1-\lambda)n(s) - \gamma]ds.$$

The level of saving, $s(t)$, therefore is[7]

$$s(t) = \rho\left[y(0)e^{\rho t/\pi} + \frac{1}{\pi}\int_0^t e^{\rho(t-s)/\pi}[(1-\lambda)n(s) - \gamma]ds\right] - \gamma - \lambda n(t). \qquad (6)$$

Assume, for simplicity, that the level of resource inflow is constant at n. Then equation (6) becomes a relatively simple function of n:

$$s(t) = [\rho y(0) - \gamma]e^{\rho t/\pi} + [e^{\rho t/\pi}(1-\lambda) - 1]n.$$

Notice that a sustained increase in n causes an initial ($t = 0$) drop in saving if $\lambda > 0$, but that saving rises monotonically thereafter, overtaking its prior path at time $t = -\pi\ln(1 - \lambda)/\rho$. If $\lambda = 0$ (the case of no leakage), saving is always higher after n rises.[8]

Consider the behavior of the saving *rate* as a fraction of GDP, given by

---

[7] The following notion of saving, as discussed further below, isn't the theoretically relevant one when n takes the form of unrequited aid, because, in that case, n becomes part of national income. In the balance of payments, n would appear as a current-account credit (a transfer from abroad) with a counterpart debit equal to additional imports in the amount n. If resources are borrowed, however, the appropriate definition of saving must subtract from GDP those interest payments due to foreign creditors. Chenery's models, as noted below, ignored the dynamics of foreign interest payments and did not clearly distinguish between foreign aid and lending.

[8] Chenery's models also considered the possibility that growth might be constrained by the availability of foreign exchange, independently of the domestic savings constraint. Thus, despite domestic savings themselves being adequate for satisfactory growth, growth could be impeded by lack of enough foreign exchange to buy necessary imported inputs. While some older empirical studies support the relevance of this "two-gap" approach (e.g., Weisskopf, 1972), it seems of secondary importance today. I therefore omit further discussion. For an exposition, see Cardoso and Dornbusch (1989).

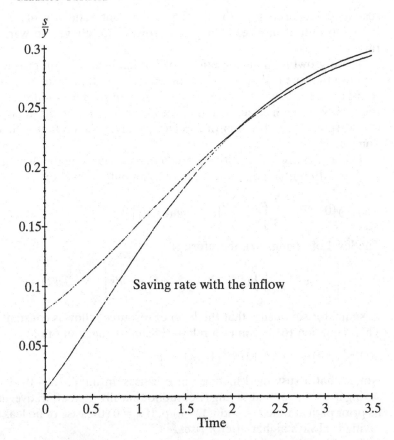

Figure 5.1. Dynamic effect of a resource inflow on the saving rate.

$$\frac{s(t)}{y(t)} = \rho - \frac{\gamma}{y(t)} - \frac{\lambda n}{y(t)}.$$

If n rises in a sustained fashion at $t = 0$, the saving rate initially falls because saving falls and $y(0)$ is given. As GDP growth accelerates, however, the saving rate eventually overtakes and passes its initial path, ultimately converging to ρ (as it would at the initial level of n). Figure 5.1 shows an example of how the saving rate with a foreign resource inflow overtakes its initial path, despite the rather large leakage parameter ($\lambda = 2/3$) assumed in the simulation.

The preceding model warrants several comments. Obviously, the welfare significance of the initial fall in saving that accompanies a foreign resource inflow is unclear a priori. In the model, the inflow augments aggregate consumption possibilities (and consumption) at every point in time; hence, welfare is increasing in the standard sense. A precise assessment of the welfare gain, however, requires a satisfactory account of individual or social preferences with regard to the level and timing of consumption. Such an account would, in general, predict a consumption function quite different from the naive Keynesian consumption function of equation (4).

Another weakness of the model is the assumption of unlimited labor supplies, or at least of no fixed factors in production. While the "new growth theory" has revived theoretical interest in such models, their empirical relevance has been increasingly questioned in recent years. (Even in a more traditional neoclassical growth model along Solow lines, however, higher investment due to a foreign resource inflow increases the economy's growth rate while the economy is in transit to its steady state.)

Finally, the model gives no adequate account of the dynamics of foreign debt when foreign resources must (at least in part) be borrowed. Such debt would affect consumption behavior; in particular, the need to service foreign obligations has strong consequences for long-run consumption possibilities. The implied interest payments to foreigners would drive a wedge between national output and national income. This last distinction is critical for assessing the long-run welfare impact of the resource inflow, since higher GDP growth may yield little domestic benefit if most of it goes to service external debts.

After a review of some useful accounting identities and of the existing empirical evidence, the next major section will take up models that remedy these deficiencies.

A Digression on Accounting

The implication of Chenery-style models, that foreign assistance would invariably promote investment and growth, and eventually raise saving, was disputed by critics who viewed development assistance programs as motivated ultimately by an alleged desire of donor countries to exercise political and economic dominance in the developing world. The ensuing empirical debate generated many studies on the links between foreign resource inflows and various aspects of macroeconomic performance by the recipients.

A preliminary digression to recall some accounting identities highlights several basic issues in the empirical assessment of the macroeconomic impact of foreign resource inflows.

Let ca denote the (per capita) current account surplus, a aid, ℓ gross foreign lending, b gross foreign borrowing at market interest rates, and int interest and dividend payments to foreigners. Then the national income identity is

$$y + a - int = c + i + g + ca$$
$$= c + i + g + \ell - b.$$

On the assumption that int is determined by the past and, thus, is unresponsive to current changes, the preceding identity gives the following responses of national saving $s = i + ca$ to exogenous changes in a and b, respectively:

$$\frac{ds}{da} = 1 + \frac{dy}{da} - \left(\frac{dc}{da} + \frac{dg}{da} \right), \quad \frac{ds}{db} = \frac{dy}{db} - \left(\frac{dc}{db} + \frac{dg}{db} \right).$$

Aid directly increases national income and, hence, national saving, and it may have an effect dy/da on output – for example, through income effects on labor supply. To the extent that private or government consumption rises, however, national saving falls. Borrowing operates through similar channels, except that the sum borrowed, unlike a sum granted outright, does not enter national income. *Domestic* saving (in contrast to national saving) could be defined as $s - a$, that is, as national saving net of unrequited transfers. Aid affects domestic saving only through its effects on y, c, and g. But national rather than domestic saving is the theoretically relevant concept from the standpoint of tracking net asset accumulation and intertemporal welfare.

The associated investment effects are

$$\frac{di}{da} = \frac{ds}{da} + \frac{db}{da} - \frac{d\ell}{da}, \quad \frac{di}{db} = \frac{ds}{db} + 1 - \frac{dl}{db}.$$

Aid affects investment by changing saving and the net inflow of borrowed foreign resources. For example, if aid raises saving, but the saving escapes abroad (capital flight), investment will not change. Gross foreign borrowing that is channeled into flight capital leaves investment unchanged, but borrowing can raise investment even if saving declines.[9]

These relations suggest that to understand how particular foreign resource inflows affect saving and investment (and growth), there are a few key questions to ask. How are government and private consumption affected, how does output respond, and, importantly, what are the induced effects on other (endogenous) gross resource inflows and outflows? (Of course, the linkage from investment and consumption to growth will depend on the specific mechanisms generating output and technical change in the economy.)[10]

---

[9] One could distinguish further between the legal and illegal components of l. Illegal capital movements accomplished through deceptive invoicing of trade flows, for example, could lead to distortions in reported saving and current account figures.

[10] My discussion assumes that aid is fungible, which seems accurate for moderately sized inflows; see Pack and Pack (1993).

Evidence

The empirical debate initially focused on the first of these issues, the impact on saving of foreign resource inflows. Later researchers have looked directly at effects on investment and growth.

Griffin (1970) pointed out that if present consumption is a normal good, additional foreign resources must in general lead to an immediate rise in consumption. This is something that the Chenery and Strout (1966) model does not allow (although it may occur in the modified model developed earlier in this section if $\lambda > 0$ is allowed). Griffin (1970) and Griffin and Enos (1970) went further, however, arguing that foreign resources do not promote saving or growth at all – in effect, that λ is 1 *or even above* 1 in the model above. They argued that, through the 1960s, foreign assistance had been negatively correlated with growth and that foreign assistance largely had supplanted domestic savings.

To support the latter contention, Griffin (1970) reported the following ordinary least squares regression (based on 1962–64 average data for a sample of 32 developing countries):

$$\frac{s}{y} = 11.2 - 0.73\frac{\Delta d}{y}, \quad R^2 = 0.54,$$
$$(0.11)$$

where $\Delta d = b - \ell$ is the current account deficit (the change in foreign debt, d). While acknowledging the lack of a clear structural interpretation of this correlation, Griffin viewed it as implying a nearly complete crowding out of domestic saving by foreign borrowing. A time-series regression on 1950–63 data from Colombia led Griffin to a similar conclusion.[11]

Studies regressing saving on the current account deficit implicitly give the correlation between investment and net foreign borrowing, of course. The identity $s = i - \Delta d$ implies that the coefficient of the regression of s/y on $\Delta d/y$ is that of the regression of i/y on $\Delta d/y$, less 1. Thus, for example, if 1 percent of GNP more foreign borrowing is estimated to reduce saving by 0.5 percent of GNP, it would be estimated to raise investment by 0.5 percent of GNP.

Weisskopf (1972) presented further times-series results along the lines of Griffin's for 17 countries, but the Weisskopf results showed weaker saving effects. In a pooled sample, he found a coefficient of -0.227 (with a t-statistic of -5.3) in a regression of saving on the foreign resource inflow and other variables.

---

[11] Earlier, Rahman (1968) had reported a cross-sectional "crowding-out" coefficient of only -0.25 using Chenery and Strout's (1966) 1964 data for 31 countries.

Papanek (1972) leveled a number of criticisms at these and similar studies. National saving, he noted, typically had been calculated as investment less total net foreign inflows. However, inflows with a grant component – for example, concessional loans – are in part gifts that should augment national income. Correspondingly, even when these gifts are entirely consumed, national saving does not decline. Papanek also noted that prior analyses erred in another way when aggregating all foreign inflows, whether pure aid, borrowing on market terms, official reserve depletion, direct foreign investment, project assistance, or the like. In principle, such inflows could have very different effects on saving and growth. The discussion of accounting above suggests that the use of net flows itself could be misleading. If gross inflows partially finance capital flight rather than domestic investment, regressions of saving or growth on net inflows could seriously overstate the impact of a dollar of foreign borrowing.

Papanek (1973) focused on the effects of foreign inflows on growth, using cross-section regressions that control for saving and break inflows down into aid, direct foreign investment, and other foreign inflows. He found some evidence that inflows, especially aid inflows, promoted growth in Asian and Mediterranean countries in the 1950s and 1960s. Less favorable results are reported for a different sample by Mosley, Hudson, and Horrell (1987), who find no convincing cross-section evidence that, conditional on saving and other variables, aid promotes growth.

Papanek's (1972) weightiest criticism of previous literature flowed from the observation that the correlations between saving or growth and inflows found in the data do not establish *causality* running from the latter variable to the former ones. For example, countries experiencing economic difficulties might receive more aid or borrow more heavily abroad. Recipient governments might even behave strategically, consuming rather than investing aid inflows in the belief that economic stagnation will elicit more future donor largesse than would robust growth (Pedersen, 1996; Svensson, 1996).

One might add that, to the extent that resource inflows are elastic, an exogenous fall in domestic saving can lead to additional foreign borrowing to finance investment: measured statistical relationships may, in large part, reflect this mechanism rather than an effect of resource inflows on saving. Similarly, an exogenous rise in the profitability of domestic investment leads to extra foreign borrowing and helps induce a negative statistical relation between investment and the current account, one that has been extensively documented (on industrial countries, see, e.g., Baxter and Crucini, 1993; on East Asia and Latin America, see Reinhart and Talvi, 1997). But it does not follow that capital inflows "cause" investment; if anything, the reverse is closer to the truth in the last example.

Papanek (1972) concluded that "for a number of countries it is plausible to conclude that exogenous factors caused both high inflows and low savings rates and generally low growth rates as well" (p. 948). The key point is that inflows are *endogenous*, in a way most likely to be quite important when a country has some discretion over the amount it borrows from abroad, but also potentially important even when it does not. Earlier researchers had failed to grapple directly with this problem.

Gupta (1975) was probably the first to account for endogeneity through explicit simultaneous equations, deriving the effects of exogenous shifts in foreign inflows from a seven-equation, life-cycle-based empirical model of the saving rate, the output growth rate, per capita income, the dependency rate, the birth rate, the female labor force participation rate, and the infant mortality rate. Gupta found that the "role of foreign resource inflows [in reducing the saving rate] is quite small" (at most a coefficient of -0.13; p. 372). Gupta also found that foreign private investment has the largest growth-enhancing effect of the types of foreign inflow considered. Unfortunately, Gupta reports no standard errors on reduced-form coefficients and offers no rationale for the appearance of foreign saving in the domestic saving function. A general drawback of multiequation approaches, of course, is that misspecification of any single equation generally will contaminate all of the multipliers derived from the estimated model.

Subsequent work by Fry (1978, 1980) and Giovannini (1983, 1985), despite some ambiguity, tends to support the negative correlation between aid inflows and saving. Chenery himself (see Chenery and Syrquin, 1975, p. 125) suggested, on the basis of a cross-section regression with 41 observations, that on average only 45 percent of external resources would translate into additional investment.

Halevi (1976) regresses investment, private consumption, and public consumption on the import surplus and individual components of the capital account, finding strong evidence of a positive correlation of inflows with investment (conditional on GNP) and weaker evidence of positive correlation with private and public consumption. Halevi's direct focus on investment and consumption, rather than saving, is quite appropriate, since these variables are directly relevant to welfare and growth. Furthermore, saving, which is calculated as a residual, is probably subject to greater measurement error than are investment and consumption. Finally, as noted above, the definition of saving has differed from study to study – some fail to include aid or foreign interest bills in income, for example. Thus, future empirical work should add consumption and investment to the list of variables to be explained.

In two studies, Levy (1987, 1988a) regresses investment rates on saving rates and the ratio of official development assistance (ODA) to GDP. He finds that, conditional on saving, ODA feeds through virtually one-for-one to investment.[12] Since this regression procedure is silent on the response of saving itself to ODA, it cannot disclose the *reduced-form* or total response of investment to ODA. Levy (1987) recognizes the potential dependence of saving on ODA in devising instrumental-variable estimates of his basic ODA equation, but he unfortunately does not report the result of his first-stage regression of the saving rate on instrumental variables including ODA. Thus, his results give no obvious answer to the question: how does aid affect investment?

Levy (1988b) observes that aid inflows are in part predictable, and that systematic, anticipated aid should have different effects from unexpected, temporary aid, such as emergency famine relief. Levy tests this hypothesis by first estimating a forecasting model in which transfers of aid resulting from previous aid commitments depend on a distributed lag of past commitments. He then regresses consumption (for a panel data set) on "permanent income" (defined as a weighted average of past income), the forecast model's prediction of the expected aid inflow based on past commitments, and unexpected aid inflows. He finds that much or all of the unexpected aid inflow feeds into consumption (with a coefficient equal to or higher than that of permanent income). Expected inflows, however, have a much smaller effect on consumption. (An alternative estimation approach yields similar results.) Levy argues that these results support the idea that systematic aid is not targeted for consumption and is less fungible than emergency aid, which often is targeted for consumption. This is not entirely convincing, since even aid targeted for investment may release resources to consumption that might have been invested in the absence of the targeted aid. Thus, Levy's results become difficult to reconcile with a consumption-smoothing model in which transitory, unexpected aid should be largely saved and systematic aid con-

---

[12] Feldstein (1994) adopts a similar cross-section regression methodology to study the effect on aggregate domestic investment of foreign direct investment (FDI) outflows and inflows. For a sample of industrial countries, he regresses the investment rate on the national saving rate plus FDI outflows and inflows, with both of the latter two variables expressed as a fraction of output. The outflows variable attracts a coefficient near -1; so does the inflows variable, in some regressions, but the evidence on inflows is much more mixed. Feldstein concludes that FDI outflows are extremely effective in lowering domestic investment, given saving. It is hard to reconcile this conclusion with a picture of perfectly integrated world capital markets, except by positing that some of the same factors (perhaps country-specific technology shocks) that lower aggregate domestic investment profitability also make foreign investment more attractive. Feldstein attempts to allow for this possibility by adding control variables to his regression equations, but reports that his initial conclusions are not substantially modified.

sumed. Levy (p. 456) recognizes this, arguing that recipients of systematic aid must, somewhat irrationally, perceive it as transitory. A partial rationale for Levy's results may come from the observation that emergency aid tends to be given when consumption urgency is especially high. Despite these ambiguities, however, the study by Levy (1988b) is important in focusing attention both on permanent-income theories of consumption and on the distinctions between expected and unexpected, and permanent and transitory, aid.

The foregoing considerations bring out the need for dynamic studies of resource inflows that go beyond the prevalent pure cross-sectional methodology. Schmidt-Hebbel, Webb, and Corsetti (1992) provide a study along these lines. Using panel data from 10 countries, they regress the *household* saving rate on a number of postulated determinants of aggregate saving, including trend income, the deviation of income from trend, the real interest rate, and the current account deficit (which they label foreign saving). They find that foreign saving has a significantly negative coefficient (equal to around -0.15) in their regressions. Since their result applies to household rather than total private saving (which includes corporate saving), it is difficult to know what the implications are for the correlation between foreign saving and investment.

While Schmidt-Hebbel et al. motivate their saving function by standard life-cycle theories, their lack of a general equilibrium framework leads to some ambiguities in interpretation. For example, they find that interest rate effects on household saving are insignificant, and attribute this to the well-known tension among income, wealth, and substitution effects. However, foreign inflows will affect saving in part through their interest rate effects, which tend to drive domestic and world interest rates into line. Thus, some of the effect of changes in domestic real interest rates could be captured by the resource-inflow variable. The effects of foreign resource inflows depend on the share going to the government and the precise mode by which the balance is allocated to the private sector.

Most recently, Boone (1994, 1996) has carried out cross-section regressions on a large sample of countries during the period 1971–90 to study the effects of aid. To address the simultaneity issue raised by Papanek (1972), he uses as instrumental variables dummies that capture donors' political interests rather than recipients' economic conditions. He also uses population as an instrument and runs regressions that control for variables that might endogenously influence aid flows (such as GNP per capita). He finds that aid has virtually no investment effect (except in countries where aid is a very large share of GNP) and no growth effect. The hypothesis that all aid goes into consumption cannot be rejected.

Interestingly, the simultaneity bias hypothesized by Papanek appears to be abundantly present in Boone's data. Ordinary least squares regression gives much higher estimates of the proportion of aid that is consumed. Boone argues that, because poorer countries have higher consumption–income ratios, this finding merely reflects the simultaneous positive effect of low per capita income on both the consumption–income and aid–income ratios.

Boone's 1994 study is unique in basing its estimation strategy on an explicit intertemporal model of consumption and growth. Boone's specification assumes that every country is in the *steady-state* equilibrium of a Ramsey-Cass-Koopmans exogenous long-run growth model of the type explored in the remaining sections of this chapter. Countries have identical rates of long-run technological efficiency gain and population growth, but investment (and, hence, consumption) as a fraction of GDP differs across countries due to different levels of distortion imposed by the domestic government or political system.

A difficulty in drawing inferences from Boone's (1994) methodology is related to the interpretation of his results. While the results may be informative about economies in steady state, they say nothing about the effects of aid on countries that are still in transition. The models introduced below will make clear that in a Ramsey-Cass-Koopmans model, aid will generate additional saving and investment *only* when the recipient economy hasn't yet reached its balanced growth path. Boone (1994, p. 13) also points this out. Thus, Boone's estimates potentially throw little or no light on the effects of aid on developing countries, which presumably are considered to be developing in part because they have not yet attained balanced-growth paths. Plainly a measure of the economy's distance from the steady state could be essential for getting an estimate of the *actual* effects of aid on consumption, saving, and investment. Boone's (1994) attempt to interpret the evidence on aid in terms of forward-looking dynamic models is, however, a very important step and is completely consistent with the perspective I adopt in this chapter.

Recent empirical work by Burnside and Dollar (1997) makes use of the instrumental variables suggested by Boone to correct for simultaneity. The work also adopts a specification in which aid flows interact with an index of policy quality in an empirical growth equation. Burnside and Dollar find that the effect of aid on growth depends on the quality of economic policies. Contrary to Boone's findings, countries following bad policies seem to experience a growth slowdown as a result of aid, whereas countries following sufficiently good policies can reap a significant growth-rate gain. The authors also try to explain policy quality, but find that aid does not make policies any better or worse.

Assessment

The weight of the accumulated empirical evidence suggests that net foreign resource inflows (especially borrowed resources) are negatively related to national saving and positively related to domestic investment. Thus, in credit-constrained economies, higher resource inflows that reach the private sector may well promote higher consumption and higher investment (at least for a time), as a market-clearing, competitive, intertemporal model would suggest. But the *magnitudes* of these consumption and investment effects are quite uncertain – the existing empirical work, none of which is tightly linked to a structural theoretical framework, yields a wide range of results that depend on the details of specification, time period, and country sample. Unfortunately, in the absence of such a theoretical framework it is hard to know how to interpret these findings. In particular, it is hard to know if they represent a causal relationship linking resource inflows to economic performance, or merely a statistical regularity devoid of a unidirectional causal interpretation.

The lack of any consistent statistical relationship between resource inflows and economic growth reinforces these doubts. As noted by Cassen and associates (1994, p. 29) in their discussion of aid:

> Intercountry statistical analyses do not show anything conclusive – positive or negative – about the impact of aid on growth. Given the enormous variety of countries and types of aid, this is not surprising. If appropriate aid is put to good use in a satisfactory policy context, and if all the other components of growth are present, the statistical relationship between aid and growth will be positive. If such a relationship does not emerge overall, it only shows the unexciting conclusion that aid may or may not be strongly related to growth, depending on circumstances.

What research strategy should one adopt, then, in seeking to understand the effects of resource inflows on saving, investment, and growth? One approach would be to pursue the cross-sectional strategy followed in much of the literature reviewed above, refining the estimating equations to encompass the additional variables to which Cassen and associates (1994) allude. These could include political and macroeconomic stability, quality of the educational system, central bank independence, the honesty of government officials, conditionality of foreign resource flows, and the like. Such analyses (e.g., in Edwards, 1995; Burnside and Dollar, 1997) can be useful in revealing stylized facts, but typically yield no structural information – notably, no account of causal mechanisms. Boone's (1994) work, discussed earlier, is unique in deriving its estimating equations from a well-specified intertemporal model, thus admitting the potential for structural interpretation.

The underlying data used in such exercises, and the statistical correlations that emerge, can also play a role in informing an alternative research strategy. That strategy is to develop medium-scale general-equilibrium intertemporal models that capture the behavior of key macroaggregates when modified to reflect institutional features of the economy under study. Schmidt-Hebbel and Servén (1995) have built a model based on just this idea. The strategy, somewhat reminiscent of Chenery's basic approach, would allow one to simulate the dynamic effects of resource inflows, but within a model that is empirically plausible and that allows for forward-looking consumption and investment behavior in a manner that Chenery and his coauthors did not. A lesson of the existing econometric work is that applications must explicitly distinguish between different forms of resource inflow, taking account of permanence and predictability as well.

The next section presents an illustrative analytical model, basic to either research strategy, within which pertinent thought experiments can be performed and the key parameters determining dynamic responses ascertained.

An Illustrative Theoretical Model

The fundamental effects of foreign resource inflows on saving, consumption, and growth are well illustrated by a stripped-down model of capital accumulation over time. The model is much too simple to capture all of the complex institutional factors governing intertemporal allocation in industrial (not to mention developing) economies. Yet the model highlights forces that will be at work in more realistic settings and serves as a springboard for more detailed exercises.

For simplicity, the model involves two factors of production only, physical capital and raw labor. Much recent research on economic growth emphasizes the role of human capital, and an impact of resource inflows on the educational system could be a crucial conduit for growth effects. The model sketched below could easily be expanded to incorporate human capital accumulation, possibly with borrowing restrictions. The next main section studies an endogenous growth model with human capital.

Foreign Aid

Let us begin by considering the case of a permanent unrequited foreign aid inflow at level a (in terms of consumption) per period. There is a representative individual in the economy who maximizes

$$\int_0^\infty u[c(t)]e^{-\delta t}dt \tag{7}$$

subject to the constraint

$$\dot{k}(t) = a + f[k(t)] - c(t). \tag{8}$$

As usual, we can think of the objective function (7) as the social welfare function of a benevolent economic planner in an economy with heterogeneous individuals, in which case the model's results have a normative interpretation. Positive conclusions concerning economies with finite lifetimes require a more detailed treatment of aggregation, as discussed below.[13] The production function $f(k)$ implicitly assumes a constant labor force, although the model can accommodate exogenous labor-force growth with k reinterpreted as the capital–labor ratio in production, $f(k)$ as output per capita net of the decline in capital intensity due to labor-force growth, and c as consumption per labor unit.

The equations necessary for an optimum plan are the capital-accumulation constraint and the intertemporal Euler condition

$$\dot{c} = -[u'(c)/u''(c)][f'(k) - \delta]. \tag{9}$$

Two specific assumptions simplify the model further so as to allow a relatively transparent analysis of the model's dynamics. These assumptions are that $u(c)$ belongs to the isoelastic class,

$$u(c) = \frac{c^{1-(1/\sigma)} - 1}{1 - (1/\sigma)},$$

where $\sigma > 0$ is the intertemporal substitution elasticity, and that the production function $f(k)$ is Cobb-Douglas,

$$f(k) = Ak^{\alpha},$$

with $\alpha < 1$. Under these assumptions the dynamic system describing the economy is given by the specialized forms of equations (9) and (8):

$$\dot{c} = \sigma c(\alpha Ak^{\alpha-1} - \delta),$$

$$\dot{k} = a + Ak^{\alpha} - c.$$

The steady state of this system consists of $\bar{c}$ and $\bar{k}$ such that

$$\bar{c} = a + A^{1/(1-\alpha)}(\alpha/\delta)^{\alpha/(1-\alpha)}, \quad \bar{k} = (\alpha A/\delta)^{1/(1-\alpha)}.$$

The second equation here is the fundamental condition determining the long-run capital stock in this model, $f'(\bar{k}) = \delta$, that is, the long-run

---

[13] Eaton (1989) contains a very interesting discussion of several alternatives along these lines. His treatment of the present model, however, is restricted to consideration of a resource transfer that occurs when the economy is in a steady state (in which case only consumption, and not investment, changes). The steady-state assumption is probably not appropriate for developing economies. Below, I therefore consider economies with capital stocks strictly below steady-state levels.

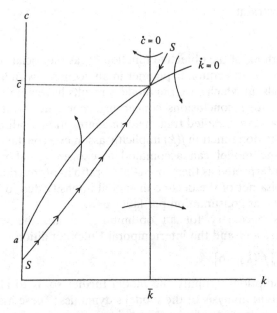

Figure 5.2. Adjustment to the steady-state capital stock.

marginal product of capital must equal the rate of time preference. Figure 5.2 shows the dynamic behavior that the equations imply. The steady state is a saddle point, and, in the present case (*a* expected to remain at a constant level forever), the relevant adjustment path is the stable saddle path labeled *SS*.

A simple way of exploring how the economy's preferences and technology interact to determine the impact of aid is to take a linear approximation to the two-equation system in a neighborhood of the steady state. The result is

$$\begin{bmatrix} \dot{c} \\ \dot{k} \end{bmatrix} = \begin{bmatrix} \sigma(\alpha A \bar{k}^{\alpha-1} - \delta) & \sigma \bar{c} \alpha(\alpha - 1)A\bar{k}^{\alpha-2} \\ -1 & \alpha A \bar{k}^{\alpha-1} \end{bmatrix} \begin{bmatrix} c - \bar{c} \\ k - \bar{k} \end{bmatrix}$$

$$= \begin{bmatrix} 0 & -\sigma(1-\alpha)\delta(\delta + a/\bar{k}) \\ -1 & \delta \end{bmatrix} \begin{bmatrix} c - \bar{c} \\ k - \bar{k} \end{bmatrix}.$$

The characteristic roots of the matrix above are real and of opposite sign, equal to

$$\lambda^{+}, \lambda^{-} = \left\{ \delta \pm \left[\delta^2 + 4\sigma(1-\alpha)\delta(\delta + a/\bar{k}) \right]^{1/2} \right\} / 2. \tag{10}$$

It is the negative, stable root λ^- alone that governs the economy's motion along *SS* in Figure 5.2.

It can be shown that, along SS, consumption and the capital stock are given (as a function of the initial capital stock, $k(0)$) by

$$c(t) - \bar{c} = (\delta - \lambda^-)[k(0) - \bar{k}]\exp(\lambda^- t),$$
$$k(t) - \bar{k} = [k(0) - \bar{k}]\exp(\lambda^- t).$$

Notice a key point: the greater the absolute value of λ^-, the faster the capital stock's convergence rate to the steady state, that is, the faster the initial discrepancy $k(0) - \bar{k}$ is eliminated. A critical determinant of $|\lambda^-|$ is σ, the elasticity of intertemporal substitution, which, loosely speaking, measures consumers' willingness to tolerate a tilted consumption path. When σ is large, $u'(c)$ doesn't vary much as consumption changes, and, so, people find it optimal to arrange for rapidly growing consumption when the marginal product of capital is high compared with δ. This, in turn, implies a relatively low level of consumption in the early phases of the development process and, correspondingly, a more rapid convergence to the steady state.

Dividing the first of the two last equations by the second shows that, near the steady state, SS is approximated by the linear equation

$$c(t) = \bar{c} + (\delta - \lambda^-)[k(t) - \bar{k}]. \tag{11}$$

This equation makes clear that changes in a affect consumption and investment through two channels: changing long-run consumption per capita, $\bar{c}$, and changing the negative root λ^- and, hence, the slope of SS and the economy's rate of convergence. (Recall that here, $\bar{k}$ is independent of a.)

The local (near the steady state) consumption effect of a change in a (given the current capital stock $k(t)$, which is predetermined by history) can be calculated as the sum of these two effects:

$$\frac{dc(t)}{da} = 1 - \frac{d\lambda^-}{da}[k(t) - \bar{k}],$$

where

$$\frac{d\lambda^-}{da} = -\sigma(1 - \alpha)\delta/(\bar{k}(\delta - 2\lambda^-)) < 0.$$

(These derivatives follow from differentiating equations (11) and (10), respectively.) If the economy is initially at its steady state $[k(0) = \bar{k}]$, all of a permanent increase in aid is consumed ($dc/da = 1$).[14] For an initial capital stock *below* the steady state $[k(0) < \bar{k}]$, however, $dc/da < 1$. Figure 5.3 illustrates this effect when a rises from 0 to a positive level; the effect basically follows from the fact that, even with zero capital, aid

---

[14] This is the application of the present model emphasized by Eaton (1989).

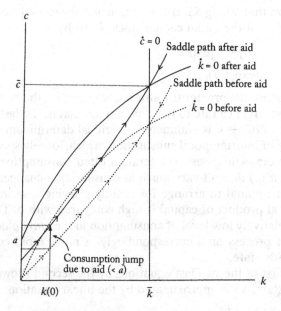

Figure 5.3. Permanent unexpected aid in the amount *a* causes consumption to jump initially by less than *a* if $k(0) < \bar{k}$.

makes possible positive levels of consumption and saving. Consumption rises by less the greater is the difference between $\bar{k}$ and the current capital stock. Furthermore, it can be shown that a higher value of σ lowers dc/da. Thus, for an economy below its steady state, a permanent increase in aid raises both consumption and investment in the short run, and raises the rate of convergence toward the steady state.

Figure 5.4 shows the effects of a temporary aid inflow *a*, which lasts from dates 0 to T.[15] The path indicated is determined by the implication of smooth consumption, that consumption not take an anticipated discrete jump on date T. Consumption jumps initially, as does investment, but the consumption growth rate subsequently declines and investment accelerates. On date T, the economy is again on the original saddle path SS; but the date T capital stock, $k(T)$, is higher than it would have been in the absence of temporary aid. Obviously, both permanent and temporary aid inflows entail higher economic welfare for the recipient country.

---

[15] Schmidt-Hebbel and Servén also consider this experiment in their simulation model.

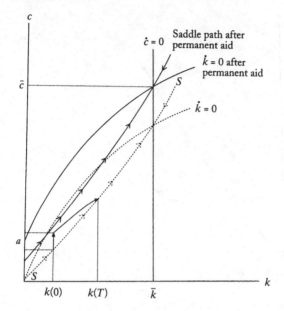

Figure 5.4. Unexpected temporary aid in the amount a causes a smaller consumption rise than equal permanent aid.

Constrained Foreign Borrowing

A more intricate analysis applies to the case of an exogenous easing in a country's foreign borrowing constraint. (Of course, the borrowing of a country whose capital-market access is constrained only by its intertemporal budget constraint is endogenous, so any additional gross capital inflow would merely generate an equal gross outflow in equilibrium.) Suppose that, at time 0, a country previously excluded from the international capital market gains the opportunity to borrow a fixed amount n per period at an interest rate $r \leq \delta$. Suppose that the government auctions these resources to the private sector at the going rate of interest.

Since $f'(k) > \delta \geq r$ as long as the capital stock is below $\bar{k}$, it will pay for the economy to borrow the full available amount n each period. The gains from fully investing n are obvious, but, in general, the economy can better satisfy its social welfare objective by consuming part of what it borrows. At the time T when k first reaches $\bar{k}$, $f'(\bar{k}) = \delta$ and foreign borrowing stops provided we make the extra assumption that $r = \delta$. Steady-state consumption is determined by the obligation to service the debt nT incurred between dates 0 and T:

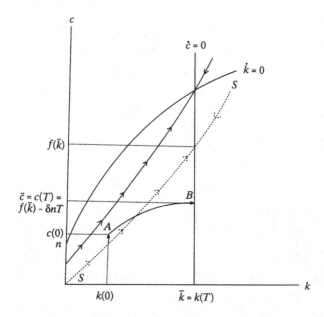

Figure 5.5. Adjustment to the steady-state capital stock with a rationed foreign credit flow of n.

$$\bar{c} = f(\bar{k}) - \delta nT. \tag{12}$$

Figure 5.5 shows the economy's path once the borrowing opportunity appears at time 0. Prior to date 0, the economy is on the saddle path SS associated with financial autarky. Once borrowing is available in the amount n, all of which is used, the equation of motion for capital is given by equation (8), with a set equal to n. Correspondingly, the phase diagram for the system's motion after time 0 corresponds to the cum-aid case in Figure 5.3, with $a = n$.

The economy's path is given by AB, the divergent path of the latter phase diagram that terminates at $\bar{c}$ in equation (12) exactly at time T. An initial consumption level above $c(0)$ would slow capital accumulation and lengthen T, thus necessitating a sharp anticipated downward jump in $c(T)$ to $\bar{c}$ when k reached $\bar{k}$. An initial consumption level below $c(0)$ would shorten T and, by similar logic, imply an expected upward jump of $c(T)$ when $k(T) = \bar{k}$. Thus, the problem has a determinate solution. Analytically, the precise path can be determined by solving for the unknowns $c(0)$ and T:

$$\bar{c} = f(\bar{k}) - \delta nT = c(0)\exp\left[\int_0^T \sigma\{f'[k(s)] - \delta\}ds\right],$$

$$\bar{k} = k(0) + \int_{0}^{T} \{f[k(s)] - c(s)\}ds + nT,$$

when c and k follow equations (9) and (8) (the latter with $a = n$) for $0 \leq s \leq T$.

More interesting than these computational questions are the qualitative properties of the path AB in Figure 5.5. Consumption rises in the short run, as does investment, but the need to service debts in the long run makes long-run consumption lower. Nonetheless, the economy is better off than under financial autarky, because it can arrange for a more nearly level consumption path over the course of its development. Furthermore, the economy's convergence to the steady state is hastened by an ability to borrow even a limited amount. Notice that $c(0)$ rises by less, and investment by more, than in the case where the foreign resource inflow is outright aid rather than a loan. This result points, once again, to the importance of distinguishing the effects of the grant and loan components of aid inflows.

As noted above, the preceding model can be viewed as one with an intergenerational structure, but in which a planning authority allocates consumption so as to maximize a social welfare function.[16] For positive purposes, it might be more appropriate to proceed with an overlapping-generations structure similar, for example, to those proposed by Blanchard (1985) or Weil (1989). The principles governing the effects of resource inflows in those models are quite similar to those sketched above. A major complication is that with an overlapping-generations structure, permanent aid inflows or any past borrowing can affect the steady-state stock of capital. Furthermore, government tax/subsidy policies associated with the disbursement of aid or the servicing of foreign debts will affect the economy's saving behavior, as stressed by Eaton (1989).[17]

Any attempt to use models such as these for predictive purposes must contend, not only with demographic complexity, but with a host of structural issues such as imperfect domestic credit markets, distorting taxes, the conditionality (or lack thereof) of foreign resource inflows, the agendas of the agents who make up the government, and the like. The role of relative prices, also ignored up until now, can be critical as well.

---

[16] See Calvo and Obstfeld (1988) for a formal justification.

[17] The economy's steady-state capital stock can be affected by permanent aid, even in the absence of overlapping generations, if some relative prices are endogenously determined, including the case in which there is an endogenous domestic labor supply. An endogenous rate of private time-preference would also lead to variable steady-state capital intensity. So would any effect of aid on the long-run rate of capital taxation.

In the next section I sketch a basic empirical analytical framework that can be adapted to account for such issues.

A Basic Framework for Investigation

This section sketches a bare-bones empirical framework suitable for examining the impact of foreign resource inflows under more realistic assumptions. Two models are examined, one a standard optimal-growth model with a set of liquidity constrained consumers, the other an endogenous-growth model. One approach to applying the general framework of this section is to construct a medium-scale macroeconomic model capturing the major determinants of consumption and investment behavior in a dynamic setting. The basic models can be tailored to the particular economy under study by modifying parameter values and institutional features to fit known empirical regularities. The approach thus can, at least potentially, answer more detailed questions than the prevalent cross-section regression methodology, and it has the definite advantage of laying bare the structural, causal mechanisms through which resource inflows operate on the economy. As mentioned earlier, the work of Schmidt-Hebbel and Servén (1995) exemplifies this use of a related but more detailed model. The basic model can also be applied to *normative* questions: for a given social welfare function, what fraction of resource inflows *should* an economy be investing domestically?

The drawback of this "calibration" approach is that, while models can be tailored to fit the most salient empirical regularities, they can never match the data perfectly, nor can we be certain that some other model doesn't underlie the empirical data-generating process. The interpretation of *any* econometric work, however, requires *some* maintained identifying assumptions, some stance on the underlying economic model. The approach I sketch here has the advantage of making the identifying assumptions explicit, hence, in principle, refutable.

A second approach to applying the framework sketched in this section is to use it as a guide to econometric specification. This is the promising tack taken by Boone (1994, 1996), whose approach could be extended in several ways, including the explicit estimation of nonbalanced-growth models.

I have deliberately kept the models described below simple – indeed, simple enough to understand intuitively and to solve without extensive computation. I examine one experiment, a permanent and unanticipated increase in aid inflow to an economy that is shut off from world capital markets. One could modify the basic model to look at more subtle capital-market imperfections.

One important message of this section's analysis is that the saving and growth dynamics induced by resource inflows are likely to be quite intricate. Cross-section econometric studies that ignore temporal factors can throw no light on these dynamics.

A Basic Model

Per capita output is produced according to the technology

$$y_t = Ak_t^\alpha,$$

and, if a is the permanent level of aid inflow and θ the depreciation rate of capital, capital evolves according to

$$k_{t+1} = (1 - \theta)k_t + y_t + a - c_t. \tag{13}$$

In actual applications, it would be important to allow for secular per capita growth in the form of a trend increase in the technology parameter A.

There are two classes of consumers. Class 1 consumers are intertemporal maximizers with access to perfect capital markets. Each class 1 consumer maximizes

$$\sum_{t=0}^{\infty} \beta^t u(c_{1t}) \quad (0 < \beta < 1),$$

subject to a standard present-value budget constraint. As usual, a condition for intertemporal optimality is the consumption Euler equation

$$u'(c_{1t}) = \beta(1 + r_{t+1})u'(c_{1t+1}), \tag{14}$$

where $r_{t+1} = \alpha Ak_{t+1}^{\alpha-1} - \theta$ is the domestic real rate of interest between periods t and $t + 1$. A class 2 consumer owns no assets and consumes all of labor income. On the assumption that aid is rebated to the population in an egalitarian fashion, the consumption of a representative class 2 consumer is

$$c_{2t} = a + (1 - \alpha)Ak_t^\alpha \tag{15}$$

(recall that $1 - \alpha$ is labor's share of GDP under a Cobb-Douglas production function).

Aggregate consumption per capita is a weighted average of c_{1t} and c_{2t}:

$$c_t = \psi c_{1t} + (1 - \psi)c_{2t}. \tag{16}$$

Assuming the earlier isoelastic form for $u(c)$, equation (14) takes the form

$$c_{1t+1} = \beta^\sigma \left[1 + \alpha Ak_{t+1}^{\alpha-1} - \theta\right]^\sigma c_{1t}. \tag{17}$$

Using equations (15) and (16), one can rewrite equation (13) in terms of c_{1t} as

$$k_{t+1} = [1 - (1 - \psi)(1 - \alpha)]Ak_t^\alpha + \psi a - \theta k_t - \psi c_{1t}. \tag{18}$$

The steady state for this system in c_1 and k is

$$\bar{c}_1 = a + (1/\psi)\{[1 - (1 - \psi)(1 - \alpha)]A\bar{k}^\alpha - \theta\bar{k}\},$$

$$\bar{k} = \left(\frac{\alpha A \beta}{1 - \beta + \beta\theta}\right)^{1/(1-\alpha)}.$$

Linearization of equations (17) and (18) near the steady state[18] yields the difference-equation system

$$\begin{bmatrix} c_{1t+1} - \bar{c}_1 \\ k_{t+1} - \bar{k} \end{bmatrix} = \begin{bmatrix} 1 - \psi\xi_{ck} & \xi_{ck}(1 + \xi_{kk}) \\ -\psi & 1 + \xi_{kk} \end{bmatrix} \begin{bmatrix} c_{1t} - \bar{c}_1 \\ k_t - \bar{k} \end{bmatrix},$$

where $\xi_{ck} = \beta\sigma\bar{c}_1\alpha(\alpha - 1)A\bar{k}^{\alpha-2}$ and $\xi_{kk} = [1 - (1 - \psi)(1 - \alpha)]\alpha A\bar{k}^{\alpha-1} - \theta$. The stable characteristic root of this system is

$$\lambda^- = \left\{2 + \xi_{kk} - \psi\xi_{ck} - \left[(2 + \xi_{kk} - \psi\xi_{ck})^2 - 4(1 + \xi_{kk})\right]^{1/2}\right\}/2.$$

In a neighborhood of the steady state, the consumption of class 1 consumers is related to the aggregate capital stock by

$$c_{1t} = \bar{c}_1 - \left(\frac{1 + \xi_{kk} - \lambda^-}{\psi}\right)(k_t - \bar{k}). \tag{19}$$

Using equations (16), (18), and (19), one can investigate the effects of changes in a for alternative parameter values. I assume below that $\alpha = 0.4$, $\psi = 0.6$, $\theta = 0.1$, $\beta = 0.97$, and $\sigma = 0.4$ (a value in line with Ostry and Reinhart's, 1992, estimates for developing countries). I also assume an initial capital–output ratio of 1 and that initial per capita output is 1,000 real 1999 dollars per year. The last assumptions imply $A = 63.1$, given that $\alpha = 0.4$. The long-run capital–output ratio is 3.06.

Dynamic Effects of Aid

The experiments look at the effects of a permanent, unexpected increase in a from 0 to 10 (which equals 1 percent of initial GDP). The variables of primary interest are consumption, net investment, and the growth rate of net output, $y - \theta k$. Because there is no opportunity to lend or borrow abroad, the net saving rate equals the net investment rate, Δk, and the current account is identically zero. Notice that, in calculating net saving, I therefore include a as a component of national income:

$$s_t = a + y_t - \theta k_t - c_t. \tag{20}$$

---

[18] An alternative approach would be to log-linearize, as in Campbell (1994).

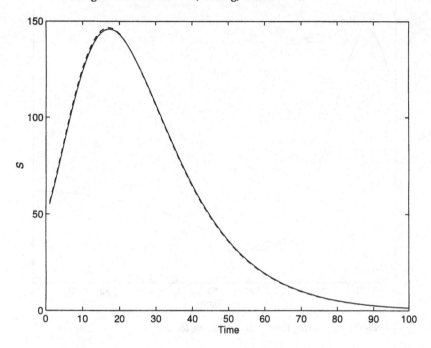

Figure 5.6. Saving (dashed for $a = 10$, solid for $a = 0$).

Figure 5.6 shows the effect on (net) saving (and, by implication, on net investment) of an unexpected permanent rise in a from 0 to 10. Saving rises slightly initially, eventually falling below its initial level. Figure 5.7 shows the difference that the aid makes to saving. Slightly more than a tenth of the aid translates initially into higher saving and investment, the balance going into consumption. Over time, however, output and savings both rise above their initial levels. After seven years, saving is about $1.60 higher than in the baseline simulation. Then it falls sharply to, and below, the baseline level.

Saving ultimately must fall because the long-run capital stock is independent of aid. Thus, because aid accelerates investment, it also accelerates the rate at which the real rate of return falls over time. Ultimately, this leads to saving below the baseline ($a = 0$) level. Asymptotically, saving converges to zero with or without aid.

The aggregate consumption effects underlying these saving results are shown in Figure 5.8. Initially, each class 1 consumer raises her consumption by about $8.22, while each class 2 consumer raises his by the full $10 of higher disposable income. Thus, the initial rise in aggregate consumption per capita is $(0.6) \times (\$8.22) + (0.4) \times (\$10) = \$8.93$. Figure 5.9 shows that aid has a greater impact on consumption in early years than

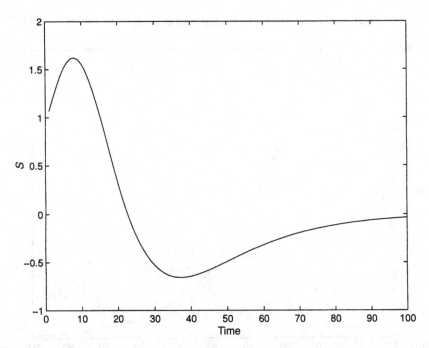

Figure 5.7. Saving for $a = 10$ less saving for $a = 0$.

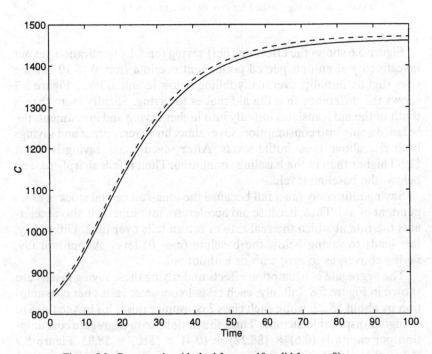

Figure 5.8. Consumption (dashed for $a = 10$, solid for $a = 0$).

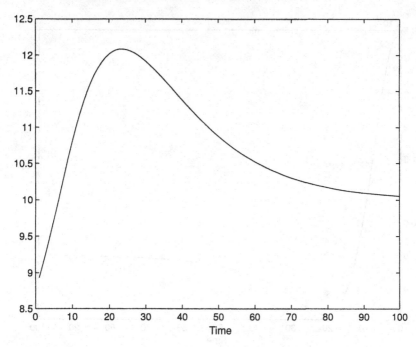

Figure 5.9. Consumption for $a = 10$ less; consumption for $a = 0$.

later on (where the positive effect on consumption asymptotes to $10).
This "bulge" simply reflects the higher level of output in the short run,
which temporarily depresses domestic real interest rates relative to their
baseline path.

In their model, which is based on the preceding optimal-growth
paradigm but allows for several of the extensions listed at the end of
this section, Schmidt-Hebbel and Servén (1995) also find that most of
a permanent aid inflow is consumed. Investment rises in the short run
because an endogenous terms-of-trade improvement raises the long-
run capital stock. Replacement investment in the steady state also is
higher.

Figure 5.10 shows the difference in the present model that aid makes
for the growth rate of net output. The additional saving of class 1 consumers promotes growth initially, but since the long-run output level is
independent of aid, this temporary acceleration of growth must be repaid
later in the form of growth below baseline. (However, positive growth
today, when consumption is low, is worth more than the same amount
of negative growth later when consumption is comparatively high.) All
growth effects are quantitatively small, but the amount of the aid is also

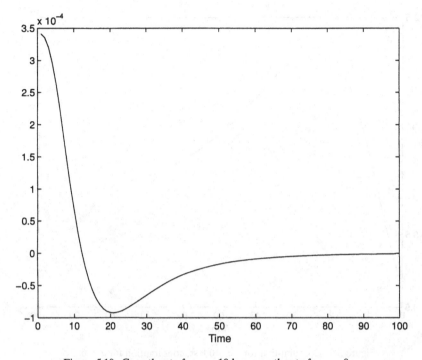

Figure 5.10. Growth rate for $a = 10$ less growth rate for $a = 0$.

quite a small fraction of GDP. Very large amounts of aid (relative to GDP) naturally could have palpable growth effects in the short run.

Net growth effects over time would require a model in which growth is endogenous, or a "big push" model (à la Murphy, Shleifer, and Vishny, 1989) with scale effects in which aid facilitates a larger market and a permanent rise in output. (An overlapping-generations model could also generate net growth effects, but at a level less likely to be quantitatively important.) The incorporation of such features into the model is feasible – examples exist in the literature on "real business cycles" – and suggests an important line of future research.

While the present model is special, the small initial effect of aid on investment seems likely to be a robust feature of any plausible model in which aid is funneled through the private sector. One could increase this investment response by raising σ, as discussed in the preceding section, but few researchers believe σ to be significantly above 1. Aid funneled through the government could have a greater impact on investment if the crowding-out effect on private investment were not too strong. But there is little evidence that, in practice, governments have a higher marginal propensity to invest than does the private sector. The result that even intertemporally optimizing consumers save far less than half of an aid inflow renders extremely implausible any causal interpretation of reduced-form regression results showing big effects of aid on aggregate investment or growth. The result also raises the question of the desirability, on welfare grounds, of a large investment response. The next model has similar implications.

An Endogenous-Growth Model

An example using an endogenous-growth model indicates how the effects of aid inflows can be evaluated in that setting. The model used is the physical/human capital model of Uzawa (1965), as exposited by Barro and Sala-i-Martin (1995, Section 5.2). The particulars of the model applied would vary with the country case at hand, but the following account exposes economic forces likely to be at work in most endogenous-growth settings.

In this model the supply of raw labor is constant and normalized at 1. Raw labor can be viewed as a fixed factor in the production of output, y, which also depends on physical capital, k, and human capital, h, according to the production function

$$y = Ak^{\alpha}(uh)^{1-\alpha}, \tag{21}$$

where $u \in [0,1]$ is the fraction of the economy's human capital stock allocated to production. The balance of the human capital, $1 - u$, is used in producing new human capital ("education"), so that the stock of human capital evolves according to

$$\dot{h} = B(1-u)h - \theta h, \tag{22}$$

where B, like A, is a productivity coefficient and θ is the capital depreciation rate. (Continuous time simplifies the derivations now.) Both A and B are assumed constant. The stocks of physical and human capital, and therefore their ratio,

$$\omega \equiv k/h,$$

are predetermined state variables of the economy.

The representative individual again maximizes equation (7), subject to equations (21), (22), and

$$\dot{k} = y + ak - c - \theta k, \tag{23}$$

where a is the aid inflow, expressed as a fraction of the capital stock. In what follows I will take a to be a permanent constant (for the purpose of having a steady state with aid), but I will assume that the dependence of total aid on k is ignored by domestic investors in making their decisions;

that is, the aid recipient takes the product ak as given. Under this assumption, consumption follows the Euler equation

$$\dot{c}/c = \sigma\left[\alpha Au^{1-\alpha}\omega^{-(1-\alpha)} - \theta - \delta\right] \tag{24}$$

when $u(c)$ is isoelastic.

Following Barro and Sala-i-Martin (1995), define

$$\chi \equiv c/k.$$

Then equations (32) and (24) imply that

$$\dot{\chi}/\chi = (\alpha\sigma - 1)z + \chi - [\theta(\sigma - 1) + \delta\sigma] - a, \tag{25}$$

while (since $\omega \equiv k/h$), equations (21), (22), and (23) imply that

$$\dot{\omega}/\omega = Au^{1-\alpha}\omega^{-(1-\alpha)} - \chi - B(1 - u) + a. \tag{26}$$

Finally, the optimality condition for u is

$$\dot{u}/u = -\chi + Bu + B\left(\frac{1-\alpha}{\alpha}\right) + a, \tag{27}$$

as a simple modification of Barro and Sala-i-Martin's discussion shows. The model has a steady-state balanced growth path in the variables $\omega = k/h$, $\chi = c/k$, and u, such that the *absolute levels* of c, k, and h grow at equal constant rates given by equation (24). The critical simplification that Barro and Sala-i-Martin suggest is to define the average product of capital (which also is constant in the steady state),

$$z \equiv Au^{1-\alpha}\omega^{-(1-\alpha)}, \tag{28}$$

and to notice that equations (26) and (27) imply

$$\dot{z}/z = (1 - \alpha)(B/\alpha - z). \tag{29}$$

This step is useful because the system consisting of equations (25), (27), and (29) is relatively easy to analyze.

To do so, solve for the steady-state values

$$\bar{z} = B/\alpha, \quad \bar{\chi} = a + [\theta(\sigma - 1) + \delta\sigma] + \frac{(1 - \sigma\alpha)B}{\alpha},$$

$$\bar{u} = 1 - \sigma + \frac{[\theta(\sigma - 1) + \delta\sigma]}{B}. \tag{30}$$

As in the standard optimal-growth model, aid affects steady-state consumption one-for-one, but has no other steady-state effect on the economy. Thus, one must look at the transition path to find effects of aid on investment. The model's linearization around the steady state is

$$
\begin{bmatrix} \dot{z} \\ \dot{\chi} \\ \dot{u} \end{bmatrix} = \begin{bmatrix} -(1-\alpha)\bar{z} & 0 & 0 \\ (\alpha\sigma-1)\bar{\chi} & \bar{\chi} & 0 \\ 0 & -\bar{u} & B\bar{u} \end{bmatrix} \begin{bmatrix} z-\bar{z} \\ \chi-\bar{\chi} \\ u-\bar{u} \end{bmatrix}.
$$

The characteristic roots of this system are apparent from inspection: they are $-(1-\alpha)\bar{z}, \bar{\chi}$, and $B\bar{u}$. The linearized model has a unique saddle path along which z, χ, and u evolve according to

$$
z(t) - \bar{z} = [z(0) - \bar{z}]\exp[-(1-\alpha)\bar{z}t], \tag{31}
$$

$$
\chi(t) - \bar{\chi} = \left(\frac{(1-\alpha\sigma)\bar{\chi}}{\bar{\chi}+(1-\alpha)\bar{z}}\right)[z(0) - \bar{z}]\exp[-(1-\alpha)\bar{z}t], \tag{32}
$$

and

$$
u(t) - \bar{u} = \left(\frac{(1-\alpha\sigma)\bar{\chi}}{\bar{\chi}+(1-\alpha)\bar{z}}\right)\left(\frac{\bar{u}}{B\bar{u}+(1-\alpha)\bar{z}}\right)[z(0) - \bar{z}]\exp[-(1-\alpha)\bar{z}t]. \tag{33}
$$

Provided that $\alpha\sigma < 1$, as conventional estimates imply, z and χ rise or fall together along the saddle path, implying that c/k rises as k/h falls. The reason is that a high initial k/h (say) implies a low real interest rate and, through the income effect, a low initial consumption level relative to the capital stock.

In simulating an unexpected shock to the model, it is important to remember that z is *not* a state variable. However, ω is, so equation (33) can be used to eliminate $u(0)$ from equation (28), allowing solution for $z(0)$ in terms of $\omega(0)$, which is predetermined at $t = 0$, and the new steady-state values of z, χ, and u.

Figure 5.11 shows the consumption effect of a permanent unexpected aid inflow equivalent to 1 percent of the capital stock. For this simulation, I set B, the steady-state marginal product of capital, at 0.18, $\alpha = 0.4$, $\sigma = 0.4$, $\theta = 0.1$, $\delta = 0.3$, and normalize $A = 1$. With an aid inflow of zero, the initial steady state is

$$
\bar{z} = B/\alpha = 0.45, \bar{\omega} = 1.06, \bar{u} = 0.33, \bar{\chi} = \overline{c/k} = 0.33.
$$

Steady-state growth, the hallmark of endogenous-growth models, is at 2 percent per year. The long-run values of z, ω, and u are unaffected by the aid, as is the long-run growth rate, but $\bar{\chi}$ rises by 0.01. In the short run, however, aid effects all the model's endogenous variables. I assume that, initially, $\omega(0)$ is given at $1.5 > \bar{\omega} = 1.06$. Thus, the economy initially is rich in physical relative to human capital. (The endogenous-growth model's impulse responses do not depend on the country's absolute wealth, just on the initial imbalance between the two types of capital.)

Figure 5.11 shows that c/k initially jumps, but by less than the full

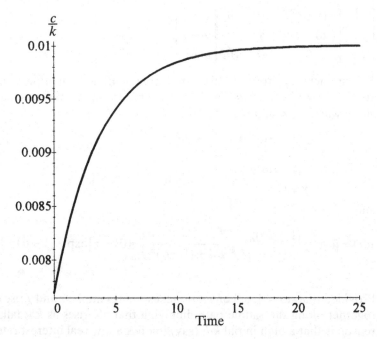

Figure 5.11. Effect of permanent aid equal to 1 percent of capital stock on the ratio c/k.

amount of the aid, 0.01. The initial jump is 0.00769: 76.9 percent of the aid is consumed initially. (The initial consumption jump would be even greater were some consumers liquidity constrained.) It is important to notice that if the economy were in a starting position with $\omega(0) < \bar{\omega}$, c/k would rise by *more than* a. Alternatively, with $\omega(0) > \bar{\omega}$ but $\alpha\sigma > 1$, c/k would jump initially by more than a. There thus is no presumption in this model that all aid will not be consumed, even in a country at a total wealth level that is low relative to developed-country total wealth levels.

Interestingly, aid that is not consumed does not go entirely into physical capital accumulation, although investment does rise slightly (see Figure 5.12). When aid is received, u immediately falls. As human capital is shifted from the final-goods sector to producing human capital, output falls and human capital accumulation accelerates.

The initial reallocation of human capital from the output to the "educational" sector lowers the initial rate of return to physical capital. According to Euler equation (24), consumption growth dips temporarily.

This endogenous-growth model confirms the earlier growth model's prediction that, optimally, most aid will and should be consumed. An

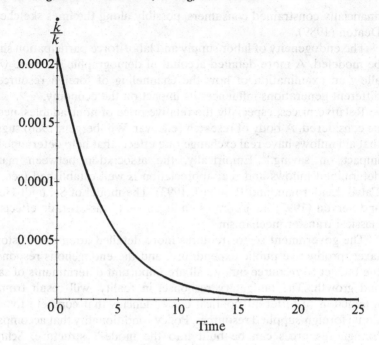

Figure 5.12. Effect of permanent aid equal to 1 percent of capital stock on capital-stock growth rate.

interesting finding is that, for the parameter constellation above, a country richly endowed with human relative to physical capital will consume more than its total marginal aid inflow. The model cautions that the effects of aid on investment may well show up in human rather than physical capital accumulation.

Extensions

This section has illustrated a basic methodology for exploring the impact of foreign resource inflows within dynamic models. The models were deliberately chosen to be rather generic. Applications to individual economies would require country-specific modeling of various technological and institutional features.

A number of modifications to the basic models might be necessary to match the features of specific economies. Stochastic elements could be introduced, allowing calibration of the model to observed moments of macrovariables or to impulse–response functions from identified vector autoregressions. Explicit recognition of the economy's stochastic structure would permit a more detailed treatment of the saving behavior of financially constrained consumers, possibly along the lines sketched by Deaton (1989).

The endogeneity of labor supply and labor-force participation should be modeled. A more detailed account of demographic structure would allow an examination of how the channeling of foreign resources to different generations influences its impact on the economy.

Relative prices, especially the relative price of nontradables, need to be considered. A body of research (e.g., van Wijnbergen, 1986) suggests that aid inflows have real exchange rate effects that help determine their impact on saving.[19] Empirically, the association between market-determined inflows and real appreciation is well established (see, e.g., Calvo, Leiderman, and Reinhart, 1993). The model of Schmidt-Hebbel and Servén (1995) incorporates endogenous terms-of-trade effects, the classical transfer mechanism.

The government sector requires more detailed attention. Distorting taxes, productive public expenditure, and the endogenous response of the budget to resource inflows all are important determinants of saving and growth. The budgetary response, in reality, will result from the interaction of different political constituencies that compete for additional foreign-supplied resources. Policy conditionality that accompanies foreign resources can be built into the model's structure. Schmidt-Hebbel and Servén (1995) consider a fairly detailed model of government activities, including government debt, money creation, consumption, and investment subsidies.

Resource leakages through capital flight probably are important in practice in determining the impact of gross inflows. An important but little-discussed empirical question is the extent to which capital flight limits the effectiveness of gross aid inflows. In addition, the model should endogenize key elements – sovereign risk, moral hazards, and the like – that may limit access to world capital markets.

The model above applied to the medium term, but its applicability to the short-run analysis of some economies would be enhanced by the addition of nominal rigidities. In general, the incorporation of monetary factors would allow an analysis of the impact of foreign resource inflows on inflation and seigniorage revenue. Schmidt-Hebbel and Servén (1995) incorporate money, as noted above, and a rigid real wage.

Finally, the preceding models have relied on *linear* solution procedures even though they may be inaccurate if (as I assumed above) the economy initially is far from the steady state. Schmidt-Hebbel and Servén (1995) solve their nonlinear model through a modified multiple-shooting algorithm.

---

[19] For a theoretical analysis, see Edwards (1989).

Conclusion

This chapter has surveyed the literature on the consumption, investment, and growth effects of foreign resource inflows. Early empirical research on the subject suffered from pervasive endogeneity of regressors, preventing a clear structural interpretation of least squares results. After surveying the empirical literature, including more recent contributions, I explored the effects of exogenous foreign resource inflows, both permanent and transitory, in dynamic representative-agent growth models. That discussion led to a description of neoclassical and endogenous growth models that might be calibrated to investigate the impact of additional foreign resource inflows, or applied in econometric testing and estimation.

An interesting and seemingly robust implication of these models is that even under intertemporal optimization by a unitary planner, much of any small resource inflow is likely to be consumed, not saved, so that even short-run growth effects are small for moderately sized inflows. From a policy perspective, the fact that aid and other inflows raise consumption in the short run is not necessarily a bad thing. After all, if the purpose of resource transfers to developing countries is to raise long-run consumption, the principle of consumption smoothing dictates that consumption also should rise in the short run.

Unfortunately, the consumption rises observed in practice often seem to be concentrated among the political elites rather than among those most in need of more resources. This suggests that in thinking about the effects of resource inflows and in designing efficient aid and lending programs, the question of who ultimately benefits from resources is as important as the question of how the resources are used.

References

Adelman, I., and H. Chenery. 1966. "Foreign Aid and Economic Development: The Case of Greece," *Review of Economics and Statistics* 48: 1–19.

Bardhan, P. 1967. "Optimum Foreign Borrowing," in K. Shell, ed., *Essays in the Theory of Optimal Economic Growth* (Cambridge, MA: MIT Press).

Barro, R., and X. Sala-i-Martin. 1995. *Economic Growth* (New York: McGraw-Hill).

Baxter, M., and M. Crucini. 1993. "Explaining Saving/Investment Correlations," *American Economic Review* 83: 416–36.

Blanchard, O. 1985. "Debts, Deficits, and Finite Horizons," *Journal of Political Economy* 93: 223–47.

Boone, P. 1994. "The Impact of Foreign Aid on Savings and Growth," mimeographed, London School of Economics, June.

   1996. "Politics and the Effectiveness of Foreign Aid," *European Economic Review* 40: 289–329.

Bruno, M. 1970. "Trade, Growth and Capital," mimeographed, MIT.

Burnside, C., and D. Dollar. 1997. "Aid, Policies, and Growth," Policy Research Working Paper 1777, World Bank, Policy and Research Department, Macroeconomics and Growth Division.

Calvo, G., L. Leiderman, and C. Reinhart. 1993. "Capital Inflows and Real Exchange Rate Appreciation in Latin America: The Role of External Factors," *IMF Staff Papers* 40: 108–51.

Calvo, G., and M. Obstfeld. 1988. "Optimal Time-Consistent Fiscal Policy with Finite Lifetimes," *Econometrica* 56: 411–32.

Campbell, J. 1994. "Inspecting the Mechanism: An Analytical Approach to the Stochastic Growth Model," *Journal of Monetary Economics* 33: 463–506.

Cardoso, E., and R. Dornbusch. 1989. "Foreign Private Capital Flows," in H. Chenery and T. N. Srinivasan, eds., *Handbook of Development Economics*, vol. 2 (Amsterdam: North Holland).

Cassen, R., and associates. 1994. *Does Aid Work?* (2d edition) (Oxford: Clarendon Press).

Chenery, H., and M. Bruno. 1962. "Development Alternatives in an Open Economy: The Case of Israel," *Economic Journal* 72: 79–103.

Chenery, H., and P. Eckstein. 1970. "Development Alternatives for Latin America," *Journal of Political Economy* 78: 966–1006.

Chenery, H., and A. Strout. 1966. "Foreign Assistance and Economic Development," *American Economic Review* 56: 679–733.

Chenery, H., and M. Syrquin. 1975. *Patterns of Development, 1950–1970* (New York: Oxford University Press, for the World Bank).

Deaton, A. 1989. "Saving in Developing Countries: Theory and Review," *Proceedings of the World Bank Annual Conference on Development Economics* 1: 61–96.

Eaton, J. 1989. "Foreign Public Capital Flows," in H. Chenery and T. N. Srinivasan, eds., *Handbook of Development Economics*, vol. 2 (Amsterdam: North Holland).

Edwards, S. 1989. *Real Exchange Rates, Devaluation, and Adjustment* (Cambridge, MA: MIT Press).

Edwards, S. 1995. "Why Are Saving Rates So Different across Countries? An International Comparative Analysis," Working Paper 5097, National Bureau of Economic Research.

Feldstein, M. 1994. "The Effects of Outbound Foreign Direct Investment on the Domestic Capital Stock," Working Paper 4668, National Bureau of Economic Research.

Fry, M. 1978. "Money and Capital or Financial Deepening in Economic Development?" *Journal of Money, Credit and Banking* 10: 464–75.

——— 1980. "Saving, Investment, Growth, and the Cost of Financial Repression," *World Development* 8: 317–27.

Giovannini, A. 1983. "The Interest Elasticity of Savings in Developing Countries: The Existing Evidence," *World Development* 11: 601–7.

——— 1985. "Saving and the Real Interest Rate in LDCs," *Journal of Development Economics* 18: 197–217.

Griffin, K. 1970. "Foreign Capital, Domestic Savings and Economic Development," *Bulletin*, Oxford University Institute of Economics and Statistics, 32: 99–112.

Griffin, K., and J. Enos. 1970. "Foreign Assistance: Objectives and Consequences," *Economic Development and Cultural Change* 18: 313–27.

Grinols, E., and J. Bhagwati. 1976. "Foreign Capital, Savings and Dependence," *Review of Economics and Statistics* 58: 416–24.

Gupta, K. 1975. "Foreign Capital Inflows, Dependency Burden, and Saving Rates in Developing Countries: A Simultaneous Equations Model," *Kyklos* 28: 358–74.

Halevi, N. 1976. "The Effects on Investment and Consumption of Import Surpluses of Developing Countries," *Economic Journal* 86: 853–8.

Levy, V. 1987. "Does Concessionary Aid Lead to Higher Investment Rates in Developing Countries?" *Review of Economics and Statistics* 69: 152–6.

1988a. "Aid and Growth in Sub-Saharan Africa: The Recent Experience,"*European Economic Review* 32: 1777–96.

1988b. "Anticipated Development Assistance, Temporary Relief Aid, and Consumption Behaviour of Low-Income Countries," *Economic Journal* 97: 446–58.

Montiel, P. 1994. "Capital Mobility in Developing Countries: Some Measurement Issues and Empirical Estimates," *World Bank Economic Review* 8: 311–50.

Mosley, P., J. Hudson, and S. Horrell. 1987. "Aid, the Public Sector and the Market in Less Developed Countries," *Economic Journal* 97: 616–41.

Mundell, R. 1968. *International Economics* (New York: Macmillan).

Murphy, K., A. Shleifer, and R. Vishny. 1989. "Industrialization and the Big Push," *Journal of Political Economy* 97: 1003–26.

Ostry, J., and C. Reinhart. 1992. "Private Saving and Terms of Trade Shocks," *IMF Staff Papers* 39: 495–517.

Pack, H., and J. Pack. 1993. "Foreign Aid and the Question of Fungibility," *Review of Economics and Statistics* 75: 258–65.

Papanek, G. 1972. "The Effect of Aid and Other Resource Transfers on Savings and Growth in Less Developed Countries," *Economic Journal* 82: 934–50.

1973. "Aid, Foreign Private Investment, Savings, and Growth in Less Developed Countries," *Journal of Political Economy* 81: 120–30.

Pedersen, K. 1996. "Aid, Investment and Incentives," *Scandinavian Journal of Economics* 98: 423–38.

Rahman, M. 1968. "Foreign Capital and Domestic Savings: A Test of Haavelmo's Hypothesis with Cross Country Data," *Review of Economics and Statistics* 50: 137–8.

Reinhart, C., and E. Talvi. 1997. "Saving and Capital Flows Reconsidered: East Asia versus Latin America," working paper, Center for International Economics, University of Maryland.

Schmidt-Hebbel, K., and L. Servén. 1995. "Dynamic Response to External Shocks in Classical and Keynesian Open Economies," in D. Currie and D. Vines, eds., *North–South Linkages and International Macroeconomic Policy* (Cambridge University Press).

Schmidt-Hebbel, K., S. Webb, and G. Corsetti. 1992. "Household Saving in Developing Countries: First Cross-Country Evidence," *World Bank Economic Review* 6: 529–47.

Svensson, J. 1997. "When Is Foreign Aid Policy Credible? Aid Dependence and Conditionality," Policy Research Working Paper 1740, World Bank, March.

1998. "Foreign Aid and Rent Seeking," Policy Research Working Paper 1880, World Bank, February.

Tornell, A., and P. Lane. 1998. "Are Windfalls a Curse? A Non-Representative Agent Model of the Current Account," *Journal of International Economics* 44: 83–112.

Uzawa, H. 1965. "Optimum Technical Change in an Aggregative Model of Economic Growth," *International Economic Review* 6: 18–31.

van Wijnbergen, S. 1986. "Macroeconomic Aspects of the Effectiveness of Foreign Aid," *Journal of International Economics* 21: 123–36.

Weil, P. 1989. "Overlapping Families of Infinitely-Lived Agents," *Journal of Public Economics* 38: 183–98.

Weisskopf, T. 1972. "The Impact of Foreign Capital Inflow on Domestic Savings in Underdeveloped Countries," *Journal of International Economics* 2: 25–38.

White, H. 1992. "The Macroeconomic Impact of Development Aid: A Critical Survey," *Journal of Development Studies* 28: 163–240.

CHAPTER 6

Aggregate Saving and Income Distribution

Klaus Schmidt-Hebbel and Luis Servén

Introduction

If all individuals were identical in all dimensions related to saving decisions (behavior, endowment, and restrictions they face), then aggregate
saving would be trivially related to individual saving – it would just equal
the saving of a representative agent multiplied by the population. To
determine society's total saving, it would suffice to know the values of
the representative agent's income, wealth, and so on. In other words,
given the total population, aggregate saving would depend only on the
aggregate values of variables such as income and wealth.

If individuals are instead heterogeneous, however, this simple relationship ceases to hold. To be more precise, only under very particular
(and restrictive) forms of heterogeneity do aggregate consumption
and saving depend exclusively on aggregate quantities.[1] In the more
general, and realistic, case in which individual heterogeneity can take
arbitrary forms, aggregate consumption and saving patterns inevitably
reflect the dissimilar behavior of heterogeneous agents that differ in
their preferences, resources, and/or institutional constraints. This, of
course, has long been recognized by consumption theory; indeed, consumption and saving are among the few areas in macroeconomics where
theoretical developments have occasionally left the safe haven of
representative-agent models to venture into the wilderness of agent
heterogeneity, collecting along the way valuable analytical and empirical
insights – such as those derived, for example, from the life-cycle consumption model.

One particular dimension of heterogeneity that has received increased attention from the macroeconomic viewpoint in recent years is
that of income distribution. Recent analytical and empirical work has

---

[1] For a formal discussion of the circumstances under which the economy can be summarized by a "representative consumer," see Mas-Colell, Whinston, and Green (1995). See
also Kirman (1992) for a recent sharp criticism of the representative-agent paradigm.

focused on the relationship between income inequality, growth, and investment.[2] Less attention has been paid, however, to the links between income distribution and saving.

It is important to clarify what distribution of income one is talking about, because different concepts have been considered in the literature. Early research focused on functional income distribution, which can behave very differently from personal income distribution. Further, among the class of personal distributions of income, household and individual income distribution typically differ significantly. Finally, the precise income definition also matters. For example, in a world of otherwise identical individuals that differ only by age (but have the same lifetime income), inequality in current income would merely reflect the different stage of the life cycle in which different individuals find themselves.

Much of the historical literature on distribution and aggregate saving – comprising both neoclassical and Keynesian growth models – has focused on functional income distribution. Yet neoclassical consumption theory brings out a number of channels through which inequality in the personal distribution of income affects directly the total volume of personal (i.e., individual or household) saving. Most of these mechanisms (but not all) result in a positive relationship between income inequality and personal saving. However, recent political economy theory underscores indirect links from inequality – through investment, growth, and public saving – to aggregate (household plus corporate plus public) saving that should result in a negative relationship. Therefore, the sign of the overall impact of inequality on aggregate saving is ambiguous on theoretical grounds and becomes largely an empirical matter.

As discussed below, most of the empirical literature on the links between personal income distribution and personal saving based on cross-section microdata suggests a positive relation between personal income inequality and overall personal saving. In turn, the evidence from aggregate (typically, cross-country) data is more mixed. Some studies also find positive effects of personal income inequality on *aggregate* saving, but others do not. Reconciling these conflicting results is difficult because empirical studies based on macrodata use widely different samples and specifications, different measures of saving and inequality, and, in most cases, income distribution information of questionable quality.

This chapter reexamines the empirical evidence from macrodata on the links between the distribution of personal income and aggregate saving, controlling for relevant saving determinants. It provides an en-

---

[2] See, e.g., Galor and Zeira (1993), Alesina and Rodrik (1994), Persson and Tabellini (1994), Perotti (1995), and Alesina and Perotti (1996).

compassing framework and a robustness check for previous empirical studies, and extends them in five dimensions: (i) testing alternative saving specifications, (ii) using alternative inequality and saving measures, (iii) making use of newer, better, and larger databases, (iv) conducting estimations jointly and separately for industrialized and developing countries, and (v) applying various estimation techniques on both cross-country and panel data. On the whole, we do not find any consistent effect of income inequality on aggregate saving – a result that accords with the theoretical ambiguity.[3]

This chapter begins with a survey of alternative mechanisms through which income distribution affects saving. Then we review previous empirical studies on the effects of income distribution on saving. A brief description of our database for income distribution, saving, and other data for a large number of industrial and developing countries is provided next, followed by new econometric evidence from cross-country and panel data estimations, using our data set. Concluding remarks close the chapter.

Analytical Overview

Aggregate saving is the result of individual saving efforts by heterogeneous members of different classes of savers. Heterogeneity may be due to the fact that different individuals determine their consumption/saving plans according to different objectives (i.e., their preferences are not identical). Alternatively, even if all individuals possess identical preferences, their behavior may differ because they face different institutional constraints (e.g., in their access to borrowing).

Heterogeneity is of course important because when agents are dissimilar the aggregate levels of those variables relevant for *individual* saving decisions are not sufficient to determine *aggregate* saving – the latter also depends on the distribution of such variables across individual savers. There are some exceptions to this rule that apply when the class of admissible individual preferences and/or admissible endowment distributions across individuals are suitably restricted (for some recent examples, see Caselli and Ventura, 1996). However, the practical relevance of those exceptions is rather limited. Even if all agents share the same

---

[3] This chapter thus extends significantly along several dimensions the preliminary cross-section evidence reported in Schmidt-Hebbel and Servén (1998), which likewise revealed little evidence of any effects of income distribution on saving. Such provisional conclusion is considerably strengthened by the empirical analysis in this chapter based on an improved and expanded database, including a systematic replication of the findings of previous empirical results obtained by other researchers, presenting results exploiting the time dimension of the available data, and performing systematic tests of the robustness of the empirical findings to alternative specifications and estimation techniques.

preferences and face identical constraints, distribution still matters as long as agents' (common) decision rule for saving is not linear in the relevant variables.

Heterogeneity among savers is a key feature that helps us understand how aggregate saving is affected by changes in saving determinants, including policies. A given change in the aggregate value of a saving determinant (such as disposable income or wealth) can have very different consequences for aggregate saving, depending on how it impacts different types of savers. Likewise, purely redistributive policies can have an impact on aggregate saving – for example, public transfers to the poor financed by taxes on the rich will reduce total saving if the former have a higher propensity to spend than do the latter.

Next we focus on the impact of changes in the distribution of income (or wealth) on aggregate saving. We examine four issues: (1) the relation between saving and the *functional* distribution of income; (2) the links between saving and the *personal* distribution of income; (3) the interaction between borrowing constraints, distribution, and saving; and (4) the indirect effects of distribution on saving. Then we briefly sum up the different mechanisms at work.

Functional Distribution and Saving

The relation between the functional distribution of income and saving (and growth) is at the core of the neoclassical growth model (Solow, 1956), as well as the neo-Keynesian growth models of Lewis (1954), Kaldor (1957), and Pasinetti (1962). By nature these are general-equilibrium models, with both saving and income distribution as endogenous variables.

In the neoclassical framework, workers and capitalists do not necessarily differ in their saving patterns. Aggregate saving behavior in conjunction with production characteristics determines income distribution. The reason is that saving influences investment and thus the capital stock. An increase in the propensity to save will increase the long-run capital–labor ratio, and capital's income share will rise or fall depending on whether the elasticity of factor substitution is greater or smaller than one, respectively.

However, as already noted in Chapter 3, the neo-Keynesian growth models of Lewis and Kaldor assume from the outset that workers and capitalists have different saving behavior. Lewis (1954) argues that most saving comes from the profits of the entrepreneurs in the modern, industrial sector of the economy, who save a high fraction of their incomes, while other groups in the economy save less. Income redistribution from the low-saving group to the entrepreneurs therefore raises aggregate saving.

Likewise, in the simplest form of Kaldor's (1957) model, workers spend what they earn (their propensity to save is zero), and the share of profits in national income depends positively on the investment–output ratio and inversely on the propensity to save of the capitalists. In turn, Pasinetti (1962) assumes that saving propensities differ among classes of individuals, rather than classes of income. Workers' saving is not zero; indeed, they are assumed to own shares on the capital stock and receive part of the profits. Nevertheless, the implications for the share of profits in income are the same obtained by Kaldor. The fact that workers save does influence the distribution of income between capitalists and workers, but does not influence the distribution of income between profits and wages.

Recent work by Bertola (1993) provides a new perspective on these neo-Keynesian models. Using an endogenous-growth framework with intertemporally optimizing agents, Bertola shows that along steady-growth paths the economy generates a saving dichotomy between owners of nonaccumulated productive inputs (e.g., labor or land) and those of accumulated factors (e.g., "capitalists"): the former do not save at all, while the latter do. The implications are thus strikingly similar to those of the neo-Keynesian models above, where the saving dichotomy is directly imposed rather than derived as a feature of the economy's growth path.

While these neo-Keynesian models establish a clear relation between the functional distribution of income and saving, it is worth noting that their implications in terms of the inequality–saving link are less automatic. The reason is that in many societies wage earners do not necessarily represent the poorer segments of the population, which are likely to include instead rural landowners with small holdings and self-employed individuals in the informal sector. As a result, the association between the functional and personal distributions of income is empirically rather weak (Atkinson, 1994).

Personal Distribution and Saving

When consumers are heterogeneous, standard consumption theories also generate links between personal income distribution and aggregate saving that, unlike the classical theories just referred to, do not depend on the exogenous distinction between savers and nonsavers. These links result from a nonlinear relationship between individual saving and income, which can have different sources.

A starting point is the life-cycle hypothesis (LCH) fathered by Modigliani and Brumberg (1954), amended to include bequests. In its original formulation, the LCH ignored bequests because they were thought insignificant, a notion that has later been reversed (Kotlikoff and Summers, 1981, 1988). The view that bequests as a saving motive are perhaps more important than life-cycle considerations, and that the elasticity of bequests with respect to lifetime resources exceeds unity, helps explain a number of empirical puzzles on the LCH model (for further discussion and references, see Deaton, 1992, and Chapter 3 in this book).

First, there is little evidence that the old dissave, as implied by the simple LCH; on the contrary, their saving rates appear to be as high or even higher than those who are young. Second, if bequests are a luxury (at least over a relevant wealth range), saving rates should be higher among wealthier consumers and richer countries than in the rest, which empirically seems to be the case. Then (lifetime) income redistribution from rich to poor will unambiguously reduce aggregate saving.

Third, the fact that saving appears to be concentrated among relatively few richer households, who may be accumulating mostly for dynastic motives, is also in agreement with a central role of bequests in driving saving. This is also consistent with the classical "capitalist spirit" model of saving, in which wealth is accumulated for its own sake (see, e.g., Zou, 1994), and higher wealth prompts further accumulation – because consumption and wealth are gross substitutes in the agent's utility function. More generally, the apparent concentration of saving in a small group of richer individuals suggests that a better understanding of their saving behavior is essential to understand aggregate saving patterns.

Becker (1975) suggested an alternative route through which income distribution may matter for aggregate saving. If there are decreasing returns to human capital, the poor will invest relatively more in human capital than will the rich. Since human capital expenditures are considered as consumption in standard national accounting, the measured saving rates of the poor will appear lower than those of the rich, even if their "overall" saving rates (including human capital accumulation) are identical.

Precautionary saving also implies a link between distribution and saving because it prompts risk-averse consumers to set aside a certain amount of resources to face uncertain changes in future income levels or other variables. Consumers with low assets tend to compress consumption to avoid running down these precautionary balances, so that their marginal propensity to consume out of income is higher than that of those consumers holding large asset stocks – they would devote most of any extra income to consumption. Thus, redistribution from the wealthy to the poor would depress overall saving. The opposite could happen, however, if the poor face greater uncertainty, are more risk-averse, or have more limited access to risk diversification than the rich; in such circumstances (which seem in principle quite realistic), a transfer from the latter to the former would lead to higher aggregate saving.

More generally, the relationship between precautionary saving and inequality may depend on the nature of the link between the latter and the income volatility faced by individual savers. For example, if inequality results mostly from unpredictable high-variance shocks to individual income, a reduction in their dispersion could lower observed inequality as well as precautionary saving. In this vein, Friedman (1957) observed that if the cross-section distribution of income reflects future income uncertainty, then greater income inequality should raise precautionary saving.

Borrowing Constraints, Distribution, and Saving

The inability of some consumers to borrow forges a powerful link between income distribution and saving. Consumption models with borrowing constraints divide consumers into savers and nonsavers. Unlike in the older models of functional income distribution, however, this does not arise from the exogenous distinction of two classes of people or preferences, but from the distribution of preferences among the population, interest rates, the variability of earnings, and their rate of growth.

Borrowing constraints act in a way similar in many respects to the precautionary saving motive. Given the inability to borrow, consumers use assets to buffer consumption, accumulating when times are good and running them down to protect consumption when earnings are low. In theoretical models, borrowing constraints mostly affect impatient consumers who face high earnings growth (Deaton, 1991).

The empirical relevance of borrowing constraints is well established. However, they help explain mostly short-term saving for consumption buffering, not long-term saving for old age or for bequests. For example, Hayashi (1985) finds that for a significant fraction of the Japanese population, the behavior of consumption over time is consistent with the existence of credit rationing and differential borrowing and lending rates. Borrowing constraints appear particularly important with regard to saving for housing purchases. Jappelli and Pagano (1994) show that credit constraints reflected in housing mortgage regulations are an important explanatory factor behind cross-country differences in saving.

In practice, borrowing constraints affect mostly poorer households, and not the rich who hold large asset stocks. Thus, like the precautionary saving motive, borrowing constraints likely are a chief force behind the saving behavior of lower- and middle-income groups, but not richer households. Income redistribution away from the latter makes the borrowing constraints less likely to bind and reduces the importance of buffer-stock saving, thus lowering aggregate saving rates.

Indirect Links

Other recent literature brings out some indirect links between distribution and saving operating through third variables that affect saving. One particularly active line of research is the political economy literature, which has underscored the positive association between income equality and economic growth in a framework of endogenous growth and endogenous economic policy. In this approach, causality runs from distribution to growth via investment. In addition, these models include a political mechanism that provides a link between income inequality and economic policy.

The main line of argument is that a highly unequal distribution of income and wealth causes social tension and political instability (violent protests, coups, etc.); the result is a discouragement of investment through increased uncertainty, along with adverse consequences for productivity and thus growth (Alesina and Rodrik, 1994; Persson and Tabellini, 1994; Perotti, 1996; Alesina and Perotti, 1996). In addition, income distribution may also affect growth through taxation and government expenditure: in a more unequal society there is greater demand for redistribution and therefore higher taxation, lower returns to investments in physical and human capital, and less investment and growth.

These arguments have received some empirical support. From the point of view of saving, the implication is that if saving is positively dependent on growth, then higher inequality will, through the above channels, depress aggregate saving – in contrast with the positive impact of inequality on saving implied by most of the theories examined so far. Additionally, distributive inequality may also tend to lower *public* saving, as governments engage more actively in redistributive expenditures – as in the populist experiences examined by Dornbusch and Edwards (1991); in the absence of strict Ricardian equivalence, this would in turn reduce aggregate saving.

The existence of an inverse relationship between inequality and investment, as suggested by the above literature, could also imply a negative association between inequality and saving through firms' earnings retention. The latter is typically the primary source of financing for private investment, so that if higher inequality lowers investment it should also reduce firm saving. What happens with *aggregate* saving, however, depends on whether firm owners (i.e., households) can pierce the "corporate veil" that separates household and firm decisions. If this were the case, a fall in firm saving could be fully offset by a rise in household saving, leaving aggregate saving unaffected.

Income Concentration Affects Household Saving Directly and	
Positively	*Negatively*
If:	
• Marginal saving propensities increase with income levels. • Bequests are luxury goods. • The poor invest relatively more in education, the rich in financial assets. • The poor engage in buffer-stock saving in response to uncertainty. • Borrowing constraints affect the poor more strongly.	• The poor face larger uncertainty, are more risk averse, or have limited access to risk diversification.
Income Concentration Affects Aggregate Saving Indirectly and	
Positively	*Negatively*
If:	
	• It raises instability that depresses corporate investment and corporate saving (and, hence, aggregate saving if households do not pierce the corporate veil), and reduces growth (and saving again). • It triggers larger distributional public spending programs, and thus reduces public saving (and, hence, aggregate saving if Ricardian equivalence is not satisfied).

Figure 6.1. Summary of mechanisms through which income concentration affects household and aggregate saving.

Summing Up

Figure 6.1 summarizes the different mechanisms through which a change in the distribution of personal income affects aggregate saving. The figure lists six ways in which income concentration affects household (and, hence, aggregate) saving *directly* – positively in five cases and negatively in one. It also lists two *indirect* links from income concentration to aggregate saving – both negative – that occur through lower corporate and lower public saving. We conclude that, in view of the opposite signs of the different mechanisms at work, the overall impact of changes in income distribution on household and aggregate saving is ambiguous on theoretical grounds and is largely an empirical matter.

Empirical Studies

Empirical tests of the impact of income distribution on saving are rather scarce. Some early studies followed the Kaldor-Lewis approach and focused on the functional distribution of income. Along these lines, Houthakker (1961), Williamson (1968), Kelley and Williamson (1968), and Gupta (1970) found some evidence that the propensity to save from nonlabor income exceeds that from labor income.

More recent empirical studies have shifted their focus from functional to personal income inequality and its effects on saving. Blinder (1975) uses U.S. time-series data for 1949–70 to estimate an equation for aggregate consumption including income distribution indicators. He finds that higher inequality appears to raise aggregate consumption (and thus lower saving), although the estimated effect is, in general, statistically insignificant. He proposes as a preferable empirical test the estimation of separate consumption equations by income class, a suggestion taken up by Menchik and David (1983), who use disaggregated U.S. data to test directly whether the elasticity of bequests to lifetime resources is larger or smaller for the rich than for other income groups. They find that the marginal propensity to bequeath is unambiguously higher for the wealthy, so that higher inequality leads to higher lifetime aggregate saving.

Data from household surveys typically show that high-income households save on average more than do low-income households. Bunting (1991), who uses U.S. consumer expenditure survey data, finds strong evidence that household spending depends on both the level and distribution of income: his estimates of the marginal propensity to save uniformly increase as the quintile share of income rises. Huggett and Ventura (1995) calibrate an overlapping-generations model to U.S. household income and saving data and conclude that age differences across households and social security transfers from young to old are important in explaining the cross-section pattern of U.S. saving rates. More recently, Dynan, Skinner, and Zeldes (1996), using U.S. household survey data, find some evidence that high-income households save a larger fraction of their (permanent) income.

Several cross-country studies have used aggregate saving data from national-accounts sources. Early contributions by Della Valle and Oguchi (1976) and Musgrove (1980) investigate the relationship between saving and income distribution using cross-country data on both industrial and developing countries. In both cases the results show no statistically significant effect of income distribution on saving. The exception are the OECD countries included in the study by Della Valle and Oguchi, for which they find some evidence that increased inequality may increase saving. In turn, Lim (1980) finds that inequality tends to raise aggregate saving rates in a cross-section sample of developing countries, but his coefficient estimates are significant at conventional levels in only some subsamples.

Venieris and Gupta (1986) use aggregate data for 49 countries to draw inferences about the average saving propensities of different income groups, using an econometric specification that also includes political instability as a saving determinant. Their results suggest that poorer households have the lowest saving propensities, while – somewhat surprisingly – the highest propensity corresponds to the middle-income group. Hence, redistribution against the rich may raise or lower the aggregate saving ratio depending on whether the favored group is the middle class or the poor, respectively. However, the interpretation of their results is somewhat unclear due to their use of constant-price saving as the dependent variable, which has no clear analytical justification.

Sahota (1993) tests a reduced-form relationship between saving and income distribution. Using data on 65 industrial and developing countries for the year 1975, he regresses the ratio of gross domestic saving to GDP (GDS/GDP) on the Gini coefficient and a quadratic polynomial in per capita income; he also includes regional dummy variables as a crude attempt to control for cultural and habit effects. The parameter estimate on the Gini coefficient is found to be positive, but the estimate is somewhat imprecise and significantly different from zero only at the 10 percent level.

More recently, Cook (1995) presents estimates of the impact of various inequality measures on the GDS/GDP ratio in 49 LDCs, using a conventional saving equation including also the level and growth rate of real income, dependency ratios, and a measure of capital inflows; the exogeneity of the latter variable is clearly questionable. A dummy for Latin American countries is also added to the regressions, although its justification is unclear since no other regional dummies are included. Using decade averages for the 1970s, he finds a positive and significant effect of inequality on saving, which appears robust to some changes in specification and to the choice of alternative indicators of income inequality.

Hong (1995) reports econometric results on the effect of the share of the top 20 percent income group on GDS/GDP ratios in cross-country samples of 56 to 64 developing and industrial countries, using 1960–85 averages for each country. He finds that the income share of the top 20 percent of the population has a positive effect on saving rates, controlling for population dependency, the level and growth of income, and education level.

Edwards (1996) estimates private saving equations using panel data for developing and OECD countries for the years 1970–92. While the main focus of the study is not the relation between income distribution and saving, he reports two regressions for mostly OECD countries that control for income inequality, finding that the latter has a significant positive effect on private saving if combined with one set of regressors, but the effect turns negative and insignificant when combined with a different set of regressors.

In summary, most empirical studies based on micro–household data show evidence for a positive effect of income concentration on household saving. Regarding the studies based on cross-country aggregate data, the results are more mixed, although some do find a positive impact of income inequality on total saving. Independent, of their results, however, most of the cross-country studies utilize inadequate saving measures and use income-distribution data of highly heterogeneous quality, mixing both income- and expenditure-based measures. Their robustness to alternative specifications and data samples is also unclear. These drawbacks justify a more systematic empirical search for the effect of income inequality on aggregate saving across different specifications, saving and income distribution measures, data samples, and estimation techniques. This task is undertaken below.

Overview of the Data

We begin with a brief summary of the data that we will use in our subsequent empirical work. Individual variable definitions and sources are reported in the Appendix. Our basic information is cross-country time-series data for the 1965–94 period from the World Bank macroeconomic and social databases, and income distribution data from a new World Bank database assembled by Deininger and Squire (1996). The cross-country data presented in this section were constructed by computing the 1965–94 country averages of the raw data. For some countries some of the variables of interest (notably those related to income distribution) are not available every year of the 1965–94 period; country averages were computed using the available observations. Finally, in some empirical experiments below, the cross-country data was complemented with information from Barro and Lee's (1994) database. Thus, apart from the income distribution data, our sources are standard and well known. Hence, we describe briefly the main features of the income distribution database, and in particular the selection of the subsample used in this chapter.

Deininger and Squire's (1996) new cross-country time-series database on income inequality measures represents a major improvement in rigor, quality, and coverage over preceding data sets – including in particular those used in the previous literature on saving and income distribution.

Unlike in other existing databases, a clear distinction is made between income-based and expenditure-based inequality measures, as well as between household-based and individual-based measures, and the underlying primary data are checked for three important quality criteria: they have to be based on household or individual surveys (not on national accounts), their coverage has to be comprehensive (i.e., based on nation-wide samples), and measurement of income (or expenditure) has to be comprehensive as well (including all income or expenditure categories).

While the total number of country-year observations in the Deininger and Squire data is 2,621, applying the three latter quality criteria reduces the number to 682 high-quality country-year observations, corresponding to 108 countries and years within the period 1890–1995. For these observations, both Gini coefficients and income shares by population quintiles are available.

Of these 682 observations, we include in our subsample only those 468 country-year observations (corresponding to 82 countries) that fall into the 1965–94 period (the one for which we have complete macroeconomic data). However, this set includes observations based on income data along with others based on expenditure data. In order to make the Gini coefficients from income- and expenditure-based data comparable (income is typically more concentrated than expenditure), we follow the simple procedure suggested by Deininger and Squire by adding a constant equal to 6.7 to the expenditure-based coefficients. The latter figure is the average difference between income- and expenditure-based Gini coefficients reported by Deininger and Squire, for those country-year observations for which both data are available. However, it is methodologically much less clear what type of correction should be applied to the expenditure-based income shares by quintiles. Hence, we opt for dropping them and restrict our database of income shares to only income-based data.

For our cross-country data set based on 1965–94 averages for each country we impose an additional requirement to achieve a minimum of time representation: countries are included only if they have at least one observation in each of the following two 15-year periods: 1965–79 and 1980–94. This leaves us with 52 country observations. Table 6.1 presents a summary of the total number of observations in terms of country-years (for our panel data set) and country averages (for our cross-country data set) for Gini coefficients and share ratios and by country groups.

Unless otherwise noted, here and in the rest of the chapter we use the terms "income inequality" and "income distribution" for all samples and statistical results, even when they refer to Gini coefficients based on both

Table 6.1. *Country Data on Income Distribution*

	Country-year Observations, 1965–94	Country Observations, 1965–94 Averages
Income- and expenditure-based data		
(for Gini coefficients)	468	52
OECD countries	209	19
Developing countries	259	33
Income-based data (for income shares)	339	40
OECD countries	187	17
Developing countries	152	23

income- and expenditure-based information.[4] Likewise, we use the terms "saving" and "saving ratio" to refer to gross national saving and its ratio to GNP. We choose national saving and national product data as the relevant variables because they are closer to the relevant units (households or individuals) for which income distribution data is available than are the domestic saving and domestic product measures. In this respect we differ from most previous empirical studies, which are based on the less adequate domestic measures.

A final caution relates to measurement error. As is well known, this is a central problem in empirical studies of saving, due not only to the inadequacy of the very saving concept used by the system of national accounts (which, for example, exclude capital gains from the definition of income, and treat human capital expenditures as consumption), but also to the unreliability of measured saving, which stems largely from the fact that saving is often computed as the residual from another residual (consumption). The upshot is that saving measures may contain large errors, particularly in developing countries where the statistical apparatus involved in the collection of household data is likely to be weaker.[5] Measurement error is likely to be an even more serious problem in the case of income distribution statistics. The latter are primarily derived

[4] The empirical results based on the smaller subsample of income-based Gini coefficients were very similar to those reported below, which are based on the larger sample comprising both income-based and adjusted expenditure-based Ginis. To save space, we only report the latter.

[5] Biases may arise in saving regressions as a result of measurement errors in saving, because the errors are likely to be correlated with saving determinants in general and income in particular. Recent discussions of measurement problems in saving data and analyses include Deaton (1989), Lipsey and Tice (1989), Srinivasan (1994), and Schmidt-Hebbel, Servén, and Solimano (1996).

Table 6.2. *Income Distribution Indicators: Descriptive Statistics*

	Number of Observations	Gini Coefficient		Income Share Ratio of Top 20% to Bottom 40%		Income Share of Middle 60%	
		Mean	Std. Dev.	Mean	Std. Dev.	Mean	Std. Dev.
World	52	0.417	0.085	3.33	1.56	0.48	0.07
OECD countries	19	0.336	0.042	2.12	0.37	0.53	0.02
Developing countries	33	0.464	0.066	4.22	1.50	0.43	0.05

Note: The summary statistics for the income shares have been computed using the income-based data only. The corresponding number of observations are: World (40), OECD (17), and developing countries (23).

from household survey data, which typically understate the income of the richer households. As a result, income inequality is likely to be underestimated – and probably more so in poorer countries.

Keeping in mind the features and limitations of the available data discussed above, we next provide summary statistics for our income distribution data (a detailed description of the full data set is in Deininger and Squire, 1996). Table 6.2 presents means and standard deviations of three conventional indicators of inequality: the Gini coefficient, the ratio between the income shares of the richest 20 percent and poorest 40 percent of the population, and the income share of the "middle class," defined as the middle 60 percent of the population (often used as an indicator of equality). The statistics are computed for the world, industrial (OECD) countries, and developing countries. As the table shows, developing countries are more unequal than industrial countries by any of the three indicators presented, and show also a larger dispersion in their levels of inequality.

Figure 6.2 presents the scatter plot of the 1965–94 averages of the saving rate and the Gini coefficient for the countries in the sample. OECD countries are placed in the left half of the figure, reflecting their lower degree of income inequality. On the whole, the figure suggests a negative partial association between saving rates and inequality.

Table 6.3 presents the full-sample cross-correlations of saving and a number of saving determinants. As can be seen from the table, the saving ratio is positively correlated with real per capita GNP and its square, real per capita growth, and the old-age dependency ratio. Saving is negatively

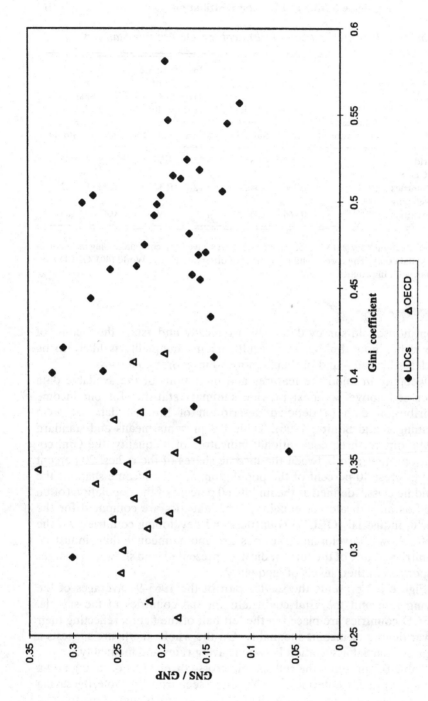

Figure 6.2. Long-term world saving and income distribution (gross national saving rate incl. net current transfers and Gini coefficient, 1965–94 country averages).

Table 6.3. Correlation Matrix of Basic Saving Determinants

	GNS/GNP	GNP per Cap.	GNP per Cap. Squared	Growth Rate GNP per Cap.	Gini Coefficient	Inc. Share Top 20%/ Bottom 40%	Inc. Share Middle 60%	Old Age Dep. Ratio
GNS/GNP								
Real GNP per capita	0.360							
Real GNP per capita squared	0.287	0.972						
Growth rate of per capita GNP	0.496	0.016	-0.023					
Gini coefficient	-0.316	-0.698	-0.653	-0.289				
Income share: top 20%/bottom 40%	-0.361	-0.661	-0.606	-0.246	0.940			
Income share of middle 60%	0.331	0.792	0.723	0.153	-0.956	-0.914		
Old-age dependency ratio	0.229	0.862	0.813	0.031	-0.715	-0.676	0.771	
Young-age dependency ratio	-0.420	-0.885	-0.814	-0.238	0.775	0.763	-0.839	-0.940

correlated with the young-age dependency ratio. Further, all these correlations (except that with the old-age dependency ratio) are significantly different from zero at the 5 percent level.

Is the association between saving and income distribution as clear-cut as that between saving and the above mentioned variables? Table 6.3 confirms that the full-sample correlation between saving and the Gini coefficient is negative ($-.32$, significant at the 5 percent level), as suggested by Figure 6.2. A closer look, however, reveals that the correlation pattern is rather different in the industrial (.10) and developing-country ($-.20$) subsamples; in neither is it significantly different from zero.

Are these correlations sensitive to our choice of the Gini coefficient as the relevant inequality statistic? A number of alternative indicators are found in the literature – for example, Theil's index, the coefficient of variation of income across households, the income share of the poorest 20 or 40 percent of the population, the ratio of the latter to the income share of the richest 20 percent, or the income share of the middle class. Analytically, among the above mentioned distribution indicators, the Gini coefficient, Theil's index, or the coefficient of variation are generally preferable because they use more information than the commonly encountered quintile-based indicators.[6] At the same time, the Gini index has the well-known drawback that it is not uniquely related to the shape of the underlying distribution, so that very different redistribution schemes can be reflected in the same change in the Gini coefficient. Finally, income shares (in levels) and Gini coefficients may pose cross-country comparability problems more severe than those derived from the use of share ratios (Deininger and Squire, 1996).

In practice, however, the informational content of all these indicators is usually very similar, as shown by the fact that they typically are very highly correlated – even though they may yield different orderings for a few sample observations (see Clarke, 1992). This applies also in our case, as reflected in Table 6.3 by the cross-correlations between the Gini coefficient and the income-share indicators just mentioned (notice however that availability of the latter is restricted to the income-based subsample totaling 40 observations), which exceed .90 in absolute value in all cases. As a result, the correlation of saving with income-share inequality indicators is virtually identical to that with the Gini coefficient.

In summary, we find a negative association between aggregate saving rates and standard measures of income inequality, but the relationship does not appear robust across subsamples. More importantly, the substantive question is whether the negative association between both variables continues to hold – or instead is reversed in sign – once other

---

[6] For a discussion of the properties of these indices see Cowell (1977).

standard saving determinants are taken into consideration. To answer this question, we need to place the latter in a broader empirical framework encompassing other relevant determinants of saving. This task is undertaken in the next section.

Econometric Results

In this section we present new empirical results on the relationship between aggregate saving and income distribution. Our aim is to examine this relationship making use of the world database introduced in the preceding section and described in more detail in the Appendix, applying a variety of specifications and econometric techniques, and conducting various robustness tests. We proceed in three stages. First, we investigate if the results of some recent cross-country studies that find a positive impact of income concentration on aggregate saving still hold when using our improved data set and alternative saving definitions. Next we introduce a simple saving specification (including measures of income distribution, among other variables), estimate it on cross-country data, and test the robustness of our empirical results to alternative specifications, income distribution measures, country groupings, and econometric techniques. Finally we apply our saving specification to a panel of annual time-series cross-country data.

Replicating Previous Cross-Country Results

For our replication we select the three most recent studies focused on the effect of income inequality on aggregate saving. We maintain the specifications used by the authors as described above: Sahota (1993), Cook (1995), and Hong (1995). The first two make use of regional dummy variables (only for Latin America in the case of Cook), while Hong does not. Our data samples are somewhat smaller in terms of country observations than the corresponding samples of the three authors because we limit ourselves to the high-quality income and expenditure distribution data subset of Deininger and Squire's database, as discussed above. However, our data set is much larger in the time dimension and includes more recent years.

We start by using the saving rate measures (GDS/GDP) adopted by the three authors and the time periods used in computing individual country observations (time averages) that come closest to those considered by them.[7] Columns 1–3 in Table 6.4 present our attempt at

---

[7] For the replication of Sahota's work we use country averages for 1972–78 (our interpretation for his observations "close to 1975"). In the case of Cook we use averages for the decade of the 1970s, and to reproduce Hong's estimation we use 1965–94 averages (which come close to his 1960–85 data).

Table 6.4. Replication of Previous Results

	Dependent Variable: GDS/GDP			Dependent Variable: GNS/GNP				
	1 Sahota (1972–78) Full	2 Cook (1970s) LDCs	3 Hong (1965–94) Full	4 Sahota (1972–78) Full	5 Cook (1970s) LDCs	6 Hong (1965–94) Full	7 Sahota (1965–94) Full	8 Cook (1965–94) LDCs
Constant	−0.037 (−0.417)	0.208 (1.035)	−0.153 (−0.735)	0.025 (0.249)	0.020 (0.120)	0.157 (0.767)	0.048 (0.681)	0.197 (1.128)
Real GDP or GNP per capita (1987 constant dollar)	4.47E-05 (5.206)	4.24E-05 (4.757)		3.68E-05 (3.035)	4.45E-05 (6.058)		2.27E-05 (3.122)	8.91E-06 (1.207)
Real GDP or GNP per capita squared	−2.05E-09 (−4.537)			−1.79E-09 (−2.947)			−9.28E-10 (−2.578)	
Real GDP or GNP growth rate		0.077 (0.136)	0.818 (1.584)		0.589 (1.592)	1.421 (4.187)		0.626 (1.749)
ln (GDP or GNP per capita)			0.030 (2.728)			0.011 (0.978)		
Old-age dependency ratio		−3.365 (−2.594)			−1.789 (−1.966)			−0.624 (−0.689)
Young-age dependency ratio		−0.211 (−0.470)			0.213 (0.589)			−0.318 (−0.806)

	(1)	(2)	(3)	(4)	(5)	(6)	(7)	(8)
Total dependency ratio	0.182		0.020			0.088		
	(0.938)		(0.060)			(0.895)		
Gini coefficient		0.384		0.158	0.244		0.161	0.363
		(1.736)		(0.815)	(1.378)		(1.149)	(1.772)
Income share of top 20%			0.221			0.088		
			(2.199)			(0.895)		
Current acct. bal./(GNP or GDP)		0.601			0.695			0.667
		(2.838)			(4.995)			(2.866)
Latin America regional dummy	0.088	−0.035		0.031	−0.045		0.007	−0.050
	(2.044)	(−1.516)		(0.577)	(−2.876)		(0.181)	(−3.110)
Africa regional dummy	0.153			0.081			0.021	
	(3.391)			(1.873)			(0.559)	
Asia regional dummy	0.131			0.088			0.081	
	(4.771)			(2.363)			(2.509)	
Adjusted R^2	0.369	0.556	0.401	0.233	0.638	0.511	0.355	0.374
Standard error	0.059	0.057	0.047	0.062	0.046	0.040	0.046	0.046
Number of observations	45	28	50	44	28	50	52	31

Note: The *t*-statistics (shown in parentheses) were computed using heteroskedasticity-corrected standard errors.

replicating their results. Our results for a full sample of 45 OECD and developing countries in column 1 are very similar to Sahota's: the parameter estimate on the Gini coefficient is positive and close to that reported by Sahota (.19), but well below conventional levels of significance. Regarding Cook's specification, applied to a sample of 28 LDCs, the effect of the Gini is also positive but barely reaches a 10 percent confidence level (column 2). Finally, in Hong's specification, applied to 50 OECD and developing countries, the relevant distributive variable is the income share of the top 20 percent, for which our results do replicate a positive effect significant at a 5 percent level.

However, domestic saving and domestic product are not good saving and income measures for open economies. As argued before, national saving and national product data are closer to the relevant units for which income distribution figures are available. Therefore, we next attempt to replicate the three authors' estimations by making use of the preferable gross national saving (GNS) and gross national product (GNP) measures, as reported in columns 4–6 in Table 6.4. The common finding across the three specifications is a general loss of precision regarding the coefficient estimates for income inequality. The point estimates are still positive but do not reach conventional levels of significance. The decline in precision is particularly strong in the case of Hong's specification, which is based on our complete sample period (1965–94).

As a final check, we expand the time dimension of the country averages by applying Sahota's and Cook's specifications to our longer 1965–94 sample period, which also allows us to add more countries to the sample, while still using GNS and GNP measures. The results show that under Sahota's specification (column 7), the Gini coefficient remains statistically insignificant, while it just reaches 10 percent significance under Cook's specification (column 8). Interestingly, however, both specifications rely on the inclusion of regional dummy variables whose justification, particularly in Cook's case, is unclear. Other empirical experiments (not reported to save space) show that dropping from the specification in column 8 the Latin America dummy or the current-account surplus – which, being the difference between saving and investment ratios, is clearly an endogenous variable – would make the parameter estimate on the Gini coefficient statistically insignificant at any reasonable level.

We conclude that the results of these three empirical studies – which found a positive effect of income concentration on aggregate saving – are not robust to alternative and better saving and income distribution measures. In two cases (Hong's and Sahota's specifications) the results vanish altogether, while in the third one they do not reach conventional significance levels and, furthermore, are dependent on a questionable empirical specification. The question that arises now is if stronger evidence on the effect of income inequality on saving could be found using more standard specifications than those used by the previous authors. This is our next topic.

Testing Alternative Specifications Using Cross-Country Data

We limit our model search to variants of simple specifications found in comparable cross-country studies of saving (see, e.g., Schmidt-Hebbel, Webb, and Corsetti, 1992; Edwards, 1996; and Masson, Bayoumi, and Samiel, 1995) and the saving distribution models tested above. Our basic specification encompasses the income, demographic, and inequality variables included by Sahota (1993) and Cook (1995) but, for the reasons already noted, excludes their more controversial variables (the current-account balance and regional dummies). The basic equation to be estimated is the following:

$$GNS/GNP = \beta_0 + \beta_1 \, gnp + \beta_2 (gnp)^2 + \beta_3 \, growth + \beta_4 \, old$$
$$+ \beta_5 \, young + \beta_6 \, distrib, \tag{1}$$

where GNS/GNP is the ratio of current-price gross national saving to current-price gross national product, gnp is real per capita gross national product, $growth$ is the (geometric) average annual rate of growth of real per capita gross national product, old is the old-age dependency ratio (ratio of population of age 65 and above to total population), $young$ is the young-age dependency ratio (ratio of population of ages 0 to 15 to total population), and $distrib$ is an income distribution variable.

The basic specification in equation (1) embeds both a linear and a quadratic term in real per capita income to encompass the nonlinear relation between the saving rate and income often encountered in empirical work; accordingly, we should expect $\beta_1 > 0$, $\beta_2 < 0$. All other variables enter linearly in our basic equation. The majority of empirical studies suggests that the coefficient on $growth$ should be positive, while those on the dependency ratios should be negative, according to standard life-cycle arguments.[8]

We broaden our empirical search by using as income distribution indicators both the Gini coefficient and the ratio of the income share of the richest 20 percent of households to that of the poorest 40 percent; we also perform some experiments using the income share of the middle 60 percent of the population. The latter variables, however, are available only for the smaller income-based sample.

---

[8] See Leff (1969) and Modigliani (1970). Gersovitz (1988) includes an analytical discussion of the effects of these and other demographic variables on saving.

We first examine the evidence from cross-country data, using country averages for the period 1965–94. The correlation matrix of our basic set of regressors was presented in Table 6.3 and shows four striking features. First, as already mentioned, all three income distribution indicators are very highly correlated. Second, the (negative) correlation between young-age and old-age dependency ratios is also very large $(-.94)$. Third, dependency ratios are closely correlated with real per capita income (the corresponding correlation coefficients exceed .86 in absolute value). Finally, the correlations between income distribution measures and dependency ratios are also high; this is to be expected since such measures reflect differences in both intragenerational and intergenerational income distribution, and the latter are also captured in part by the dependency ratios. It will be important to keep in mind these features of the data for the discussion of the empirical results below.

Table 6.5 shows estimation results using the basic specification for a variety of samples. As a benchmark, column 1 reports parameter estimates for the full sample of OECD and developing countries using a specification that excludes income distribution indicators. As expected, the second and third rows in column 1 show that saving ratios rise with income levels (a result also found by Carroll and Weil, 1994, and Edwards, 1996) but taper off at high income, as indicated by the negative coefficient on squared GNP.

In turn, the fourth row in the table indicates that saving ratios are positively associated across countries with per capita GNP growth rates. A 1 percent increase in real growth raises the national saving ratio by about .9 percentage points. Finally, it can be seen from the fifth and sixth rows in column 1 that both old- and young-age dependency ratios have the expected negative effect on national saving rates, although only the former reaches a high level of significance.

The simple specification in column 1 accounts for nearly 50 percent of the observed cross-country variation in national saving rates. However, the estimated coefficients on per capita income and its square, as well as on the young-age dependency ratio, exhibit large standard errors. The obvious reason for this lack of precision is the just-described cross-correlation between age-dependency ratios, real income, and its square.[9] Indeed, a joint F-test of the null hypothesis that real income and its square have no impact on saving rates can be rejected with a p-value of .04; adding the restriction that young-age dependency also has no effect further reduces the p-value to .009, overwhelmingly rejecting the null.

[9] Note from Table 6.3 that the correlation between real per capita GNP and its square equals .98.

Table 6.5. *Cross-Section Estimates of Saving Equation – Dependent Variable: GNS/GNP*

	OLS							2SLS	
	1 Full	2 Full	3 OECD	4 LDC	5 Full	6 OECD	7 LDC	8 Full	9 Full
Constant	0.397 (2.636)	0.367 (2.375)	0.394 (2.214)	0.392 (2.410)	0.488 (2.620)	0.526 (2.762)	0.669 (1.994)	0.079 (0.346)	-0.032 (-0.108)
Real GNP per capita (1987 constant dollar)	1.19E-05 (1.356)	1.20E-05 (1.356)	1.01E-05 (1.306)	6.05E-05 (4.527)	6.70E-06 (0.791)	5.80E-06 (0.792)	6.43E-05 (5.305)	2.43E-05 (2.837)	3.26E-05 (2.860)
Real GNP per capita squared	-4.51E-10 (-1.134)	-4.41E-10 (-1.112)	-3.34E-10 (-0.947)	-6.46E-09 (-4.778)	-2.33E-10 (-0.656)	-2.25E-10 (-0.668)	-7.02E-09 (-5.648)	-9.10E-10 (-2.272)	-1.20E-09 (-2.420)
Real GNP growth rate	0.878 (2.132)	0.947 (2.195)	3.085 (3.251)	0.575 (1.247)	1.106 (2.061)	2.754 (2.937)	0.435 (0.781)	2.020 (2.934)	2.317 (2.763)
Old-age dependency ratio	-1.264 (-2.469)	-1.244 (-2.487)	-1.181 (-2.547)	-2.167 (-3.510)	-1.382 (-2.539)	-1.343 (-2.896)	-4.59 (-1.958)	-0.778 (-1.185)	-0.654 (-0.836)
Young-age dependency ratio	-0.468 (-1.542)	-0.511 (-1.666)	-0.819 (-1.919)	-0.387 (-1.200)	-0.753 (-1.883)	-1.157 (-2.549)	-0.950 (-1.548)	-0.025 (-0.059)	0.286 (-0.477)
Gini coefficient		0.095 (0.864)	0.066 (0.708)	-0.067 (-0.471)				0.154 (1.268)	
Income share ratio of top 20%/bottom 40%					0.005 (0.654)	0.016 (0.955)	-0.005 (-0.094)		0.006 (0.719)
Adjusted R^2	0.423	0.4186	0.555	0.569	0.491	0.56	0.663	0.453	0.356
Standard error	0.043	0.043	0.027	0.041	0.042	0.028	0.039	0.041	0.047
Number of observations	52	52	19	33	40	17	23	46	38

Note: The *t*-statistics (shown in parentheses) were computed using heteroskedasticity-corrected standard errors. The equations using the top 20% to bottom 40% ratio (columns 5–7 and 9) as the relevant distribution measure were estimated using only observations with income-based distribution data.

Columns 2–4 in Table 6.5 augment the specification in column 1 using the Gini coefficient as income distribution indicator, both for the full country sample and separately for the 19 OECD and 33 developing countries. The sign pattern of the parameter estimates in the first six rows remains unchanged, and the full-sample estimates in column 2 are virtually identical to those in column 1. However, the saving–income and saving–growth relationships do not appear robust across country groups. The saving–per capita GNP relationship is weak among industrial countries (column 3) but very strong among developing countries (column 4). The opposite is true for the saving–growth relationship, which appears strong among OECD countries but weak among LDCs – the same cross-country pattern found by Carroll and Weil (1994). Controlling for other factors, a 1 percent increase in the growth rate raises national saving ratios by 3.1 percentage points among OECD countries, and by only .6 percentage point among LDCs (and the latter effect is not significantly different from zero). In both country groups the influence of demographic dependency on saving is negative, although the size and statistical significance differs among country groups.

The seventh row reports the parameter estimates for the Gini coefficient. They are positive for the full sample and the OECD subsample, and negative for LDCs – the same sign pattern encountered earlier in the simple correlations. In all three cases, however, the estimates are insignificantly different from zero.

Columns 5 through 7 use as an alternative income distribution indicator the ratio of the income shares of the top 20 and bottom 40 percent of the population. This results in a loss of 12 observations (2 industrial countries and 10 developing countries) due to unavailability of the income-based data for those countries. Despite the smaller sample size, however, the estimation results are very similar to those obtained using the Gini coefficient, an unsurprising result in view of the very high correlation between the two income distribution indicators. The inequality variable remains statistically insignificant, and its estimated coefficient has opposite signs for developing and industrial countries.

One potential source of bias in these regressions is the possible endogeneity of right-hand-side variables. For example, it is possible that income levels and growth rates are affected by saving ratios through the conventional saving–investment–output link discussed in preceding sections. In order to address this possible simultaneous-equation bias, columns 8 and 9 of Table 6.5 report results of two-stage least squares estimations on the full country sample, using the Gini coefficient and the income-share ratio, respectively. The instruments used for the level, square, and growth rate of real per capita GNP were chosen among the variables found to be most significant in empirical cross-country growth regressions.[10] Due to instrument data unavailability for some countries, this results in a loss of 6 and 2 observations, respectively.

As the table shows, the results from instrumental-variable estimation are qualitatively similar to those obtained from OLS, particularly in regard to the sign pattern of individual regressors. Note, however, that the coefficients of the three instrumented GNP measures roughly double relative to their OLS counterparts (in columns 2 and 5), and their individual significance levels are now very high. This contrasts with the loss in precision of the coefficients of the (noninstrumented) dependency ratios. Finally, and most important, these results confirm the previous lack of significance of both income distribution measures. As a more formal check on the validity of the OLS estimates, we performed Hausman tests for the endogeneity of the three GNP-related variables. The computed test statistics were 6.098 (with an associated p-value of 0.107) and 5.792 (p-value of 0.122) for the specifications in columns 8 and 9, respectively. Thus, we do not find strong evidence against the OLS estimates, although this may be partly due to the low power of the test.

Overall, the above results are consistent in suggesting that income inequality does *not* significantly affect aggregate saving. To investigate their robustness, we explore a number of alternative specifications and income inequality measures found in previous studies. Table 6.6 presents some results using the full country sample.

The first two columns investigate alternative inequality indicators: column 1 uses the income share of the middle class (to verify Venieris and Gupta's 1986 finding that the middle class is the highest-saving group), while column 2 uses the income share of the top 20 percent of population (which is Hong's 1995 income concentration measure). In neither case do we find any significant effects of income inequality on saving. Next we explore possible nonlinear effects of income distribution, adding to the Gini coefficient an interaction term between the Gini and real per capita GNP (column 3), and the square of the Gini (in column 4). Neither specification proved successful.[11]

Finally, we test the role of income inequality by considering two alternative specifications based on the inclusion of additional saving regressors. While these regressors seem popular in the empirical saving

[10] The instrument list included initial conditions and demographic and institutional variables (see the Appendix for details). This choice was based on the results of standard cross-country growth regressions. See, e.g., Barro and Sala-i-Martin (1995) and Barro (1996).

[11] F-tests of the joint significance of the Gini coefficient and its product with GNP per capita (for column 3) and the Gini coefficient and its square (for column 4) yield marginal significance levels of .887 and .680, respectively, so that both variables can be safely dropped from the respective specifications.

Table 6.6. *Cross-Section Estimates of Alternative Specifications – Dependent Variable: GNS/GNP*

	1 Full	2 Full	3 Full	4 Full	5 Full	6 Full
Constant	0.6037 (2.933)	0.394 (2.009)	0.361 (2.236)	0.189 (0.954)	0.266 (1.784)	0.302 (1.874)
Real GNP per capita (1987 constant dollar)	9.59E-06 (1.161)	8.90E-06 (1.075)	1.39E-05 (1.301)	1.26E-05 (1.364)	1.10E-05 (1.379)	1.48E-05 (1.838)
Real GNP per capita squared	-3.39E-10 (-0.996)	-3.22E-10 (-0.935)	-4.64E-10 (-1.252)	-4.61E-10 (-1.118)	-4.50E-10 (-1.216)	-5.66E-10 (-1.539)
Real GNP growth rate	1.154 (2.154)	1.171 (2.182)	0.958 (2.109)	0.963 (2.283)	0.941 (2.409)	0.572 (1.224)
Old-age dependency ratio	-1.328 (-2.463)	-1.316 (-2.430)	-1.258 (-2.593)	-1.154 (-2.340)	-0.787 (-1.476)	-1.107 (-2.070)
Young-age dependency ratio	-0.741 (-1.968)	-0.770 (-2.025)	-0.512 (-1.662)	-0.474 (-1.530)	-0.315 (-0.999)	-0.551 (-1.771)
Gini coefficient			0.112 (0.667)	0.863 (1.610)	0.154 (1.213)	0.249 (1.792)
Income share of middle 60%	-0.250 (-1.257)					

	(1)	(2)	(3)	(4)	(5)
Income share of top 20%	0.2193 (1.312)				
GNP* Gini coefficient		-4.37E-06 (-0.193)			
Gini coefficient squared			-0.902 (-1.400)		
Current acct. bal./GNP				0.561 (2.443)	
Latin America regional dummy					-0.016 (-0.428)
Africa regional dummy					0.005 (0.143)
Asia regional dummy					0.038 (1.090)
Adjusted R^2	0.5083	0.5116	0.4057	0.4173	0.4114
Standard error	0.0414	0.0413	0.0437	0.0433	0.0422
Number of observations	40	40	52	52	48

Note: The *t*-statistics (shown in parentheses) were computed using heteroskedasticity-corrected standard errors.

literature, we excluded them from our basic specification because of their severe endogeneity problems and/or their ad hoc nature. Column 5 of Table 6.6 reports the results when the ratio of the current-account balance to GNP is included. As in other saving studies (i.e., Edwards, 1996; Hong, 1995; Masson, Bayoumi, and Samiei, 1995), the corresponding coefficient is large and highly significant – a hardly surprising result because by definition the current-account balance equals national saving minus investment, and hence a coefficient equal to unity should be expected (in fact, the 95 percent confidence region for our point estimate does include 1). Further, in an open economy with access to international lending (as is the case for most OECD countries throughout 1965–94, and for many developing countries during much of that time), the current account simply reflects national saving and investment decisions and is therefore endogenous, so that the OLS estimator is inconsistent. Whatever the interpretation of this equation, however, the Gini coefficient estimate remains far below conventional levels of significance.

Finally, in column 6 we follow some of the previous literature by introducing regional dummy variables, with OECD countries as the omitted category. The parameter estimate on the Gini coefficient now reaches 10 percent significance. However, quite apart from the (obscure) interpretation of the dummies, this weak result seems suspect, because the dummies are not significant individually or jointly (an F-test of their joint significance yields a p-value of .273, so they could be safely removed from the equation).

To summarize, our extensive[12] empirical tests on cross-sectional data find little evidence of income inequality affecting aggregate saving, after controlling for standard saving determinants. Arguably, however, our results are based only on part of the available information, because we have ignored the time-series dimension of the data. Further, ad hoc regional dummies seem to affect the significance of the inequality indicators, which suggests that, like in other cross-country empirical work,

---

[12] We tried a number of additional experiments not reported here. In one case we added income variability to the basic set of regressors (with variability measured by the standard deviation of real per capita GNP around trend relative to the average GNP level). According to the precautionary saving motive, it should have a positive impact on saving. In fact, the estimated coefficient was negative and insignificant, possibly because aggregate income variability is very different from – actually much lower than – individual income variability, as shown by Pischke (1995). We also experimented with the ratio of domestic credit to GNP as a measure of the extent of borrowing constraints. Its coefficient had the expected positive sign but it was insignificantly different from zero. Finally, we reestimated our basic specifications using the least absolute deviation estimator (see, e.g., Koenker and Basset, 1978), to control for the possible influence of extreme observations. Our results were materially unaffected.

country heterogeneity could be a potential problem in the regressions. The best way to address these two concerns is by exploiting the full panel dimension of our data.

Panel Data Results

As we noted earlier, not all variables (especially the income distribution indicators) are available for each country every year within our sample period, and therefore our panel data set is unbalanced. Table 6.7 reports the results of eight unbalanced-panel regressions for OECD and developing countries, jointly and separately, and applying alternative estimation techniques.[13]

The first two columns report simple OLS estimates on the pooled data for the full sample (468 observations), using our basic specification. Unlike in the cross-section regressions above, now all the parameters are strongly significant, with the notable exception of the Gini coefficient. In column 1, its point estimate is negative and, more importantly, small and insignificantly different from zero. The basic specification accounts for a respectable 48 percent of the observed variation in saving ratios.

Column 2 adds regional dummies to the regression, thus reproducing the specification in column 6 of Table 6.6; while the dummies are individually insignificant, they are strongly significant when taken together (the corresponding F-test yields a p-value of 0.014). The estimated parameter on the Gini coefficient turns positive, but remains small and insignificant.

Do the regional dummies satisfactorily capture whatever country heterogeneity may exist in the sample? To answer this question, column 3 in Table 6.7 reports fixed-effect estimates on the full sample. The addition of country-specific effects raises dramatically the explanatory power of the regression, which now accounts for over 88 percent of the variation in the dependent variable. All the coefficients remain strongly significant, again with the exception of the inequality variable, whose point estimate is now very close to zero. Further, some of the estimates change substantially relative to the OLS results: the coefficient on real income growth falls, while that on its level more than doubles. The country effects are extremely significant, as shown by the F-test reported at the bottom of the table. Finally, we can test if the heterogeneity captured by the country effects can be adequately summarized by regional dummies. This amounts to testing a set of linear restrictions (specifically, 78 of them) on the estimated country dummies. The computed

---

[13] Initially, all the specifications also included a set of year dummies. However, they were never significant either individually or jointly, and therefore were dropped from the estimations.

Table 6.7. *Panel Estimates of Saving Equation – Dependent Variable: GNS/GNP*

	Simple Pooled Estimates		Panel Estimates with Fixed Effects					
	1	2	3	4	5	6	7	8
Estimation Procedure	Full	Full	Full	OECD	LDCs	Full	OECD	LDCs
Constant	0.644 (15.442)	0.550 (10.151)	NA	NA	NA	NA	NA	NA
Real GNP per capita (1987 constant dollar)	6.38E-06 (2.633)	9.72E-06 (3.172)	2.15E-05 (4.820)	-2.79E-06 (-0.631)	5.87E-05 (5.202)	2.04E-05 (4.770)	2.37E-06 (0.492)	4.51E-05 (4.285)
Real GNP per capita squared	-2.45E-10 (-2.301)	-3.61E-10 (-2.924)	-5.69E-10 (-4.331)	1.28E-10 (0.991)	-3.02E-09 (-3.299)	-5.99E-10 (-4.495)	-5.77E-11 (-0.376)	-1.19E-09 (-1.230)
Real GNP growth rate	0.542 (7.402)	0.502 (6.789)	0.368 (7.641)	0.362 (6.375)	0.357 (5.416)	0.335 (6.666)	0.409 (6.940)	0.250 (3.502)
Old-age dependency ratio	-1.947 (-11.341)	-1.746 (-8.758)	-2.903 (-6.340)	-0.725 (-2.016)	-4.578 (-4.137)	-3.144 (-7.034)	-0.883 (-2.350)	-7.489 (-5.80)
Young-age dependency ratio	-0.953 (-11.235)	-0.863 (-9.676)	-0.525 (-6.147)	0.221 (1.917)	-0.575 (-4.290)	-0.670 (-7.722)	0.149 (1.279)	-1.067 (-6.658)

Gini coefficient	−0.048 (−1.157)	0.037 (0.697)	0.014 (0.217)	0.020 (0.299)	0.047 (0.489)			
Income share ratio of top 20%/ bottom 40%						−0.0046 (−1.723)	−0.0084 (−1.268)	−0.0015 (−0.471)
Latin America regional dummy		−0.002 (−0.128)						
Africa regional dummy		−0.009 (−0.441)						
Asia regional dummy		0.028 (1.515)						
F-test for joint significance of fixed country effects (p-value)			0.000	0.000	0.000	0.000	0.000	0.000
Adjusted R^2	0.470	0.478	0.861	0.876	0.868	0.881	0.887	0.906
Standard error	0.062	0.062	0.032	0.020	0.037	0.027	0.019	0.030
Number of observations	468	468	468	209	259	339	187	152

Note: t-Statistics are shown in parentheses. The equations using the top 20% to bottom 40% ratio (columns 6–8) as the relevant distribution measure were estimated using only observations with income-based distribution data.

F-statistic was 17.18, with a marginal significance level below .001, reject-ing overwhelmingly the regional-dummy in favor of the fixed-effect specification.

In view of this result, columns 4 and 5 report fixed-effect estimates using separately the industrial and developing country subsamples. In both cases the explanatory power of the regressions is very high, and the adjusted R^2 exceeds .86. Also in both cases the estimated parameter on the Gini coefficient is very small and altogether insignificant. There are also some differences across the two subsamples. In the OECD sample (209 observations) we find that neither the level nor the square of per capita income is significant, a result that we also encountered in the cross-section regressions in Table 6.5. Further, the young-age depend-ency ratio carries a surprising positive sign and is close to 5 percent significance. By contrast, in the developing country subsample (259 ob-servations) all the regressors except the Gini coefficient are strongly significant and carry the expected signs.

Finally, columns 6–8 are analogous to columns 3–5 but use the ratio of the income share of the top 20 percent to the bottom 40 percent of the population as the relevant income inequality measure. With the exception of the latter variable, the results remain basically unchanged for all other saving determinants. Interestingly, the income inequality variable carries a negative (albeit again very small) coefficient across the three samples, and even reaches 10 percent significance in the full sample.

We have come to the end of a wide empirical search for evidence on the influence of income inequality on aggregate saving, controlling for other saving determinants. Only exceptionally have we found a (barely) significant effect: a positive one in cross-country data when using ad hoc regional dummies (alone or in combination with another highly suspect variable, the current account deficit), and a negative one in panel data when controlling for country-specific effects and using the ratio of income shares as the relevant inequality measure. In every other specification, income concentration does not affect aggregate saving at a statistically significant level. This conclusion is consistent with the theoretical ambiguity on the saving effects of income inequality.[14]

Concluding Remarks

Both the historical literature on distribution and aggregate saving based on functional income distribution and neoclassical consumption theory based on the personal distribution of income bring out a number of

---

[14] One should note, however, that strong empirical results may be obtained even when theory makes only ambiguous predictions.

channels through which inequality affects personal saving. Several of these mechanisms (but not all) suggest positive direct effects of income inequality on overall personal saving. However, recent political economy research brings out negative indirect links from inequality (through investment, growth, and public saving) to aggregate saving. Taken together, these two strands of the literature imply that the overall impact of inequality on aggregate saving is ambiguous and can only be assessed empirically.

The empirical literature on the links between personal income distribution on personal saving based on household data typically finds a positive relation between personal income inequality and overall personal saving. In turn, some empirical studies based on macro–saving data from national accounts, typically conducted on cross-country samples, also report positive effects of personal income inequality on *aggregate* saving while other studies find the opposite result or no effect whatsoever. Reconciling these conflicting results is difficult because macrovariable-based empirical studies use widely different samples and specifications, different measures of saving and inequality, and, in most cases, income distribution information of questionable quality.

This chapter has reexamined the empirical evidence from macrodata on the links between the distribution of personal income and aggregate saving, controlling for relevant saving determinants, providing an encompassing framework and a robustness check for previous empirical studies, and extending them in five dimensions: (i) testing alternative saving specifications, (ii) using alternative inequality and saving measures, (iii) making use of newer, better, and larger databases, (iv) conducting estimations jointly and separately for industrialized and developing countries, and (v) applying various estimation techniques on both cross-country and panel data. On the whole, after taking into account other standard saving determinants, we do not find any consistent effect of income inequality on aggregate saving. This result is in agreement with the theoretical ambiguity.

While our findings are robust to a variety of changes in sample, specification, and econometric procedure, they are still tentative in that they are obtained mostly from (semi-)reduced-form saving models. In reality, income distribution is determined jointly with saving and growth, so feedback effects from saving to inequality are theoretically possible. However, we doubt that allowing for such effects in a more general model of saving and inequality would change in any material way the empirical results reported here.

Appendix

The basic variables used in the estimations along with their definitions and sources are listed next.

Variable	Source
Gross national saving ratio	GNS/GNP ratio, each series in current prices and local currency. Source: GNS accounts, World Bank National Accounts (WBNA)
Gross domestic saving ratio	GDS/GDP ratio, each series in current prices and local currency. Source: WBNA
Real GNP per capita	In constant 1987 U.S. dollars. Source: WBNA
Real GDP per capita	In constant 1987 U.S. dollars. Source: WBNA
Growth rate of real GNP per capita	Annual growth rate computed from real GNP per capita
Growth rate of real GDP per capita	Annual growth rate computed from real GDP per capita
Gini coefficient	The income-based Gini coefficients were taken directly from the source. The expenditure-based Ginis were adjusted by adding the mean difference between income- and expenditure-based Gini coefficients reported in the source. Source: Deininger and Squire (1996)
Ratio of income share of top 20% to bottom 40% of population and income share of middle 60%	Source: Deininger and Squire (1996)
Old-age (young-age) dependency ratio	Population aged 65 and over (14 and below) as a share of the total population. Data available every five years only. Data interpolated for panel estimates. Source: World Bank Social Indicators
Current-account balance ratio	Ratio to GNP. Both series in current U.S. dollars. Source (for current-account balance): International financial statistics, IMF

The variables used as instruments for the level of GNP per capita, its square, and the growth rate of GNP per capita in the two-stage least squares estimates of Table 6.5 follow.

Variable	Source
Initial level of GNP per capita (in 1965)	Source: WBNA
Square of initial (1965) GNP per capita. Average years of schooling in the total population over the age of 25	Average of 1960 and 1965 figures. Source: Barro and Lee (1994)
Secondary school enrollment rate	Average of 1960 and 1965 figures. Source: Barro and Lee (1994)
Initial trade share	Sum of exports/GDP and imports/GDP ratios. Averaged over the 1960–64 period. Source: Barro and Lee (1994)
Black market premium	Black market exchange rate/official exchange rate-1. Averaged over 1960–89. Source: Barro and Lee (1994)
Terms of trade shocks	Averaged over 1960–85. Source: Barro and Lee (1994)
Life expectancy (initial)	Average for the 1960–64 period. Source: Barro and Lee (1994)
Average population growth rate	Average for 1965–94 period. Source: World Bank social indicators
Measure of political instability	Average over 1960–85. Source:Barro and Lee (1994)
Index of civil liberties	Average over 1972–89. Source: Barro and Lee (1994)

Cross-Country Sample

Averages over 1960–94 were used for the following variables: GDS/GDP ratio, real GDP per capita, and growth rate of real GDP per capita. For all other variables, averages over 1965–94 were used, except where indicated otherwise.

Countries are included in each of the cross-section samples only if they have at least one observation in each of the following two 15-year periods: 1965–79 and 1980–94. In the full cross-section sample, the distribution of countries according to the number of annual Gini observations is the following 37 countries with less than 10 observations, 12 countries with 10 to 20 observations, and 3 countries with more than 20 observations.

The following 52 countries are included in the full cross-country sample. LDCs: Bahamas, Bangladesh, Brazil, Chile, Colombia, Costa Rica, Dominican Republic, Egypt, Guatemala, Honduras, Hong Kong, India, Indonesia, Iran, Jamaica, Korea, Malaysia, Mexico, Pakistan, Panama, Peru, Philippines, Seychelles, Singapore, Sri Lanka, Taiwan, Tanzania, Thailand, Trinidad, Tunisia, Turkey, Venezuela, Zambia. OECD countries: Australia, Belgium, Canada, Denmark, Finland, France, Germany, Greece, Ireland, Italy, Japan, Netherlands, New Zealand, Norway, Portugal, Spain, Sweden, United Kingdom, United States.

The following 40 countries are included in the "income-based only" cross-country sample. LDCs: Bahamas, Bangladesh, Brazil, Chile, Colombia, Costa Rica, Dominican Republic, Guatemala, Honduras, Hong Kong, Korea, Malaysia, Mexico, Panama, Peru, Philippines, Singapore, Sri Lanka, Taiwan, Thailand, Trinidad, Turkey, Venezuela. OECD countries: Australia, Belgium, Canada, Denmark, Finland, France, Germany, Ireland, Italy, Japan, Netherlands, New Zealand, Norway, Portugal, Sweden, United Kingdom, United States.

Panel Data Sample

The panel data sample comprises annual time series of variable length and coverage during the 1965–94 period for different countries.

The following 82 countries are included in the full panel sample. LDCs: Algeria, Bahamas, Bangladesh, Bolivia, Botswana, Brazil, Central African Republic, Cameroon, Chile, China, Colombia, Costa Rica, Cote d'Ivoire, Dominican Republic, Ecuador, Egypt, El Salvador, Fiji, Ghana, Guatemala, Guinea Bissau, Guyana, Honduras, Hong Kong, India, Indonesia, Jamaica, Jordan, Kenya, Korea, Lesotho, Madagascar, Malaysia, Mauritania, Mauritius, Mexico, Morocco, Nepal, Niger, Nigeria, Pakistan, Panama, Peru, Philippines, Rwanda, Senegal, Sierra Leone, Singapore, South Africa, Sri Lanka, Sudan, Taiwan, Tanzania, Thailand, Trinidad, Tunisia, Turkey, Uganda, Venezuela, Zambia, Zimbabwe. OECD countries: Australia, Belgium, Canada, Denmark, Finland, France, Germany, Greece, Ireland, Italy, Japan, Luxembourg,

Netherlands, New Zealand, Norway, Portugal, Spain, Sweden, United Kingdom, United States.

Not all countries have Gini coefficients available for each year. In the 82-country sample the distribution of countries according to the number of annual Gini observations is as follows: 47 countries with less than 5 observations, 21 countries with 5 to 9 observations, 11 countries with 10 to 20 observations, and 3 countries with more than 20 observations.

References

Alesina, A., and R. Perotti. 1996. "Income Distribution, Political Instability, and Investment," *European Economic Review* 40: 1203–28.

Alesina, A., and D. Rodrik. 1994. "Distributive Politics and Economic Growth," *Quarterly Journal of Economics* 109: 465–90.

Atkinson, A. 1994. "Seeking to Explain the Distribution of Income," *Discussion Paper WSP* 106, London School of Economics.

Barro, R. 1996. "Democracy and Growth," *Journal of Economic Growth* 1: 1–27.

Barro, R., and J. Lee. 1994. "Data Set for a Panel of 138 Countries," http://www.nber.org/pub/barro.lee, January.

Barro, R., and X. Sala-i-Martin. 1995. *Economic Growth*. New York: McGraw-Hill.

Becker, G. 1975. *Human Capital*. Cambridge: NBER.

Bertola, G. 1993. "Factors Shares and Savings in Endogenous Growth," *American Economic Review* 83: 1184–98.

Blinder, A. 1975. "Distribution Effects and the Aggregate Consumption Function," *Journal of Political Economy* 87: 608–26.

Bunting, D. 1991. "Savings and the Distribution of Income," *Journal of Post Keynesian Economics* 14: 3–22.

Carroll, C., and D. Weil. 1994. "Saving and Growth: A Reinterpretation," *Carnegie-Rochester Conference Series on Public Policy* 40: 133–92.

Caselli, F., and J. Ventura. 1996. "A Representative Consumer Theory of Distribution," unpublished manuscript, MIT.

Clarke, G. 1992. "More Evidence on Income Distribution and Growth," Policy Research Working Paper 1064, The World Bank.

Cook, C. 1995. "Savings Rates and Income Distribution: Further Evidence from LDCs," *Applied Economics* 27: 71–82.

Cowell, F. 1977. *Measuring Inequality: Techniques for the Social Sciences*. New York: Wiley.

Deaton, A. 1989. "Saving in Developing Countries: Theory and Review," *Proceedings of the World Bank Annual Conference on Development Economics*. Washington, DC: The World Bank.

—— 1991. "Saving and Liquidity Constraints." *Econometrica* 59: 1121–42.

—— 1992. *Understanding Consumption*. Oxford: Clarendon Press.

Deininger, K., and L. Squire. 1996. "A New Data Set Measuring Income Inequality," *World Bank Economic Review* 10: 565–91.

Della Valle, P., and N. Oguchi. 1976. "Distribution, the Aggregate Consumption Function, and the Level of Economic Development: Some Cross-Country Results," *Journal of Political Economy* 84: 1325–34.

Dornbusch, R., and S. Edwards. 1991. "The Macroeconomics of Populism," in R. Dornbusch and S. Edwards (eds.): *The Macroeconomics of Populism in Latin America*. Chicago: University of Chicago Press.

Dynan, K., J. Skinner, and S. Zeldes. 1996. "Do the Rich Save More?" Unpublished manuscript.

Edwards, S. 1996. "Why Are Latin America's Saving Rates So Low? An International Comparative Analysis," *Journal of Development Economics* 51(1): 5–44.

Friedman, M. 1957. *A Theory of the Consumption Function*. Princeton: Princeton University Press.

Galor, O., and J. Zeira. 1993. "Income Distribution and Macroeconomics." *Review of Economic Studies* 60: 35–52.

Gersovitz, M. 1988. "Saving and Development," in H. Chenery and T. N. Srinivasan (eds.): *Handbook of Development Economics*. Amsterdam: North Holland, 381–424.

Gupta, K. 1970. "Personal Saving in Developing Nations: Further Evidence," *Economic Record* 46(0): 243–9.

Hayashi, F. 1985. "Tests for Liquidity Constraints: A Critical Survey." *NBER Working Paper* 1720.

Hong, K. 1995. "Income Distribution and Aggregate Saving." Unpublished manuscript, Harvard University, Cambridge, MA, November.

Houthakker, H. 1961. "An International Comparison of Personal Saving," *Bulletin of the International Statistical Institute* 38: 55–69.

Huggett, M., and G. Ventura. 1995. "Understanding Why High Income Households Save More Than Low Income Households." Manuscript, Department of Economics, University of Illinois, Champaign, IL, October.

Jappelli, T., and M. Pagano. 1994. "Saving, Growth, and Liquidity Constraints," *Quarterly Journal of Economics* 109: 83–109.

Kaldor, N. 1957. "A Model of Economic Growth," *Economic Journal* 57: 591–624.

Kelley, A. C., and J. G. Williamson. 1968. "Household Savings Behavior in Developing Countries: The Indonesian Case," *Economic Development and Cultural Change* 16(3): 385–403.

Kirman, A. 1992. "Whom or What Does the Representative Individual Represent?" *Journal of Economic Perspectives* 2: 117–36.

Koenker, R., and G. Bassett. 1978. "Regression Quantiles," *Econometrica* 46: 33–50.

Kotlikoff, L., and L. Summers. 1981. "The Role of Intergenerational Transfers in Aggregate Capital Accumulation," *Journal of Political Economy* 90: 706–32.

    1988. "The Contribution of Intergenerational Transfers to Total Wealth: A Reply," in D. Kessler and A. Masson (eds.): *Modeling the Accumulation and Distribution of Wealth*. Oxford: Clarendon Press.

Leff, N. H. 1969. "Dependency Rates and Savings Rates," *American Economic Review* 59: 886–96.

Lewis, W. A. 1954. "Economic Development with Unlimited Supplies of Labor," *The Manchester School* 22: 139–91.

Lim, D. 1980. "Income Distribution, Export Instability and Savings Behavior," *Economic Development and Cultural Change* 26: 359–64.

Lipsey, R. E., and H. S. Tice (eds.). 1989. *The Measurement of Saving, Investment, and Wealth*, NBER Studies in Income and Wealth, vol. 52. Washington, DC: NBER.

Mas-Colell, A., M. Whinston, and J. Green. 1995. *Microeconomic Theory*. Oxford University Press.

Masson, P., T. Bayoumi, and H. Samiel. 1995. Saving Behavior in Industrial and Developing Countries," in *International Monetary Fund: Staff Studies for the World Economic Outlook* 5: 1–27, September.

Menchik, P., and M. David. 1983. Income Distribution, Lifetime Savings, and Bequests," *American Economic Review* 73: 672–90.

Modigliani, F. 1970. "The Life Cycle Hypothesis of Savings and Intercountry Differences in the Savings Ratio," in W. A. Eltis, M. F. G. Scott, and J. N. Wolfe (eds.): *Induction, Growth and Trade*. Oxford University Press.

Modigliani, F., and R. Brumberg. 1954. "Utility Analysis and the Consumption Function," in K. K. Kurihara (ed.): *Post-Keynesian Economics*. Rutgers University Press.

Musgrove, P. 1980. "Income Distribution and the Aggregate Consumption Function," *Journal of Political Economy* 88: 504–25.

Pasinetti, L. 1962. "Rate of Profit and Income Distribution in Relation to the Rate of Economic Growth," *Review of Economic Studies* 29: 267–79.

Perotti, R. 1996. "Growth, Income Distribution, and Democracy: What the Data Say." *Journal of Economic Growth* 1: 149–87.

Persson, T., and G. Tabellini. 1994. "Is Inequality Harmful for Growth? Theory and Evidence," *American Economic Review* 84: 600–21.

Pischke, J.-S. 1995. "Individual Income, Incomplete Information, and Aggregate Consumption," *Econometrica* 63(4): 805–40.

Sahota, G. 1993. "Saving and Distribution," in J. H. Gapinski (ed.): *The Economics of Saving*. Boston: Kluwer Academic, 193–231.

Schmidt-Hebbel, K., and L. Servén. 1998. "Income Inequality and Saving," in A. Solimano (ed.): *Social Inequality, Growth and the State*. University of Michigan Press.

Schmidt-Hebbel, K., L. Servén, and A. Solimano. "Saving and Investment: Paradigms, Puzzles, Policies," *World Bank Research Observer* 11: 87–117.

Schmidt-Hebbel, K., S. Webb, and G. Corsetti. 1992. "Household Saving in Developing Countries: First Cross-Country Evidence," *World Bank Economic Review* 6: 529–47.

Solow, R. 1956. "A Contribution to the Theory of Economic Growth," *Quarterly Journal of Economics* 70: 65–94.

Srinivasan, T. N. 1994. "Data Base for Development Analysis: An Overview," *Journal of Development Analysis* 44(1): 3–27.

Venieris, Y., and D. Gupta. 1986. "Income Distribution and Sociopolitical Instability as Determinants of Savings: A Cross-Sectional Model, *Journal of Political Economy* 94: 873–83.

Williamson, J. 1968. "Personal Saving in Developing Nations: An Intertemporal Cross-Section from Asia," *Economic Record* 44: 194–202.

Zou, Heng-Fu. 1994. "The Spirit of Capitalism and Long-Run Growth," *European Journal of Political Economy* 10: 279–93.

Index

accounting: and Chenery-style growth models, 113–14. *See also* methodology
Adelman, I, 109n6
Africa. *See* Middle East and North Africa; Sub-Saharan Africa; *specific countries*
age: and consumption, 58–9, 60; and income, 58–9; and life-cycle hypothesis, 41–3, 44–5. *See also* elderly; retirement; social security
aggregate saving: borrowing constraints, income distribution, and saving, 153; cross-country studies of income distribution and, 158–77, 180–4; definition of, 149; empirical studies of, 156–8; financial flows and estimation of, 99–101; and functional distribution of income, 150–1; and indirect links between growth and income distribution, 154–5; panel studies of income distribution and, 177–80, 184–5; and personal distribution of income, 151–3
AK model: of economic growth, 36–7, 54
Aleem, I., 77–8n7
Algeria, 184
Alesina, A., 148n2
Alessie, R. A., 77n5
annuities: financial institutions and saving, 90–1
Arrow, Kenneth J., 37
assets: accumulation of and flow-of-funds accounts, 99–101
Atkinson, A. B., 90
Attiyas, I., 25, 101n30
Australia, 184
Azariadis, C., 84n12

Baccheta, P., 15, 33
Bahamas, 184
balance sheets: and financial institutions as source of data on saving, 94

Balassa, B., 83
Banca d'Italia, 75–6, 96
Bangladesh, 184
banking. *See* financial systems
Bank of International Settlements, 20, 101
Bardhan, P., 108n3
Barro, R., 37, 137, 138, 158, 173n10
Barro-type regressions, 54
Becker, G., 152
behavior: tax incentives for saving and irrational, 89. *See also* habits; psychology
Belarus, 11n2
Belgium, 184
bequests: collection of data on, 65; and correlation between saving and growth, 56–9; and life-cycle hypothesis, 45, 63; and personal distribution of income, 151–2
Bernheim, B. D., 56, 89
Berry, A., 20
Bertola, G., 151
Betancourt, R. R., 97n26
Bewley, T., 51
Bhagwati, J., 109
Bhalla, S. S., 58, 97n26
big-push growth models, 136
Blanchard, O., 129
Blinder, A., 156
Blundell, R., 83n10
Boadway, R., 89
Bolivia, 184
bonds: saving and rates of return on, 85
Boone, P., 109n5, 119–20, 121, 130
borrowing, constraints on: and buffer stock models, 50–2; consumption and fixed ceilings, 78; exogenous easing of as form of foreign aid, 127–30; and housing, 53; and income distribution, 153. *See also* credit; interest
Börsch-Supan, A., 57
Bosworth, B. P., 64